PROCEEDINGS

OF THE

Oxford Union Society.

OXFORD,

PRINTED BY W. BAXTER.

MDCCCXLI.

LIST OF MEMBERS.

LIST OF MEMBERS.

*Acland, A. H. D. Ch. Ch.
*Acland, T. D. All Souls, M.P.
*Acres, J. Lincoln
*Adair, H. E. St. John's
*Adair, T. B. Exeter
*Adams, A. R. St. John's
*Adams, H. C. Magdalen
*Adams, H. G. Ch. Ch.
*Adams, J. Ch. Ch.
*Adams, W. C. Balliol
*Addison, W. F. Wadham
*Addison, W. G. S. Magdalen Hall
*Ady, Rev. W. Exeter
Akenhead, D. University
Alban, W. J. St. John's
*Alderson, Rev. R. J. Exeter
*Alexander, G. Trinity
Algar, J. C. University
*Allen, H. G. Ch. Ch.
*Allen, J. C. Brase-nose
*Allen, T. Balliol
*Allfrey, H. W. Exeter
*Allies, Rev. T. Wadham
*Alston, R. G. Ch. Ch.
*Anderson, D. Exeter
*Anderson, H. L. St. John's
*Andrewes, G. H. Magdalen Hall
*Andrew, Rev. S. Lincoln
Anson, G. Exeter
*Anstey, Rev. A. Worcester
*Anstis, Rev. M. Exeter
*Antrobus, G. Brase-nose
*Archdale, W. H. Exeter
*Archer, C. H. Balliol
Archer, S. H. Exeter
*Armitage, Rev. R. Worcester
*Armstrong, Rev. J. Balliol

*Armytage, Sir G. Oriel
*Arnold, C. T. Magdalen Hall
*Arnott, S. B. St. John's
*Ashhurst, W. H. Ch. Ch.
*Ashley, Hon. W. All Souls
*Ashurst, J. H. Exeter
*Atcherley, D. F. University
Atkinson, R. St. John's
*Athlone, Earl of, Ch. Ch.
*Attwood, E. W. Jesus
*Auchmuty, S. F. Brase-nose
*Austen, J. F. Ch. Ch.
*Austen, R. A. C. Oriel
Awdry, A. Magdalen Hall
*Awdry, W. H. Magdalen Hall

*Bainbridge, A. F. New Inn Hall
*Baker, C. F. Exeter
*Baker, G. T. Ch. Ch.
Baldwin, L. St. John's
*Baldwin, Rev. C. F. St. John's
Ballard, E. H. Wadham
*Balston, F. Ch. Ch.
*Balston, Rev. H. Magdalen
Bampfield, R. Trinity
*Bannatyne, Rev. C. Balliol
*Baring, Rev. C. Ch. Ch.
*Barker, A. A. Magdalen
*Barker, Rev. F. Oriel
*Barker, Rev. T. Brase-nose
*Barlow, C. G. Balliol
Barlow, J. Ch. Ch.
*Barne, Rev. H. Exeter
*Barnes, Rev. R. Ch. Ch.
*Barnes, Walter, Ch. Ch.
*Barney, S. Exeter

* Honorary Members.

*A

*Barrington, Hon. and Rev. L. I. Oriel
Barry, H. B. Queen's
*Bassett, Rev. J. M. Exeter
*Bathurst, R. New College
*Baugh, Rev. F. All Souls
*Bayley, W. H. Ch. Ch.
*Bayly, C. G. V. Exeter
*Bayntun, W. W. T. Balliol
*Bazalgette, Rev. S. Balliol
*Beach, M. H. H. Ch. Ch.
*Beach, W. H. Oriel
Beale, T. Brase-nose
Beckett-Turner, W. Queen's
*Beck, C. Balliol
*Bellamy, J. St. John's
*Bell, E. Merton
*Berkeley, Rev. G. C. Pembroke
*Berkeley, Rev. G. T. Queen's
*Bernard, Hon. and Rev. C. B. Ball.
*Bernard, Hon. H. B. Balliol
Bernard, M. Trinity
*Bernard, T. D. Exeter
*Bernard, Viscount, Oriel
*Berners, Rev. R. Magdalen
*Berry, J. G. M. Brase-nose
*Bevan, C. Balliol
*Bevan, Rev. T. Balliol
*Bigge, H. University
*Bigge, J. F. Oriel
*Bigge, Rev. E. T. Merton
Bignold, S. T. Balliol
*Bingham, Rev. C. W. New Coll.
*Birch, W. J. New Inn Hall
*Biscoe, Rev. F. Ch. Ch.
*Bishop, F. H. Trinity
Bittleston, H. St. John's
*Blachford, F. Brase-nose
*Black, A. Ch. Ch.
*Black, P. Ch. Ch.
*Blackall, Rev. H. Ch. Ch.
Blackett, J. B. Ch. Ch.
*Blackett, Rev. J. A. Ch. Ch.
*Blackstone, W. S. Ch. Ch. M.P.
*Blake, Rev. W. J. Ch. Ch.
*Bland, T. Ch. Ch.
*Blencowe, J. G. Ch. Ch.
*Bliss, Rev. Dr. St. John's
*Bliss, Rev. J. Oriel

*Blissett, G. Ballioi
*Blunt, Rev. E. P. Corpus
*Bode, J. E. Ch. Ch.
Bolland, W. University
*Bolton, C. N. St. Edmund Hall
*Boodle, A. Exeter
*Boodle, R. Oriel
*Borradaile, Rev. A. Ch. Ch.
*Borrer, C. H. Oriel
*Borrett, C. W. Magdalen
Boucherett, H. University
*Boulton, W. H. Trinity
Bourke, J. Worcester
Bowen, G. F. Trinity
*Bower, J. H. Exeter
Bowles, F. S. Exeter
*Boyle, P. Oriel
Boyle, J. Balliol
*Braikenridge, G. W. University
*Braikenridge, W. J. Exeter
*Bramston, Rev. J. Exeter
*Brancker, H. Wadham
*Brancker, Rev. T. Wadham
*Brandreth, W. H. Ch. Ch.
Brewster, W. St. John's
*Brickdale, M. Ch. Ch.
*Bridges, Rev. B. E. Merton
*Bright, J. E. Ch. Ch.
*Brigstock, W. Merton
Brine, J. G. St. John's
*Brock, Rev. O. Brase-nose
*Brock, Rev. T. Oriel
*Brodie, B. C. Balliol
*Brodrick, W. University
*Brooke-Jones, R. Wadham
Brooks, H. Brase-nose
*Brooks, Rev. J. H. Brase-nose
*Brown, Rev. F. Exeter
*Brown, H. Corpus
Browne, C. Worcester
*Browne, R. C. Brase-nose
*Browne, Rev. R. W. St. John's
*Browne, G. L. St. John's
*Bruce, Hon. J. Merton
*Bruce, Rev. W. Oriel
Brune, C. J. Prideaux, Ch. Ch.
*Bruxner, Rev. G. E. Ch. Ch.
*Brydges, H. J. J. Merton

*Buck, W. Balliol
*Buckley, W. E. Brase-nose
*Buckland, J. Ch. Ch.
*Bucknall-Estcourt, E. Balliol
Bucknill, G. Trinity
*Buddicom, Rev. R. J. Brase-nose
*Buller, Rev. A. Oriel
*Bulley, Rev. F. Magdalen
*Bullock, Rev. G. M. St. John's
*Bulteel, E. Exeter
*Bunsen, H. G. Oriel
*Burder, G. Magdalen Hall
*Burges, Rev. F. St. John's
*Burgh, F. Exeter
Burn, W. Ch. Ch.
*Burnett-Stuart, A. Brase-nose
*Burney, E. Magdalen Hall
Burney, H. B. Oriel
*Burney, Rev. C. Magdalen
*Burningham, T. Trinity
*Burr, H. Ch. Ch.
Burrowes, J. University
Burrowes, L. Wadham
*Burrows, H. W. St. John's
Butler, G. Exeter
Butler, P. Ch. Ch.
*Butler, Rev. J. Trinity
*Butterworth, Rev. J. H. Exeter
*Byng, Rev. J. Merton

*Caldwell, G. Merton
Calley, C. B. Worcester
*Calvert, F. Merton
*Cameron, A. St. Mary Hall
*Campbell, A. R. Balliol
*Campbell, C. Exeter
*Campbell, Rev. J. J. Balliol
*Cane, E. Trinity
*Capes, Rev. J. M. Balliol
*Carden, J. Merton
Carden, L. University
Cardwell, C. St. Alban Hall
*Cardwell, E. Balliol
*Carew, W. H. Pole, Oriel
*Carey, H. Oriel
Carey, O. Oriel
*Carnegie, Hon. J. Oriel

*Carr, H. B. University
*Carr, Rev. C. Exeter
*Carter, Rev. G. St. John's
*Casson, Rev. G. Brase-nose
*Caswall, Rev. E. Brase-nose
Cave, S. Balliol
Cazenove, J. G. Brase-nose
*Chadwick, E. Worcester
*Chaffers, Rev. T. Brase-nose
*Chamberlain, Rev. T. Ch. Ch.
Chambers, O. University
*Champernowne, R. Ch. Ch.
*Champneys, M. H. S. Brase-nose
*Champneys, Rev. T. P. A. Merton
*Chandler, Rev. J. Corpus
Chapman, E. J. Wadham
*Chapman, J. St. Mary Hall
Charrington, N. G. Oriel
Chase, D. P. Oriel
*Chase, T. H. Queen's
*Chelsea, Lord, Oriel
*Chesshyre, Rev. W. J. Balliol
*Chester, W. University
*Chetwynd, G. Ch. Ch.
Cherry, T. Ch. Ch.
*Chichester, Rev. R. H. Exeter
Child, A. Exeter
*Childers, Rev. C. Ch. Ch.
*Chittenden, T. K. St. John's
*Cholmeley, R. Corpus
Chretian, C. P. Brase-nose
*Church, Rev. R. W. Oriel
*Churchill, G. Worcester
*Churton, Rev. H. W. B. Brase-nose
*Clare, Rev. G. T. St. John's
*Clark, J. D. University
*Clarke, Rev. H. D. Exeter
*Clarke, R. G. Wadham
Clarke, W. G. Oriel
*Clarke, W. J. Balliol
*Claughton, Rev. T. L. Trinity
*Claughton, Rev. P. C. University
*Claughton, H. C. Brase-nose
*Clements, Hon. and Rev. F. N. Oriel
Clements, J. Oriel
Clifford, C. C. Ch. Ch.
*Clonbrock, Lord, Ch. Ch.
*Clough, A. H. Balliol

*Cobb, Rev. S. W. Oriel
*Cockin, Rev. W. Brase-nose
*Cocks, C. R. S. Ch. Ch.
*Cocks, R. T. Ch. Ch.
*Coffin, R. A. Ch. Ch.
*Coke, Rev. E. F. Brase-nose
Colborne, E. Exeter
*Cole, E. St. Mary Hall
*Cole, F. B. Ch. Ch.
*Cole, J. G. Exeter
Cole, J. H. Balliol
*Cole, O. B. Ch. Ch.
*Cole, Viscount, Ch. Ch. M.P.
Coleridge, J. D. Balliol
Collett, W. L. Queen's
*Collins, Rev. C. M. Exeter
*Collins, Rev. W. L. Jesus
*Collis, Rev. J. D. Worcester
*Collyns, C. H. Ch. Ch.
*Colquhon, W. L. Oriel
Comins, J. Queen's
*Congreve, R. Wadham
*Connell, Rev. J. Balliol
*Connellan, J. C. Oriel
*Conroy, E. Ch. Ch.
Conybeare, C. R. Ch. Ch.
Cooke, J. E. Brase-nose
*Cooke, S. H. Ch. Ch.
*Cookes, H. W. Worcester
*Coope, Rev. J. R. Ch. Ch.
Cooper, A. St. John's
*Cooper, Rev. J. Wadham
Coore, H. J. Worcester
*Coote, A. Brase-nose
*Cope, W. Trinity
*Copeland, Rev. W. J. Trinity
*Corbett, Rev. T. W. Merton
*Cornish, J. R. Ch. Ch.
*Cornish, T. B. Oriel
*Cosserat, Rev. G. P. Exeter
*Cotes, Rev. P. Wadham
*Cother, D. Brase-nose
*Cother, W. Ch. Ch.
Cotton, H. Ch. Ch.
*Cotton, Rev. W. C. Ch. Ch.
*Courtenay, F. Exeter
*Courtenay, Hon. and Rev. H. H. Merton

*Courtenay, Hon. C. L. Ch. Ch.
*Courtenay, Lord, All Souls
*Courtenay, R. Magdalen Hall
*Courthope, G. C. Ch. Ch.
*Courthope, W. Ch. Ch.
Coventry, J. Magdalen Hall
Cowburn, A. Exeter
Cox, C. Exeter
Cox, J. Trinity
*Coxe, Rev. H. O. Worcester
Coyle, M. Trinity
*Cranley, Viscount, Ch. Ch.
*Crawley, Rev. J. L. Trinity
*Crichton, Rev. W. J. Merton
*Cripps, H. W. New Coll.
*Cripps, W. Trinity
Cross, J. E. Ch. Ch.
*Crosse, Rev. J. D. O. Exeter
*Crosse, R. Balliol
Crosse, T. F. Exeter
*Crouch, W. Exeter
*Cruttwell, Rev. H. E. Worcester
Cummings, C. J. Brase-nose
*Cunningham, C. T. Ch. Ch.
Cunningham, G. Oriel

*Dalhousie, Lord, Ch. Ch.
Dalison, J. B. Merton
*Dalton, Rev. C. Wadham
*Dalton, Rev. R. University
*Daniel, J. Ch. Ch.
*Dann, H. St. John's
Darling, J. Ch. Ch.
*Dasent, G. W. Magdalen Hall
David, E. St. Mary Hall
*Davies, D. S. Balliol
*Davison, H. Trinity
Dawson, H. Balliol
Dawson, J Exeter
*Day, Rev. J. D. Brase-nose
*Dayman, Rev. P. D. Balliol
*Dean, C. K. Queen's
*Deane, J: P. St. John's
*Deane, J. W. St. John's
*Deane, W. C. St. John's
*Debary, T. Lincoln
*Dene, Rev. A. Exeter
*Denison, S. C. Balliol

*De Paravicini, F. Worcester
*De Salis, R. J. L. Oriel
*De Salis, Rev. W. A. Oriel
*De Tabley, Lord, Ch. Ch.
*De Visme, Rev. L. D. Balliol
*Dewar, Rev. E. Exeter
*Dewdney, W. G. Queen's
*Dewhurst, J. Worcester
Dickerson, R. C. Worcester
*Dickinson, W. W. Brase-nose
*Dickson, S. F. Brase-nose
*Dillon, Hon. A. D. Trinity
*Dixon, E. Worcester
*Dodgson, H. H. Ch. Ch.
Dodson, P. A. Worcester
*Dolignon, J. W. Balliol
*Domvile, H. B. University
*Domville, J. G. Ch. Ch.
Douglas, C. R. G. Exeter
Douton, C. Ch. Ch.
*Downes, R. Trinity
*Downie, R. Trinity
*Doyle, Sir F. H. All Souls
D'Oyley, T. Ch. Ch.
*Driffield, Rev. G. T. Brase-nose
Driffield, V. G. Brase-nose
*Drummond, G. H. Ch. Ch.
*Drummond, Rev. H. Balliol
Drummond, R. Ch. Ch.
*Duckworth, Sir J. Bart. Oriel
*Dudding, Rev. H. Exeter
*Duke, R. Queen's
*Dunbar, Rev. Sir W. Bart. Magdalen Hall
*Duncombe, Hon. and Rev. A. Worcester
*Durnford, Rev. R. Magdalen
*Dyer, H. S. Worcester
*Dyke, Rev. W. Jesus
*Dymock, Rev. T. F. Balliol
*Dyne, Rev. J. B. Wadham

Easum, R. Lincoln
Eddy, C. W. Brase-nose
*Edgell, Rev. W. C. St. John's
*Edmonston, Rev. C. W. Ch. Ch.
*Edwards, A. O. Trinity
*Ellerton, G. M. K. Brase-nose

*Ellis, F. J. Merton
*Ellison, H. Ch. Ch.
Ellison, H. University
*Ellison, J. Ch. Ch.
*Ellison, R. Ch. Ch.
*Elton, E. Balliol
*Elton, J. M. Balliol
*Elwes, G. C. All Souls
*Emeris, Rev. J. University
*Empson, J. Brase-nose
*Errington, Rev. J. R. Worcester
*Erskine, H. Balliol
*Estcourt, E. Exeter
*Estcourt, W. J. Balliol
Evans, E. T. Jesus
Evans, J. W. Trinity
*Evans, L. Wadham
*Evans, O. L. St. Mary Hall
*Evans, R. Jesus
Evetts, T. Corpus
Ewart, W. Exeter
*Eyre, Rev. E. Merton
*Eyre, R. H. University

*Faber, J. C. Ch. Ch.
*Fagan, Rev. G. H. U. Oriel
*Faithfull, J. G. Exeter
*Falconer, Rev. W. Exeter
Falkner, T. A. St. John's
*Fane, A. Exeter
*Farquhar, Sir W. M. Bart. Ch. Ch.
Farrer, H. R. Merton
Faulder, R. University
*Fawcett, R. T. University
*Feild, Rev. E. Queen's
Feilden, H. Ch. Ch.
*Fellowes, Rev. T. L. Ch. Ch.
Fenwick, G. University
*Fincham, G. T. St. John's
*Fisher, J. Exeter
*Fisher, T. Exeter
*Fisher, Rev. J. Magdalen
*Fitz-Gerald, Rev. A. O. Balliol
*Fitz-Gerald, R. Exeter
*Fitz-Gerald, Seymour W. R. Oriel
*Fitzharris, Viscount, Oriel
Fitzhugh, W. H. Ch. Ch.
Forbes, A. P. Brase-nose

Forbes, C. W. Oriel
*Ford, G. J. Exeter
*Formby, H. Brase-nose
*Forster, C. Worcester
*Fortescue, Rev. E. Wadham
*Fortescue, T. Exeter
*Foster, A. H. Trinity
Foster, F. Oriel
Foster, J. M. Lincoln
Foster, J. St. Mary Hall
*Foulkes, E. Jesus
*Foulkes, Rev. H. P. Balliol
*Foulkes, J. J. Jesus
*Fowle, Rev. W. C. Wadham
*Fowler, Rev. C. Oriel
*Fowler, J. C. Pembroke
*Fox, H. W. Wadham
Fox, R. S. University
*Fox, W. Balliol
*Frankland, R. University
*Franklin, W. New Inn Hall
*Fraser, J. Oriel
*Freeland, H. W. Ch. Ch.
*Freeman, Rev. T. Brase-nose
*French, Rev. M. D. Brase-nose
Frith, M. K. Exeter
*Fursdon, Rev. E. Oriel
*Furneaux, W. Exeter

*Garbett, C. Brase-nose
*Garbett, Rev. J. Brase-nose
Gardiner, H. Magdalen Hall
*Garnett, F. W. Balliol
*Garrard, C. D. Brase-nose
*Garrard, T. St. John's
*Garratt, J. Ch. Ch.
*Garside, C. B. Brase-nose
*Gaselee, B. Balliol
*Gaskell, C. T. Trinity
*Gaskell, J. M. Ch. Ch. M.P.
*Geary, Sir W. R. P. Bart. Ch. Ch.
 M.P.
*Gee, Rev. R. Wadham
George, C. F. St. Mary Hall
Gibbs, J. C. Trinity
*Giffard, W. University
*Gilbert, J. Davies, Pembroke
*Gilbertson, Rev. L. Jesus

Giles, J. Balliol
*Giles, J. D. Corpus
*Giles, J. E. Magdalen Hall
Gladstone, J. E. Magdalen Hall
*Gladstone, W. E. Ch. Ch. M.P.
*Glanville, Rev. E. F. Exeter
*Gleg, B. Merton
*Glover, W. H. University
Glyn, C. Ch. Ch.
*Glynne, Sir Steph. Bart. Ch. Ch. M.P.
*Goodenough, Rev. R. Ch. Ch.
*Goodhart, C. E. Brase-nose
*Gordon, J. Brase-nose
*Gossett, Rev. J. H. Exeter
*Goulburn, E. Merton
*Goulburn, F. A. Merton
*Gould, Rev. J. N. Wadham
*Govett, H. Worcester
*Graham, W. Ch. Ch.
*Graham, Rev. W. B. Magdalen Hall
*Graham, Rev. W. P. Queen's
Grant, J. St. John's
Grant, L. A. Balliol
*Grant, Rev. A. New College
Granville-Bradley, G. University
*Graves, Rev. E. T. Worcester
Gray, J. D. Balliol
*Gray, Rev. R. H. Ch. Ch.
*Grazebrook, Rev. T. W. S. Brase-nose
*Greaves, R. W. St. Edmund Hall
*Greenhill, Dr. W. A. Trinity
*Gregory, H. St. Mary Hall
Gregory, R. Corpus
Grenside, J. D. Exeter
*Gresley, Rev. J. M. St. Mary Hall
*Gresley, R. N. Ch. Ch.
*Griffith, A. New Coll.
*Grimston, Viscount, Ch. Ch. M.P.
*Grove, Rev. E. H. Brase-nose
*Guillemard, Rev. H. P. Trinity
*Gwilt, C. P. Ch. Ch.

*Haddan, T. H. Exeter
*Haddan, Rev. A. W. Trinity
*Hadow, P. D. Balliol
*Hall, A. H. Balliol
*Hall, Rev. G. C. Magdalen
*Hall, Rev. J. C. Ch. Ch.

*Hall, Rev. J. R. Ch. Ch.
*Hall, Rev. C. R. Ch. Ch.
*Hall, Rev. W. R. Balliol
*Hale, R. Brase-nose
Hambrough, A. J. St. Mary Hall
*Hamilton, A. Cole, St. Mary Hall
*Hamilton, Rev. W. K. Merton
Hampden, J. St. Mary Hall
Handcock, F. St. Mary Hall
*Hanmer, Sir J. Bart. Ch. Ch. M.P.
*Hanmer, H. New Inn Hall
*Hanmer, T. Brase-nose
*Hannah, J. Lincoln
*Hansell, H. Magdalen
*Hansell, Rev. P. University
*Harcourt, E. Vernon, Ch. Ch. M.P.
*Harding, J. D. Oriel
*Harding, G. S. Brase-nose
*Harding, J. S. Exeter
*Hardy, Rev. J. Oriel
*Hardy, Rev. R. Balliol
*Hardy, G. Oriel
*Harington, Rev. R. Brase-nose
*Harris, Hon. G. F. R. All Souls
*Harris, Hon. C. A. All Souls
*Harrison, Rev. B. Ch. Ch.
*Harrison, J. P. Ch. Ch.
*Harter, Rev. G. G. Trinity
*Harvey, E. Oriel
*Harvey, Rev. W. M. Wadham
*Hastings, Marquis of, Ch. Ch.
*Hatchard, T. G. Brase-nose
*Hathaway, E. P. Queen's
*Hathaway, F. Worcester
*Hatsell, J. Oriel
Hawkins, C. S. Magdalen Hall
Hawkins, J. Worcester
*Hawkins, H. Jesus
*Hawtayne, Rev. W. G. Magd. Hall
*Heathcote, Rev. G. E. New Coll.
*Hedley, W. Queen's
*Hemming, Rev. J. St. John's
*Henderson, G. Magdalen
*Henderson, R. Wadham
*Henry, Rev. C. E. Oriel
*Herbert, Hon. S. Oriel, M.P.
*Heron, Rev. G. Brase-nose
*Hessey, Rev. J. A. St. John's

*Hetherington, W. Trinity
Hewitt, Hon. J. Balliol
*Hewitt, Hon. J. Ch. Ch.
*Hewitt, T. S. Worcester
*Hext, G. Corpus
*Hicks, E. Corpus
*Highton, Rev. H. Queen's
*Higgins, M. J. New College
*Hill, Rev. J. R. University
*Hill, G. St. Edmund Hall
*Hill, Rev. R. Balliol
*Hill, H. Wadham
*Hinxman, C. Balliol
*Hippisley, J. Oriel
*Hippisley, R. W. Exeter
*Hobhouse, R. Balliol
*Hobhouse, T. Balliol
*Hobhouse, H. Balliol
*Hodges, Rev. T. F. New College
*Hodson, Rev. J. S. Merton
*Holdich, Rev. T. P. Balliol
*Hole, Rev. W. B. Exeter
*Holland, Rev. W. Lincoln
*Holland, C. University
Holmes, H. Brase-nose
*Holmes, T. K. Ch. Ch.
*Holmes, S. Magdalen Hall
Holt, R. B. Corpus
*Holthouse, Rev. C. S. St. John's
*Honywood, Rev. P. J. Trinity
*Honywood, P. University
*Hope, Hon. C. Merton
*Hopton, R. Brase-nose
Horman-Fisher, R. Ch. Ch.
*Hornby, R. A. Oriel
*Hornby, W. Ch. Ch.
*Horner, Rev. J. S. H. Exeter
*Horton, R. E. W. Ch. Ch.
*Hoskyns, H. Oriel
*Hoskyns, Rev. J. L. Magdalen
*Hotham, G. F. Ch. Ch.
*Howard, Hon. W. Ch. Ch.
*Hughan, T. Balliol
*Hughes, E. W. Worcester
*Hughes, Rev. H. Trinity
*Hughes, W. Hughes, Ch. Ch.
Hughes, J. Oriel
*Hull, Rev. H. W. Oriel

Hull, W. W. Ch. Ch.
*Hulme, Rev. G. Balliol
*Hulme, W. Balliol
*Hulse, E. All Souls
*Hulton, Rev. A. H. Brase-nose
Humbert, L. M. St. John's
*Humphreys, J. J. H. Exeter
*Hunt, R. S. Exeter
*Huntley, O. C. Oriel
Huntsman, F. Queen's
*Hussey, W. Balliol
*Hussey, R. H. Ch. Ch.
*Hussey, T. Brase-nose
Hutchings, R. C. Ch. Ch.
Hutchins, W. T. Worcester

*I'Anson, Rev. W. University
*Ingram-Winnington, A. H. Ch. Ch.
*Irby, Hon. W. D. Balliol
*Irby, F. W. Balliol
*Irwin, J. L. Ch. Ch.
Ivory, T. Balliol

*Jackson, Rev. F. G. Trinity
*Jackson, T. Brase-nose
Jackson, W. Queen's
*James, T. Ch. Ch.
James, E. B. Queen's
*Janvrin, J. H. Oriel
*Jeffray, Rev. L. W. Balliol
*Jeffreys, Rev. H. Ch. Ch.
*Jelf, Rev. W. E. Ch. Ch.
*Jenkins, J. D. E. Jesus
Jenkins, W. J. Balliol
Jervis, T. New Inn Hall
*Jones, C. W. J. Oriel
*Jones, E. R. Brase-nose
*Jones, Rev. C. R. Oriel
*Jones, W. Balliol
Jones, W. H. Queen's
*Joyce, J. W. Ch. Ch.
*Joyce, W. H. University
*Joynes, R. Corpus

*Karslake, E. K. Ch. Ch.

*Kay, W. Lincoln
*Kebbel, Rev. C. D. University
*Kelley, A. Corpus
Kemble, C. Wadham
*Kemble, T. Oriel
*Kemble, W. Oriel
*Kemmis, T. Brase-nose
*Kempson, W. H. Ch. Ch.
*Kensington, E. Balliol
*Kenyon, J. R. All Souls
Kerr, W. W. Oriel
*Kildare, Marquis of, Ch. Ch.
*King, H. Wadham
*King, Rev. B. Brase-nose
*King, R. J. Exeter
Kinlock, A. St. Mary Hall
Kitcat, J. Oriel
*Kitson, Rev. E. Balliol
*Kitson, Rev. F. P. St. John's
*Kitson, E. P. Balliol
*Knatchbull, N. J. Ch. Ch.
Knight, H. Exeter
*Knight, Rev. C. R. Wadham
*Knight, W. Worcester
*Knighton, Sir W. W. Ch. Ch.
Knox, T. St. John's
*Kynaston, Rev. H. Ch. Ch.
*Kynderley, L. Balliol
*Kynnersley, Rev. E. C. S. Trinity

*Lake, W. C. Balliol
*Lakin, T. C. Oriel
*Lakin, J. Worcester
*Lamb, J. D. St. Mary Hall
*Lambert, Rev. A. L. Trinity
*Lambert, W. Exeter
*Landon, J. T. B. Worcester
*Lane-Fox, W. E. Balliol
*Langham, H. B. St. Alban Hall
*Latouche, C. J. Magdalen Hall
*Latouche, P. Corpus
*Latouche, W. R. Exeter
*Law, G. S. Oriel
*Lawrence, Rev. C. W. Brase-nose
*Lawford, H. S. Ch. Ch.
*Leach, T. Merton
*Le Breton, Rev. W. C. Exeter

*Lee, Rev. S. Queen's
*Legard, Rev. D. C. University
*Legh, Rev. H. C. Brase-nose
Leigh, F. Magdalen Hall
*Le Mesurier, J. Ch. Ch.
*Lempriere, C. St. John's
*Leslie, C. Ch. Ch.
*Leslie, J. Charles W. Exeter
*Leveson Gower, W. Ch. Ch.
Levien, E. Trinity
Levien, J. Wadham
*Le Warner, B. New Inn Hall
*Lewin, A. Trinity
*Lewin, T. Trinity
*Lewis, Rev. D. Jesus
*Lewis, W. H. Trinity
Lewthwaite, G. University
*Ley, Rev. J. Ch. Ch.
*Lillingston, Rev. G. Worcester
*Lincoln, Earl of, Ch. Ch. M.P.
Lingen, R. Trinity
*Linwood, Rev. W. Ch. Ch.
*Linzee, Rev. E. H. Ch. Ch.
Linzee, R. Ch. Ch.
*Little, T. P. Trinity
*Littledale, C. Ch. Ch.
Littlehales, J. C. New College
*Litton, Rev. E. A. Oriel
*Lloyd, B. C. St. John's
*Lloyd, H. J. Jesus
*Lloyd, T. Ch. Ch.
Lockhart, W. Exeter
*Loftus, Lord Adam, Balliol
*Loftus, A. J. Worcester
*Lonsdale, J. G. Balliol
*Lonsdale, W. Oriel
Lopes, R. Ch. Ch.
Lopes, M. Oriel
*Lott, F. E. St. Alban Hall
Lott, W. B. Balliol
Lowder, C. F. Exeter
*Lowe, R. Magdalen
*Lowe, Rev. F. P. Magdalen
*Lowe, Rev. T. Oriel
Luard, T. G. Wadham
*Lucas, R. G. University
Lucas, S. Queen's
Lucas, W. H. Merton

*Lundy, Rev. F. J. University
*Lushington, Rev. C. Ch. Ch.
*Lyall, J. E. Balliol
*Lyons, B. Ch. Ch.

*Maberly, J. J. Brase-nose
*Maberly, Rev. T. A. Ch. Ch.
*Maberly, E. Ch. Ch.
*Macdonald, N. H. All Souls
Mac Douall, W. Ch. Ch.
*Machen, E. Exeter
Mackarness, J. F. Merton
Mackenzie, L. Exeter
Mackintosh, E. University
*Mackintosh, R. J. New College
*Mackworth, W. H. Balliol
Maclachlan, C. Exeter
*Maclean, C. H. Balliol
*Maclean, D. Balliol, M.P.
*M'Geachy, A. Balliol
*Mahon, Viscount, Ch. Ch. M.P.
*Maitland, T. F. Ch. Ch.
Mallet, H. Balliol
*Mangin, Rev. E. N. Wadham
*Manning, Rev. H. E. Merton
Mansel, H. L. St. John's
*Mant, F. W. New Inn Hall
*Mant, Rev. W. B. Oriel
*Marjoribanks, E. Ch. Ch.
*Marriott, G. R. Oriel
*Marriott, Rev. J. Oriel
*Marriott, Rev. F. A. Oriel
*Marriott, Rev. C. Oriel
*Marsden, Rev. C. J. Ch. Ch.
*Marsh, M. H. Ch. Ch.
*Marsh, R. Wadham
*Marsh, Rev. W. T. Oriel
*Marsh, Rev. G. J. Ch. Ch.
*Marshall, G. Ch. Ch.
Marshall, J. Ch. Ch.
*Martelli, C. H. A. Trinity
*Martelli, T. Brase-nose
*Martin, F. P. B. Wadham
*Martin, F. W. W. Balliol
*Martyn, C. C. Ch. Ch.
*Massie, Rev. E. Wadham
*Masserene, Viscount, Ch. Ch.

*B

*Maskell, Rev. W. University
*Matthew, Rev. H. Balliol
*Maule, G. Ch. Ch.
*Maule, G. University
*Maule, J. B. Ch. Ch.
*Maule, Rev. T. C. St. John's
*Maunsell, W. T. Ch. Ch.
*Maurice, Rev. T. Merton
*Maynard, Rev. R. Wadham
Mayo, A. F. Oriel
*Mayow, Rev. M. W. Ch. Ch.
*Mayow, R. W. Magdalen Hall
*Meawell, B. Balliol
*Meade, R. Ch. Ch.
Meade, W. Balliol
*Medlycott, W. C. Trinity
*Mellish, G. University
*Melville, Rev. D. Brase-nose
*Menzies, F. N. University
Menzies, R. University
Mercer, W. T. Exeter
Mercier, L. P. University
*Merivale, H. Balliol
*Merriman, Rev. N. J. Brase-nose
*Messiter, G. M. Wadham
*Methuen, H. H. Exeter
*Meyrick, J. Queen's
Mildmay, A. St. John, Merton
Miller, J. H. Wadham
*Mills, A. Balliol
Milman, H. Merton
*Milman, R. Exeter
*Milne, H. Brase-nose
*Mitchell, C. Wadham
*Mitford, W. T. Oriel
*Moberly, Rev. Dr. G. Balliol
*Moberly, C. Balliol
*Moncreiff, Rev. G. R. Balliol
*Moncrieff, Rev. H. New College
*Monro, Rev. E. Oriel
*Monro, H. Oriel
Montagu, G. Worcester
Montgomery, C. W. Oriel
Montgomery, H. Ch. Ch.
*Montgomery, Rev. R. Lincoln
*Moore, G. Ch. Ch.
*Moore, C. R. Ch. Ch.
*Moore, Rev. E. Ch. Ch.

*Moore, Rev. J. W. Exeter
*Moore-Stephens, J. Ch. Ch.
Moorsom, J. R. University
*Mordaunt, Sir J. Bart. Ch. Ch. M.P.
*Moreton, Hon. A. H. Merton, M.P.
Morgan, C. J. Lincoln
*Morgan, J. Trinity
*Morgan, N. Brase-nose
*Morland, W. C. Ch. Ch.
*Morley, Earl of, Ch. Ch.
*Morpeth, Viscount, Ch. Ch. M.P.
*Morrell, Rev. G. K. St. John's
*Morrell, Rev. T. B. Balliol
Morrice, J. W. Exeter
*Morris, R. Ch. Ch.
*Morris, Rev. J. B. Exeter
*Morris, Rev. T. E. Ch. Ch.
*Mortimer, Rev. G. F. W. Queen's
*Mozley, Rev. J. B. Magdalen
*Mozley, Rev. T. Oriel
*Muirhead, J. P. Balliol
Munro, A. G. Brase-nose
*Murray, Hon. C. All Souls
*Murray, Rev. G. W. Merton
*Murray, F. H. Ch. Ch.
*Murray, G. E. Ch. Ch.
*Murray, H. S. Ch. Ch.

Naghten, F. Corpus
*Neale, E. V. Oriel
*Nesbitt, T. C. Brase-nose
*Nesfield, W. M. University
*Neve, Rev. F. R. Oriel
Nevill, J. Y. Oriel
*Nevinson, Rev. C. Wadham
*Newcombe, Rev. G. C. Oriel
Newman, C. Wadham
*Newman, Rev. W. J. Oriel
Newman, W. J. Wadham
*Newman, Rev. W. S. Wadham
*Newton, C. Ch. Ch.
*Nicholson, Rev. W. Trinity
*Nicolls, J. H. Oriel
*Norbury, Earl of, Brase-nose
*Norman, J. P. Exeter
Norreys, G. W. J. Exeter
*North, Rev. J. Brase-nose

*Northcote, G. B. Exeter
*Northcote, J. S. Corpus
*Northcote, S. H. Balliol

*Oakes, C. H. Merton
*Odell, E. Ch. Ch.
Offley, C. University
*Offley, W. University
*Oke, Rev. W. S. Wadham
*Oldham, Rev. J. R. Oriel
*Oldfield, E. Wadham
*Ord, J. T. Exeter
*Ormerod, Rev. J. A. Brase-nose
*Ormerod, Rev. T. J. Brase-nose
Ormerod, S. A. Exeter
*Onslow, A. C. Ch. Ch.
*Ossory, Earl of, Ch. Ch.
Oswell, E. W. Ch. Ch.
*Oxenden, A. University
*Oxenham, Rev. N. Exeter

*Padley, C. J. Exeter
*Page, Rev. V. Ch. Ch.
*Paget, Rev. F. E. Ch. Ch.
*Palairet, Rev. C. Queen's
*Palmer, Rev. C. A. Ch. Ch.
*Palmer, F. Ch. Ch.
*Palmer, Rev. W. Magdalen
*Papillon, J. University
Parke, C. J. Oriel
Parker, J. Townley, Magdalen
*Parker, J. O. Oriel
*Parker, M. E. N. Oriel, M.P.
Parnell, P. St. John's
Parsons, H. Balliol
*Partington, H. Ch. Ch.
*Partridge, W. Ch. Ch.
*Paterson, G. Wadham
*Pattison, Rev. M. Lincoln
Paxton, A. Trinity
*Payne, Rev. P. S. H. Balliol
*Peake, Rev. J. R. Magdalen Hall
*Peard, J. W. Exeter
*Pearse, T. Magdalen
*Pearson, H. Balliol
*Pearson, Rev. C. B. Oriel

*Pearson, Rev. G. C. Ch. Ch.
*Pearson, W. University
*Pearson, J. Balliol
*Pearson, Rev. W. Exeter
Pedder, E. Brase-nose
*Pedder, W. Brase-nose
*Peel, E. Brase-nose
*Pell, J. Exeter
*Pennefather, Rev. W. Balliol
*Penrose, Rev. J. Lincoln
*Perceval, R. Brase-nose
*Perkins, A. Oriel
*Peter, J. T. H. Merton
*Petley, Rev. H. Wadham
*Pettat, Rev. C. R. University
*Peyton, T. G. St. Mary Hall
Phillimore, G. Ch. Ch.
Phillimore, R. Ch. Ch.
*Phillips, J. H. Oriel
*Phillips, Rev. H. J. Worcester
*Phillott, Rev. H. W. Ch. Ch.
*Phinn, T. Exeter
*Phipps, Hon. E. Trinity
Pickering, E. Brase-nose
*Pigot, E. Brase-nose
Pigott, F. C. Ch. Ch.
*Pigott, J. D. Ch. Ch.
Pigou, H. C. University
*Plumer, Rev. J. J. Balliol
Plummer, C. Oriel
Plumptre, E. H. University
*Plunkett, Hon. R. Ch. Ch. M.P.
*Pole, W. E. Ch. Ch.
*Polhill, H. W. O. University
*Pollard, Rev. H. S. Lincoln
Poole, J. Ch. Ch.
*Poole, W. Oriel
*Poore, D. Exeter
*Popham, F. L. All Souls
*Popham, W. Oriel
Portal, M. Ch. Ch.
Powles, R. C. Exeter
*Powell, J. C. Trinity
*Poynder, Rev. F. Wadham
*Poynder, E. S. Brase-nose
*Poynder, T. H. A. Brase-nose
*Pratt, Rev. H. E. University
*Prendergast, W. P. Trinity

*Prescott, Rev. P. Oriel
*Preston, W. T. Brase-nose
*Pretyman, Rev. J. R. Trinity
*Pretyman, H. G. Oriel
*Prevost, Rev. Sir G. Bart. Oriel
*Price, B. Worcester
Prichard, C. E. Balliol
Prichard, T. Oriel
Prior, J. L. Exeter
*Pritchard, H. Corpus
Proctor, G. H. Balliol
Prothero, G. Brase-nose
*Prout, J. W. Wadham
*Puckle, Rev. J. Brase-nose
*Puller, C. Ch. Ch.
*Pugh, Rev. J. W. Balliol
*Pulling, Rev. W. Brase-nose
*Pusey, Rev. W. B. Oriel

*Raikes, R. Exeter
Rainier, Rev. G. Brase-nose
*Randolph, J. J. Merton
Rashleigh, H. B. Exeter
Rashleigh, J. Balliol
*Rathbone, J. Oriel
*Rawlinson, Rev. G. Exeter
*Rawlinson, Rev. H. St. John's
Rawlinson, G. St. John's
*Rawnsley, E. Brase-nose
*Rawnsley, R. D. Magdalen
Rawstone, W. E. Ch. Ch.
*Reeves, Rev. F. J. H. Merton
*Reid, D. University
Reiby, T. Trinity
*Renaud, Rev. G. Corpus
*Renaud, W. Exeter
Repton, G. W. University
*Reynolds, C. W. Brase-nose
*Richards, Rev. T. M. Wadham
*Richards, H. Ch. Ch.
Richards, E. V. Ch. Ch.
Richards, R. M. Merton
*Richardson, J. J. Oriel
*Richardson, Rev. J. Queen's
Richardson, W. H. Oriel
*Rickards, G. Queen's
*Rickards, Rev. R. Balliol

*Ridley, G. Ch. Ch.
*Ridley, Rev. H. University
*Ridley, M. W. Ch. Ch.
*Ridley, Rev. W. H. Ch. Ch.
Ridley, N. J. Ch. Ch.
*Risley, Rev. J. H. New College
*Robartes, T. J. A. Ch. Ch.
*Robarts, A. G. Ch. Ch.
*Roberts, T. W. Trinity
*Robin, P. R. Brase-nose
Robson, T. U. Magdalen Hall
*Rogers, Rev. J. Balliol
*Rogers, F. Oriel
*Rogers, T. E. Corpus
*Rogers, W. Exeter
*Rogers, E. Ch. Ch.
Rogers, H. St. A. Exeter
*Rooke, Rev. W. J. E. Brase-nose
*Rooke, F. J. Oriel
*Rolls, J. E. Ch. Ch.
Roope, R. Wadham
*Roper, R. New Inn Hall
Rosseter, R. G. Ch. Ch.
*Round, F. P. Balliol
*Round, J. Balliol
Round, E. Balliol
*Rous, Hon. T. M. Balliol
*Rowlandson, A. Brase-nose
*Royds, Rev. J. L. Wadham
*Rudd, Rev. L. Pembroke
Rusher, W. E. Magdalen Hall
*Rushout, G. Ch. Ch.
Ruskin, J. Ch. Ch.
*Russell, W. St. Mary Hall
*Ryder, T. D. Oriel
*Ryder, W. D. Exeter
Ryder, R. C. Oriel
*Ryle, J. C. Ch. Ch.
Ryle, F. Ch. Ch.

*Sale, C. J. Lincoln
*Salmon, T. D. Exeter
*Salmon, E. Exeter
*Salt, Rev. J. Balliol
*Sandbach, G. Brase-nose
Sanderson, W. St. Mary Hall
*Sankey, P. St. John's

*Saunders, Rev. A. P. Ch. Ch.
Saunders, G. E. Wadham
*Savage, W. Queen's
*Sawbridge, E. H. Balliol
*Sayres, J. Wadham
Scobell, S. G. Oriel
*Sconce, R. K. Brase-nose
*Scott, C. Brase-nose
*Scott, G. D. Trinity
*Scott, Rev. R. Balliol
*Scott, M. D. University
Scott, W. H. Trinity
*Scott-Murray, C. R. Ch. Ch.
*Scratchley, Rev. C. J. Brase-nose
Scratton, T. Ch. Ch.
Seaham, Lord, Balliol
*Sealy, E. U. Ch. Ch.
Sealy, W. St. Alban Hall
Senior, N. Ch. Ch.
*Sewell, Rev. J. E. New College
*Seymer, H. K. All Souls
*Seymer, J. G. St. Alban Hall
Seymour, C. F. University
Seymour, E. R. Oriel
Seymour, H. Ch. Ch.
Seymour, J. B. Balliol
Shand, G. Queen's
*Sheppard, T. Oriel
*Sheppard, W. Oriel
*Sheppard, Rev. J. G. Wadham
*Sheppard, Rev. J. L. Wadham
Sheppard, H. J. Queen's
Shiffner, G. Ch. Ch.
*Shirreff, Rev. R. St. John, Wadham
*Short, Rev. A. Ch. Ch.
*Shortland, Rev. J. Oriel
Sibthorp, H. A. M. W. Queen's
*Sillifant, W. T. Exeter
*Simcox, Rev. T. G. Wadham
*Simpkinson, Rev. T. Balliol
Simpson, J. Exeter
*Sinclair, Rev. W. St. Mary Hall
*Skinner, A. M. Balliol
*Skrine, H. Wadham
*Skrine, H. D. Wadham
*Sladen, Rev. E. H. M. Balliol
Slater, J. Oriel
Slegg, J. Queen's

Slessor, G. H. University
*Smith, A. Ch. Ch.
*Smith, Rev. B. Magdalen
*Smith, C. G. Wadham
*Smith, E. B. Queen's
*Smith, J. Exeter
*Smith, Rev. J. F. Brase-nose
Smyth, C. D. Brase-nose
Smyth, W. H. Ch. Ch.
*Smythe, W. B. Corpus
*Smythies, C. N. Trinity
*Sneyd, Rev. W. Ch. Ch.
*Snowden, Rev. C. Worcester
*Soltau, W. F. Balliol
Sotham, F. Magdalen Hall
*Spooner, W. Oriel
*Stanley, Rev. A. P. University
Stanhope, H. S. Balliol
*Starkey, Rev. A. B. C. St. John's
St. Clair, Hon. J. Ch. Ch.
*Steele, J. M. Brase-nose
*Stephens, H. L. Oriel
*Stephens, E. Exeter
Stephenson, J. H. Queen's
*Sterling, Rev. C. J. St. Mary Hall
*Steuart, C. New College
Stevenson, S. W. Exeter
*Stewart, E. Oriel
*Stewart Mackenzie, R. W. St. John's
*St. John, A. Ch. Ch.
*St. Ledger, A. F. B. Brase-nose
*Stoddart, Rev. W. W. St. John's
*Stokes, W. H. Wadham
Stokes, E. Ch. Ch.
*Stone, J. S. Ch. Ch.
Strange, R. Ch. Ch.
*Strangways, S. F. Ch. Ch.
*Street, Rev. A. W. Pembroke
*Strong, Rev. C. Wadham
*Stuart, H. Trinity
*Sugden, E. St. Alban Hall
*Sullivan, Rev. H. W. Balliol
*Sumner, C. Balliol
*Sumner, Rev. J. Balliol
Sumner, J. H. R. Balliol
Sumner, R. Balliol
*Surtees, S. V. University
*Surtees, W. E. University

*Surtees, S. F. University
*Surtees, Rev. H. R. St. Mary Hall
*Sutherland, A. J. Ch. Ch.
*Sutton, R. S. Exeter
Swire, S. University
Sydenham, L. W. Balliol

*Tait, Rev. A. C. Balliol
*Tallents, Rev. P. W. Wadham
*Tancred, T. Merton
*Tancred, W. Ch. Ch.
*Tarbutt, Rev. A. Wadham
*Tate, F. University
*Tawke, A. Trinity
*Tawney, A. R. Merton
*Taylor, A. Trinity
*Taylor, S. W. Ch. Ch.
Taylor, R. J. Trinity
Teesdale, C. B. Ch. Ch.
*Thomas, G. T. St. Mary Hall
*Thomas, J. Trinity
*Thomas, Rev. R. J. F. Ch. Ch.
*Thomas, G. Trinity
*Thompson, Rev. W. Queen's
*Thornton, Rev. C. Ch. Ch.
*Thornton, E. Ch. Ch.
*Tickell, G. Balliol
Tickell, E. Balliol
Tickell, H. Queen's
*Tillard, P. Brase-nose
Tipping, F. G. Brase-nose
*Tooze, Rev. H. J. Brase-nose
*Torrens, H. Ch. Ch.
*Tottenham, P. Exeter
*Touchit, J. H. Exeter
*Townend, J. Oriel
*Townsend, Rev. J. F. University
*Tracy, Rev. J. Oriel
*Tracy, Rev. E. H. Exeter
Travers, C. H. Queen's
*Trench, Rev. F. Oriel
*Trevor, Rev. G. Magdalen Hall
*Tripp, H. Worcester
Tristrem, E. R. Lincoln
*Trollope, J. Pembroke
Trower, A. Lincoln
*Tufnell, E. C. Balliol

*Tufnell, Rev. E. W. Wadham
*Tufnell, H. Ch. Ch.
Tufnell, F. Wadham
*Tupper, C. W. Exeter
*Tupper, D. Brase-nose
*Turner, D. Magdalen
*Twemlow, T. F. Ch. Ch.
*Twining, A. Oriel
*Twining, W. Balliol
*Twiss, T. University
*Twisleton, E. B. Balliol
*Twiss, E. R. University
Twopeny, T. N. Oriel
*Tyers, J. St. Mary Hall
*Tylden, W. Balliol
Tyler, O. B. Trinity
*Tyndale, J. W. Ch. Ch.
*Tyndale, Rev. H. Wadham
*Tyrwhitt, R. E. Brase-nose

*Upton, W. J. New College
*Usborne, H. Balliol
*Utterton, Rev. J. S. Oriel

*Valpy, R. H. Balliol
Vale, W. S. Worcester
Vansittart, C. Oriel
*Vaughan, H. H. Oriel
*Vaughan, Rev. J. J. Merton
*Vaughan, Rev. J. Balliol
*Vaughan, Rev. E. P. Balliol
*Vaux, W. S. W. Balliol
*Venables, W. Exeter
Vernon, E. H. H. University
*Vesey, Hon. T. Ch. Ch.
*Villiers, Hon. E. E. Merton
*Villiers, Viscount, Ch. Ch. M. P.
*Villiers, Hon. and Rev. H. M.
  Ch. Ch.
*Vipan, F. J. Wadham
Vizard, A. Exeter

*Walker, J. E. Oriel
*Walker, J. University
*Walker, Rev. J. Wadham

*Walker, Rev. S. H. Balliol
*Walker, W. S. St. Mary Hall
*Walker, R. O. St. John's
*Walker, T. W. Exeter
*Wall, H. E. New College
*Wall, Rev. H. St. Alban Hall
*Waller, Rev. S. R. Brase-nose
*Walter, J. Exeter
Walters, H. Ch. Ch.
*Ward, G. A. Ch. Ch.
*Ward, Rev. H. Exeter
*Ward, Rev. W. G. Balliol
*Ward, W. R. Balliol
*Ward, Rev. W. H. P. Oriel
*Ward, Rev. R. Oriel
Ward, Lord, Trinity
*Warner, G. B. L. Balliol
*Warter, Rev. J. W. Ch. Ch.
Wasey, J. S. Trinity
Waters, E. Worcester
Watson, G. W. Merton
*Watt, F. University
*Way, Rev. H. H. Merton
Wayte, S. W. Trinity
*Weare, Rev. T. W. Ch. Ch.
*Webber, W. F. Merton
*Webster, Rev. J. Trinity
Webster, M. Lincoln
Weekes, F. A. Wadham
*Weir, J. G. Brase-nose
*Welch, J. Queen's
*West, Hon. R. W. Balliol
*West, Rev. T. W. Magdalen Hall
*Wetherell, Rev. C. Worcester
*Whalley, J. P. University
*Whately, W. Ch. Ch.
*Whately, Rev. C. S. St. Mary Hall
*Whatman, J. Ch. Ch.
*Whatman, W. Ch. Ch.
*Wheeler, Rev. G. D. Wadham
*Wheler, Rev. H. T. Merton
*Whipman, T. W. Balliol
*Whitbread, G. Brase-nose
*White, J. Lincoln
*White, W. F. Trinity
*White, W. Ch. Ch.
*Whitehorne, H. Wadham
*Whitmore, T. C. Ch. Ch. M. P.

*Whitter, T. A. Brase-nose
*Whittaker, J. University
*Whorwood, Rev. T. H. Magdalen
*Wickens, J. Balliol
*Wigan, A. St. John's
Wiggin, W. Exeter
*Wilberforce, Rev. H. W. Oriel
*Wilberforce, Rev. R. I. Archdeacon
  of York
*Wilberforce, Rev. S. Oriel, Arch-
  deacon of Surrey
Wildbore, R. Brase-nose
*Williams, Rev. J. H. St. Mary Hall
*Williams, R. Oriel, M. P.
*Williams, P. Ch. Ch.
*Williams, Rev. H. B. New College
*Williams, P. P. Ch. Ch.
*Williams, Rev. E. T. Exeter
*Williams, M. Balliol
Willock, W. C. Balliol
*Wilmot, J. E. Balliol
Wilson, T. Brase-nose
Wilson, J. H. Exeter
*Wilson, F. W. New Inn Hall
*Wilson, Rev. R. F. Oriel
Wilson, W. Wadham
*Winchester, Rev. W. Ch. Ch.
*Wing, J. University
*Wingfield, Rev. W. F. Ch. Ch.
*Winnington, T. Ch. Ch. M. P.
*Wiseman, W. H. Balliol
*Wither, Rev. L. B. Oriel
*Wodehouse, T. Balliol
Wodehouse, W. Exeter
*Wood, Rev. J. R. Ch. Ch.
*Wood, R. Oriel
*Wood, S. F. Oriel
Wood, A. Ch. Ch.
*Woodall, Rev. H. E. Exeter
*Woodcock, Rev. C. Ch. Ch.
*Woollcombe, Rev. E. C. Balliol
*Woollcombe, Rev. W. W. Exeter
*Woollcombe, E. Lincoln
*Woolley, Rev. J. University
*Wordsworth, Rev. C. Ch. Ch.
*Worsley, Rev. J. H. Magdalen
Worthington, G. St. John's
*Wortley, Hon. J. S. Merton, M. P.

*Wrangham, D. C. Brase-nose
*Wrench, Rev. F. Trinity
*Wrench, Rev. O. Worcester
*Wright, E. Oriel
*Wright, Rev. T. B. Wadham
*Wrightson, T. B. Brase-nose
*Wrottesley, Rev. E. University
Wyatt, C. F. Ch. Ch.
*Wykeham, A. W. Trinity
*Wylie, W. M. Merton
Wynne-Edwards, J. C. Brase-nose

*Yard, A. Exeter
*Yard, Rev. T. Exeter
Yearwood, S. St. Alban Hall
*Yeatman, H. F. Balliol
*Yonge, C. D. St. Mary Hall
*Young, Rev. J. C. Worcester
*Young, J. Corpus, M. P.
*Young, R. P. Exeter
*Young, Rev. R. Oriel

*Zincke, Rev. F. B. Wadham

LIST OF MEMBERS

WHO HAVE SERVED ON COMMITTEES.

LIST OF MEMBERS

WHO HAVE SERVED ON COMMITTEES.

———

Those marked with an Asterisk were elected in consequence of resignations.

———

LENT TERM, 1826.

MR. DODGSON, Ch. Ch. PRESIDENT.
*MR. WRANGHAM, Brase-nose, PRESIDENT.

Hon. T. S. Wortley, Ch. Ch. *Treasurer*
Mr. D. C. Wrangham, Brase-nose
Mr. R. A. Hornby, Oriel
Mr. S. Wilberforce, Oriel
Mr. E. E. Villiers, Merton
Mr. T. Macdonald, Oriel
Mr. H. Merivale, Trinity
Mr. J. R. Wood, Ch. Ch.
Mr. R. Durnford, Magdalen   *Mr. D. Smith, Ch. Ch.

EASTER TERM, 1826.

MR. R. DURNFORD, Magdalen, PRESIDENT.
*MR. E. E. VILLIERS, Merton, PRESIDENT.

Mr. H. Merivale, Trinity, *Treasurer*
Mr. T. B. Hobhouse, Balliol
Mr. S. Wilberforce, Oriel
Hon. C. Murray, All Souls
Mr. E. Feild, Queen's
Mr. O. B. Cole, Ch. Ch.
Mr. T. Macdonald, Oriel, *Secretary*

MICHAELMAS TERM, 1826.

MR. T. MACDONALD, Oriel, PRESIDENT.

Mr. H. Merivale, Trinity, *Treasurer*
Mr. R. A. Hornby, Oriel
Mr. T. B. Hobhouse, Balliol
Mr. F. Trench, Oriel
Mr. E. E. Villiers, Merton
Mr. S. Wilberforce, Oriel
Mr. C. Puller, Ch. Ch.
Hon. C. Murray, All Souls
Mr. O. B. Cole, Ch. Ch.
Mr. H. Tufnell, Ch. Ch. *Secretary*

LENT TERM, 1827.

MR. DOUGLAS SMITH, Ch. Ch. PRESIDENT.
*MR. H. TUFNELL, Ch. Ch. PRESIDENT.

Mr T. Macdonald, Oriel, *Treasurer*
Mr D. Smith, Ch. Ch.
Mr C. Puller, Ch. Ch.
Mr. T. B. Hobhouse, Balliol
Mr. E. B. Twistleton, Trinity
Mr. H. Merivale, Trinity
Mr. E. E. Villiers, Merton
Mr. F. Trench, Oriel
Mr. J. Pearson, Balliol
Mr. T. B. Tufnell, Ch. Ch. *Secretary*

EASTER TERM, 1827.

MR. J. PEARSON, Balliol, PRESIDENT.

Mr. Douglas Smith, *Treasurer*
Mr. H. Tufnell, Ch. Ch.
Mr. F. Trench, Oriel
Mr. C. Puller, Ch. Ch.
Mr. Maberley, Magdalen
Mr. T. B. Hobhouse, Balliol
Mr. R. A. Hornby, Oriel
Mr. C. Courtenay, Ch. Ch.
Mr. E. B. Twistleton, Trinity
Mr. W. J. Crichton, Merton, *Secretary*

MICHAELMAS TERM, 1827.

MR. H. MERIVALE, Trinity, PRESIDENT.

Mr. D. Smith, Ch. Ch. *Treasurer*
Mr. C. Puller, Ch. Ch.
Mr. E. B. Twistleton, Trinity
Mr. J. Pearson, Balliol
Mr. F. Trench, Oriel
Mr. Maberley, Magdalen
Mr. E. P. Price, Lincoln
Mr. S. Wilberforce, Oriel
Mr. C. Baring, Ch. Ch.
Mr. T. B. Hobhouse, Balliol, *Secretary*

*Mr. W. K. Hamilton, Ch. Ch.
*Mr. A. Grant, New Coll.
*Mr. R. G. Mackintosh, Balliol

LENT TERM, 1828.

MR. DOUGLAS SMITH, Ch. Ch. PRESIDENT.

Mr. T. B. Hobhouse, Balliol, *Treasurer*
Mr. C. Wordsworth, Ch. Ch.
Sir Stephen Glynne, Ch. Ch.
Mr. E. B. Twistleton, Trinity
Mr. R. A. Hornby, Oriel
Mr. A. Grant, New Coll.
Mr. R. G. Mackintosh, New Coll.
Mr. H. Merivale, Trinity
Mr. C. Puller, Ch. Ch. *Secretary*

EASTER TERM, 1828.

MR. T. B. HOBHOUSE, Balliol, PRESIDENT.

Mr. C. Wordsworth, Ch. Ch. *Treasurer*
Mr. R. G. Mackintosh, New Coll.
Mr. H. Merivale, Trinity
Mr. S. Wilberforce, Oriel
Mr. A. Grant, New Coll.
Mr. H. Tufnell, Balliol
Mr. J. D. Harding, Oriel
Mr. E. B. Twistleton, Trinity
Mr. W. K. Hamilton, Ch. Ch. *Secretary*

MICHAELMAS TERM, 1828.

MR. C. BARING, Ch. Ch. President.

Mr. S. Wilberforce, Oriel, *Treasurer*
Mr. W. K. Hamilton, Ch. Ch.
Mr. E. V. Neale, Oriel
Mr. W. B. Smythe, Corpus
Mr. J. Young, Corpus
Sir J. Hanmer, Ch. Ch.
Mr. J. D. Harding, Oriel
Mr. B. Harrison, Ch. Ch.
Mr. T. D. Acland, Ch. Ch. *Secretary*

LENT TERM, 1829.

MR. S. WILBERFORCE, Oriel, President.
*MR. T. D. ACLAND, Ch. Ch. President.

Mr. J. D. Harding, Oriel, *Treasurer*
Mr. C. Puller, Ch. Ch.
Mr. E. P. Price, Worcester
Mr. W. S. Blackstone, Ch. Ch.
Mr. H. Hughes, Trinity
Mr. R. F. Wilson, Oriel
Mr. E. V. Neale, Oriel
Mr. W. B. Smythe, Corpus
Mr. A. H. D. Acland, Ch. Ch. *Secretary*

EASTER TERM, 1829.

MR. G. R. MONCRIEFF, New Coll. President.

Mr. A. H. D. Acland, Ch. Ch. *Treasurer*
Mr. J. D. Harding, Oriel
Mr. S. Wilberforce, Oriel
Mr. J. Anstice, Ch. Ch.
Mr. R. F. Wilson, Oriel
Mr. T. Chamberlain, Ch. Ch.
Sir John Hanmer, Ch. Ch.
Mr. W. S. Blackstone, Ch. Ch.
Mr. H. C. Manning, Balliol, *Secretary*

*Sir John Hanmer, Ch. Ch. *Treasurer*
*Mr. Vaughan, Balliol
*Mr. J. M. Gaskell, Ch. Ch.
*Mr. F. H. Doyle, Ch. Ch.
*Mr. J. Hope, Ch. Ch.

*Mr. Neale, Oriel, *Secretary*

MICHAELMAS TERM, 1829.

MR. H. C. MANNING, Balliol, PRESIDENT.

Mr. J. M. Gaskell, Ch. Ch.
Treasurer
Hon. S. Herbert, Oriel
Mr. R. F. Wilson, Oriel
Mr. J. Odell, Ch. Ch.
Mr. G. R. Moncrieff, New Coll.
Sir John Hanmer, Ch. Ch.
Mr. F. H. Doyle, Ch. Ch.
Mr. A. H. D. Acland, Ch. Ch.   *Marquis of Abercorn, Ch. Ch.
Mr. H. C. Manning, Balliol,   *Mr. Vaughan, Balliol
Secretary

LENT TERM, 1830.

HON. SIDNEY HERBERT, Oriel, PRESIDENT.

Mr. J. Odell, Ch. Ch. *Treasurer*
Sir John Hanmer, Ch. Ch.   *Marquis of Abercorn, Ch. Ch.
Mr. F. H. Doyle, Ch. Ch.
Mr. W. E. Gladstone, Ch. Ch.
Mr. C. Thornton, Ch. Ch.
Mr. R. F. Wilson, Oriel
Mr. Vaughan, Balliol
Mr. H Moncrieff, New Coll.
Mr. J. M. Gaskell, Ch. Ch.
Secretary

EASTER TERM, 1830.

MR. J. M. GASKELL, Ch. Ch. PRESIDENT.

Mr. A. H. D. Acland, Ch. Ch. *Treasurer*
Mr. C. Thornton, Ch. Ch.
Hon. J. Bruce, Ch. Ch.
Mr. R. F. Wilson, Oriel
Mr. Vaughan, Balliol
Mr. R. Williams, Oriel
Mr. J. R. Oldham, Oriel
Mr. J. E Lyall, Balliol
Mr. W. E. Gladstone, Ch. Ch. *Secretary*

MICHAELMAS TERM, 1830.

MR. W. E. GLADSTONE, Ch. Ch. PRESIDENT.

Mr. T. D. Acland, Ch. Ch. *Librarian*
Mr. A. H. D. Acland, Ch. Ch. *Treasurer*
Mr. C. Thornton, Ch. Ch.
Mr. Vaughan, Balliol
Earl of Lincoln, Ch. Ch.
Mr. R. Williams, Oriel
Mr. R. G. Alston, Ch. Ch.
Mr. W. E. Jelf, Ch. Ch.
Mr. E. J. Lyall, Balliol, *Secretary.*

*Mr. G. Rickards, Trinity
*Mr. F. Rogers, Oriel
*Mr. S. C. Denison, Balliol

LENT TERM, 1831.

HON. J. BRUCE, Ch. Ch. PRESIDENT.

Mr. G. Rickards, Trinity, *Librarian*
Mr. J. E. Lyall, Balliol, *Treasurer*
Earl of Lincoln, Ch. Ch.
Mr. J. Anstice, Ch. Ch.
Hon. J. Hewitt, Ch. Ch.
Mr. R. Scott, Ch. Ch.
Mr. C. Thornton, Ch. Ch.
Mr. S. C. Denison, Balliol, *Secretary*

EASTER TERM, 1831.

MR. J. E. LYALL, Balliol, PRESIDENT.

Mr. B. Harrison, Ch. Ch. *Librarian*
Mr. A. H. D. Acland, Ch. Ch. *Treasurer*
Mr. C. H. Knatchbull, Trinity
Mr. J. Anstice, Ch. Ch.
Mr. Vaughan, Balliol
Hon. S. Herbert, Oriel
Mr. H. Moncrieff, New College
Mr. R. Palmer, Trinity
Mr. G. Rickards, Trinity, *Secretary*

*Mr. E. Massie, Wadh. *Librarian*

*Earl of Lincoln, Ch. Ch.
*Mr. W. E. Jelf, Ch. Ch.
*Mr. A. C. Tait, Balliol
*Mr. W. F. White, Trin. *Secretary*

*Mr. C. H. Oakes, Merton
*Mr. F. J. H. Reeves, Merton
*Mr. R. Lowe, Univ.

MICHAELMAS TERM, 1831.

EARL OF LINCOLN, Ch. Ch. PRESIDENT.

Mr. R. G. Alston, Ch. Ch. *Librarian*
Mr. C. H. Oakes, Merton, *Treasurer*
Mr. J. Anstice, Ch. Ch.
Mr. Vaughan, Ch. Ch.
Mr. R. Williams, Oriel
Mr. R. Scott, Ch. Ch.
Mr. G. Rickards, Trinity
Mr. C. H. Knatchbull, Trinity
Mr. W. E. Jelf, Ch. Ch. *Secretary*

LENT TERM, 1832.

MR. G. RICKARDS, Trinity, PRESIDENT.

Mr. L. D. Goldsmid, Balliol,
  Librarian
Mr. F. J. H. Reeves, Merton,
  Treasurer
Mr. E. Massie, Wadham
Mr. R. Palmer, Trinity
Mr. B. Harrison, Ch. Ch.
Mr. E. Cardwell, Balliol
Mr. A. H. D. Acland, Ch. Ch.
Mr. W. E. Jelf, Ch. Ch.   *Mr. W. G. Ward, Ch. Ch.
Mr. A. C. Tait, Balliol, *Secretary*

EASTER TERM, 1832.

MR. R. PALMER, Trinity, PRESIDENT.

Mr. L. D. Goldsmid, Balliol,
  Librarian
Mr. F. J. H. Reeves, Merton,   *Mr. W. G. Ward, Ch. Ch.
  Treasurer   *Treasurer*
Mr. W. G. Ward, Ch. Ch.
Mr. A. C. Tait, Balliol
Mr. A. H. D. Acland, Ch. Ch.
Hon. J. Hewitt, Ch. Ch.
Mr. E. Massie, Wadham
Mr. R. Lowe, University   *Mr. M. W. Mayow, Ch. Ch.
Mr. E. Cardwell, Balliol, *Secretary*

C

MICHAELMAS TERM, 1832.

MR. W. G. WARD, Ch. Ch. PRESIDENT.

Mr. L. D. de Visme, Balliol,
Librarian
Mr. W. G. Brandreth, Ch. Ch.
Treasurer
Mr. E. Cardwell, Balliol
Mr. R. Palmer, Trinity   *Mr. T. Allies, Wadham
Mr. A. C. Tait, Balliol
Mr. M. W. Mayow, Ch. Ch.
Mr. J. Puckle, Brase-nose
Mr. R. G. Alston, Ch. Ch.
Mr. E. Massie, Wadham, *Secretary*.

LENT TERM, 1833.

MR. E. CARDWELL, Balliol, PRESIDENT.

Mr. R. Palmer, Trinity, *Librarian*   *Mr. T. Allies, Wadham, *Librarian*
Mr. W. G. Ward, Ch. Ch. *Trea-*   *Mr. G. Tickell, Balliol
surer   *Mr. A. C. Tait, Balliol
Mr. T. Allies, Wadham   *Mr. N. Oxnam, Exeter
Mr. M. W. Mayow, Ch. Ch.
Mr. J. Puckle, Brase-nose
Mr. E. Massie, Wadham
Mr. G. Rickards, Trinity
Mr. L. D. de Visme, Balliol
Mr. W. G. Brandreth, Ch. Ch.
Secretary

EASTER TERM, 1833.

MR. A. C. TAIT, Balliol, PRESIDENT.

Mr. G. Rickards, Trinity, *Libra-*   *Mr. E. Cardwell, Balliol, *Librarian*
rian   *Mr. W. C. Cotton, Ch. Ch.
Mr. W. G. Ward, Ch. Ch. *Trea-*
surer
Mr. E. Cardwell, Balliol
Mr. M. W. Mayow, Ch. Ch.
Mr. G. Tickell, Balliol
Mr. L. D. de Visme, Balliol
Mr. W. W. Woollcombe, Exeter
Mr. J. Puckle, Brase-nose
Mr. H. Barne, Exeter, *Secretary*

MICHAELMAS TERM, 1833.

MR. E. MASSIE, Wadham, PRESIDENT.

Mr. F. P. Lowe, University, *Librarian*

Mr. W. G. Ward, Ch. Ch. *Treasurer*

Mr. W. W. Woollcombe, Exeter

Mr. T. Allies, Wadham

Mr. J. Adams, Ch. Ch.

Mr. C. Marriott, Oriel

Mr. W. H. Awdry, Exeter

Mr. E. Simpson, Corpus

Mr. T. Brancker, Wadham, *Secretary*

*Mr. G. E. Bruxner, Ch. Ch. *Treasurer*

*Mr. W. Twining, Balliol

*Mr. W. C. Cotton, Ch. Ch.

*Mr. G. F. Thomas, Ch. Ch.

*Mr. C. W. Bingham, New Coll.

LENT TERM, 1834.

MR. C. MARRIOTT, Oriel, PRESIDENT.

Mr. G. Rickards, Trinity, *Librarian*

Mr. G. C. Pearson, Ch. Ch. *Treasurer*

Mr. E. Marjoribanks, Ch. Ch.

Mr. W. W. Stoddart, St. John's

Mr. J. Adams, Ch. Ch.

Mr. W. Twining, Balliol

Mr. H. Rawlinson, St. John's

Mr. W. W. Woollcombe, Exeter

Mr. A. R. Campbell, Balliol, *Secretary*

EASTER TERM, 1834.

MR. H. SINCLAIR, St. Mary Hall, PRESIDENT.

Mr. G. Rickards, Trinity, *Librarian*

Mr. E. Marjoribanks, Ch. Ch. *Treasurer*

Mr. J. Adams, Ch. Ch.

Mr. A. R. Campbell, Balliol

Mr. J. Puckle, Brase-nose

Mr. C. J. Sterling, St. Mary Hall

Mr. A. C. Tait, Balliol

Mr. W. C. Cotton, Ch. Ch.

Mr. F. W. Faber, Balliol, *Secretary*

MICHAELMAS TERM, 1834.

MR. J. ADAMS, Ch. Ch. PRESIDENT.

Mr. G. C. Pearson, Ch. Ch.
Librarian
Mr. J. M. Capes, Balliol, *Trea-
surer*
Mr. W. C. Cotton, Ch. Ch.
Mr. W. G. Ward, Lincoln
Mr. G. Tickell, Balliol
Mr. F. W. Faber, Balliol   *Mr. Marsh, Oriel
Mr. A. C. Tait, Balliol
Mr. H. Rawlinson, St. John's
Mr. J. R. Cornish, Ch. Ch.
Secretary

LENT TERM, 1835.

MR. W. G. WARD, Balliol, PRESIDENT.

Mr. H. Sinclair, St. Mary Hall, *Librarian*
Mr. J. A. Hussey, Balliol, *Treasurer*
Mr. A. C. Tait, Balliol
Mr. J. M. Capes, Balliol
Mr. J. Adams, Ch. Ch.
Mr. W. C. Cotton, Ch. Ch.
Mr. W. Marsh, Oriel
Mr. H. Rawlinson, St. John's
Mr. J. R. Cornish, Ch. Ch. *Secretary*

EASTER TERM, 1835.

MR. J. M. CAPES, Balliol, PRESIDENT.

Mr. W. G. Ward, Balliol, *Librarian*
Mr. J. A. Hussey, Balliol, *Treasurer*
Mr. W. C. Cotton, Ch. Ch.
Mr. J. Adams, Ch. Ch.
Mr. J. R. Cornish, Ch. Ch.
Mr. G. K. Morrell, St. John's
Mr. G. Mellish, University
Mr. G. E. Bruxner, Ch. Ch.
Mr. W. Marsh, Oriel, *Secretary*

MICHAELMAS TERM, 1835.

MR. E. CARDWELL, Balliol, PRESIDENT.

Mr. G. E. Brancker, Wadham, *Librarian*
Mr. G. Mellish, University, *Treasurer*
Mr. W. C. Cotton, Ch. Ch.
Mr. W. Marsh, Oriel
Mr. J. R. Cornish, Ch. Ch.
Mr. H. Barne, Exeter
Mr. J. Puckle, Brase-nose
Mr. E. Massie, Wadham
Mr. G. K. Morrell, St. John's, *Secretary*

LENT TERM, 1836.

MR. T. BRANCKER, Wadham, PRESIDENT.

Mr. J. R. Cornish, Ch. Ch. *Librarian*
Mr. G. Mellish, University, *Treasurer*
Mr. W. C. Cotton, Ch. Ch.
Mr. W. Marsh, Oriel
Mr. G. K. Morrell, St. John's
Mr. G. R. Moncrieff, Balliol
Mr. T. Phinn, Exeter
Mr. W. H. Ridley, Ch. Ch.
Mr. H. W. Cripps, New Coll. *Secretary*

EASTER TERM, 1836.

MR J. R. CORNISH, Wadham, PRESIDENT.

Mr. W. Marsh, Oriel, *Librarian*
Mr. G. R. Moncrieff, Balliol, *Treasurer*
Mr. H. W. Cripps, New Coll.
Mr. G. Mellish, University
Mr. W. H. Ridley, Ch. Ch.
Mr. H. W. Phillott, Ch. Ch.
Mr. T. Brancker, Wadham
Mr. E. Salmon, Exeter
Mr. T. Phinn, Exeter, *Secretary*

MICHAELMAS TERM, 1836.

MR. W. MARSH, Oriel, PRESIDENT.

Mr. G. Mellish, University, *Librarian*
Mr. G. R. Moncrieff, Balliol, *Treasurer*
Mr. T. D. Bernard, Exeter
Mr. J. R. Cornish, Ch. Ch.
Mr. H. W. Cripps, New Coll.
Mr. J. A. Hessey, St. John's
Mr. E. Monro, Oriel
Mr. H. W. Phillott, Ch. Ch.
Mr. W. H. Ridley, Ch. Ch. *Secretary*

LENT TERM, 1837.

MR. H. W. CRIPPS, New Coll. PRESIDENT.

Mr. G R. Moncrieff, Balliol, *Librarian*
Mr. J. A. Hessey, St. John's, *Treasurer*
Mr. W. H. Ridley, Ch. Ch.
Mr. H. W. Phillott, Ch. Ch.
Mr. C. Campbell, Exeter
Mr. G. C. Fowler, Pembroke
Mr. J. S. Utterton, Oriel
Mr. E. Monro, Oriel
Mr. G. L. Browne, St. John's, *Secretary*

EASTER TERM, 1837.

MR. G. R. MONCRIEFF, Balliol, PRESIDENT.

Mr. G. C. Fowler, Pembroke, *Librarian*
Mr. J. A. Hessey, St. John's, *Treasurer*
Mr. G. L. Browne, St. John's
Mr. G. H. U. Fagan, Oriel
Mr. W. C. Lake, Balliol
Mr. F. Poynder, Wadham
Mr. H. W. Phillott, Ch. Ch.
Mr. E. Salmon, Exeter
Mr. C. Campbell, Exeter, *Secretary*

MICHAELMAS TERM, 1837.

MR. J. A. HESSEY, St. John's, PRESIDENT.

Mr. W. W. Woollcombe, Exeter, *Librarian*
Mr. W. C. Lake, Balliol, *Treasurer*
Mr. G. R. Moncrieff, Balliol
Mr. C. Campbell, Exeter
Mr. H. W. Phillott, Ch. Ch.
Mr. W. Newman, Oriel
Mr. E. Salmon, Exeter
Mr. S. H. Northcote, Balliol
Mr. F. Poynder, Wadham, *Secretary*

LENT TERM, 1838.

MR. W. H. RIDLEY, Ch. Ch. PRESIDENT.

Rev. W. C. Cotton, Ch. Ch. *Librarian*
Mr. S. H. Northcote, Balliol, *Treasurer*
Mr. W. Buckley, Brase-nose
Mr. F. Courtenay, Exeter
Mr. H. Highton, Queen's
Mr. J. S. Hodson, Merton
Mr. W. Lonsdale, Oriel
Mr. H. W. Phillott, Ch. Ch.
Mr. W. H. Sulivan, Balliol, *Secretary*

EASTER TERM, 1838.

MR. W. C. LANE, Balliol, PRESIDENT.

Rev. W. C. Cotton, Ch. Ch. *Librarian*
Mr. H. Highton, Queen's, *Treasurer*
Mr. G. H. U. Fagan, Oriel
Mr. W. H. Ridley, Ch. Ch.
Mr. H. W. Sulivan, Balliol
Mr. F. Courtenay, Exeter
Mr. W. Newman, Oriel
Mr. G. R. Moncrieff, Balliol
Mr. W. Buckley, Brase-nose, *Secretary*

MICHAELMAS TERM, 1838.

MR. H. HIGHTON, Queen's, PRESIDENT.

Rev. W. C. Cotton, Ch. Ch. *Librarian*
Mr. W. Buckley, Brasen-nose, *Treasurer*
Mr. W. C. Lake, Balliol
Mr. G. R. Moncrieff, Balliol
Mr. J. Ruskin, Ch. Ch.
Mr. R. J. Buddicom, Brasen-nose
Mr. F. W. Robertson, Brasen-nose
Mr. C. T. Arnold, Magdalen Hall
Mr. H. Fox, Wadham

LENT TERM, 1839.

MR. G. R. MONCRIEFF, Balliol, PRESIDENT.

Mr. W. C. Lake, Balliol, *Librarian*
Mr. F. W. Robertson, Brase-nose, *Treasurer*
Mr. W. Buckley, Brase-nose
Mr. G. H. U. Fagan, Oriel
Mr. H. Fox, Wadham
Mr. G. B. Northcote, Exeter
Mr. C. T. Arnold, Magdalen Hall, *Secretary*

EASTER TERM, 1839.

MR. H. W. SULIVAN, Balliol, PRESIDENT.

Mr. W. C. Lake, Balliol, *Librarian*
Mr. G. B. Northcote, Exeter, *Treasurer*
Mr. J. S. Hodson, Merton
Mr. S. H. Northcote, Balliol
Mr. F. Courtenay, Exeter
Mr. W. Buckley, Brase-nose
Mr. J. F. B. Landon, Worcester
Mr. C. T. Arnold, Magdalen Hall
Mr. J. B. Blackett, Ch. Ch. *Secretary*

MICHAELMAS TERM, 1839.

MR. W. E. BUCKLEY, Brase-nose, PRESIDENT.

Mr. J. E. Bode, Ch. Ch. *Librarian*
Mr. C. T. Arnold, Magdalen Hall, *Treasurer*
Mr. G. Rawlinson, Trinity
Mr. G. B. Northcote, Exeter
Mr. J. B. Blackett, Ch. Ch.
Mr. J. C. Moore-Stevens, Ch. Ch.
Mr. F. Courtenay, Exeter
Mr. R. Congreve, Wadham, *Secretary*

LENT TERM, 1840.

MR. J. B. BLACKETT, Ch. Ch. PRESIDENT.

Mr. J. E. Bode, Ch. Ch. *Librarian*
Mr. G. Rawlinson, Trinity, *Treasurer*
Mr. F. Courtenay, Exeter
Mr. C. T. Arnold, Magdalen Hall
Mr. G. B. Northcote, Exeter
Mr. R. Congreve, Wadham
Mr. H. W. Fox, Wadham
Mr. R. C. Powles, Exeter
Mr. C. Lempriere, St. John's, *Secretary*

EASTER TERM, 1840.

MR. G. RAWLINSON, Trinity, PRESIDENT.

Mr. F. Courtenay, Exeter, *Librarian*
Mr. R. Congreve, Wadham, *Treasurer*
Mr. J. B. Blackett, Ch. Ch.
Mr. J. F. B. Landon, Worcester
Mr. J. C. Moore-Stevens, Ch. Ch.
Mr. C. Lempriere, St. John's
Mr. J. Clements, Oriel
Mr. W. T. Alban, St. John's
Mr. R. C. Powles, Exeter, *Secretary*

D

MICHAELMAS TERM, 1840.

MR. C. T. ARNOLD, Magdalen Hall, PRESIDENT.

Mr. F. Courtenay, Exeter, *Librarian*
Mr. R. C. Powles, Exeter, *Treasurer*
Mr. G. B. Northcote, Exeter
Mr. R. Congreve, Wadham
Mr. J. B. Blackett, Ch. Ch.
Mr. M. Portal, Ch. Ch.
Mr. H. D. Seymour, Ch. Ch.
Mr. G. Phillimore, Ch. Ch.
Mr. J. Clements, Oriel, *Secretary*

LENT TERM, 1841.

MR. R. C. POWLES, Exeter, PRESIDENT.

Mr. R. Congreve, Wadham, *Librarian*
Mr. J. Clements, Oriel, *Treasurer*
Rev. G. Rawlinson, Exeter
Mr. F. Courtenay, Exeter
Mr. G. B. Northcote, Exeter
Mr. J. B. Blackett, Ch. Ch.
Mr. M. Portal, Ch. Ch.
Mr. P. Parnell, St. John's
Mr. W. Clerk, Trinity, *Secretary*

EASTER TERM, 1841.

MR. J. F. B. LANDON, Worcester, PRESIDENT.

Mr. R. Congreve, Wadham, *Librarian*
Mr. M. Portal, Ch. Ch. *Treasurer*
Rev. G. Rawlinson, Exeter
Mr. R. C. Powles, Exeter
Mr. J. B. Blackett, Ch. Ch.
Mr. J. E. Cross, Ch. Ch.
Mr. J. Clements, Oriel
Mr. J. E. Gladstone, Magdalen Hall
Mr. P. Parnell, St. John's, *Secretary*

LIST OF MEMBERS

WHO HAVE TAKEN PART IN THE DEBATES

LIST OF MEMBERS

WHO HAVE TAKEN PART IN THE DEBATES.

Abercorn, Marquis of, Ch. Ch.

Acland, A. H. D. Ch. Ch.

Acland, T. D. Ch. Ch. afterwards Fellow of All Souls

Adams, J. Ch. Ch.

Alban, W. J. St. John's

Allen, T. Balliol

Allies, Rev. T. Wadham

Alston, R. G. Ch. Ch.

Anderson, H. L. St. John's

Andrew, S. Exeter, afterwards of Lincoln

Anstice, J. Ch. Ch.

Armitage, Rev. R. Worcester

Armstrong, Rev. J. Lincoln

Arnold, C. T. Magdalen Hall

Austin, R. A. C. Oriel

Awdry, W. H. Exeter, afterwards of Magdalen Hall

Bannatyne, Rev. C. Balliol

Baring, Rev. C. Ch. Ch.

Barne, Rev. H. Exeter

Barnes, Rev. R. Ch. Ch.

Baugh, Rev. F. Exeter, afterwards of All Souls

Bayntun, W. W. T. Balliol

Bernard, T. D. Exeter

Berry, J. G. M. Brase-nose

Bingham, Rev. C. W. New Coll.

Blackett, J. B. Ch. Ch.

Blackstone, W. S. Ch. Ch. M.P.

Bliss, Rev. J. Oriel

Boyle, P. Oriel

Brancker, Rev. T. Wadham

Brandreth, W. H. Ch. Ch.

Brine, J. G. St. John's

Brodie, B. Balliol

Brooke, Jones R. Wadham

Brown, H. Corpus

Browne, G. L. St. John's

Browne, R. C. Brase-nose

Bruce, Hon. J. Ch. Ch.

Bruxner, Rev. G. E. Ch. Ch.

Buckley, W. Brase-nose

Bucknill, C. Trinity

Buddicom, Rev. R. J. Brase-nose

Burke, —, King's College, Camb.

Burney, C. Magdalen

Burrows, H. W. St. John's

Butterworth, J. H. Exeter

Calvert, F. Ch. Ch. afterwards of Merton

Campbell, A. R. Balliol

Campbell, C. Exeter

Capes, Rev. J. M. Balliol

Carden, L. University

Cardwell, E. Balliol

Carey, O. Oriel

Cazenove, J. G. Brase-nose

Chadwick, E. Worcester

Chamberlain, Rev. T. Ch. Ch.
Chapman, T. Exeter
Chase, D. P. Oriel
Chase, T. H. Trinity
Chesshyre, Rev. W. J. Balliol
Christie, A. Oriel
Clarke, Rev. H. D. Exeter
Clarke, W. J. Balliol
Clements, J. Oriel
Clerk, W. Trinity
Clifford, C. C. Ch. Ch.
Coke, Rev. E. F. Brase-nose
Cole, Lord, Ch. Ch. M.P.
Cole, O. B. Ch. Ch.
Coleridge, J. D. Balliol
Collyns, C. H. Ch. Ch.
Congreve, R. Wadham
Connell, J. Balliol
Cornish, J. R. Ch. Ch.
Cosserat, G. P. Exeter
Cother, W. Ch. Ch.
Cotton, Rev. W. C. Ch. Ch.
Courtenay, F. Exeter
Courtenay, W. R. All Souls
Cox, G. New College
Crichton, W. J. Merton
Cripps, H. W. New College
Croft, J. Balliol
Cross, J. E. Ch. Ch.

Dalton, Rev. C. Wadham
Daniel, J. Ch. Ch.
Davis, J. Brase-nose
Davison, H. Trinity
Debary, T. Lincoln
Denison, S. C. Balliol
De Salis, R. J. L. Oriel
Dewar, Rev. E. H. Exeter
Dewdney, W. G. Queen's
Dickerson, R. C. Brase-nose, after-
    wards of Worcester
Dodgson, H. H. Ch. Ch.
Domville, J. G. Ch. Ch.
Donaldson, —, Trinity Coll. Cam-
    bridge
Doughton, —, Ch. Ch.
Douglas, C. R. G. Exeter
Downie, R. Trinity

Doyle, F. H. Ch. Ch. afterwards
    of All Souls
Dupuis, —, King's College, Camb.
Durnford, Rev. R. Magdalen

Emeris, J. University
Entwistle, A. Oriel, afterwards of
    Brase-nose
Evans, R. Jesus
Evans, J. W. Trinity

Faber, F. W. Balliol, afterwards
    Fellow of University
Fagan, G. H. U. Oriel
Farquhar, Sir W. M. Bart. Ch. Ch.
Fawcett, R. T. University
Fooks, W. Exeter
Forster, C. Worcester
Forsyth, —, Trinity Coll. Cambridge
Fortescue, E. Wadham
Fowle, W. C. Wadham
Fowler, G. C. Pembroke
Fox, H. W. Wadham
Fox, J. Worcester
Frith, M. K. S. Exeter

Garnier, J. Exeter
Gaskell, J. M. Ch. Ch. M.P.
Gee, R. Wadham
Giffard, W. University
Giles, J. E. Magdalen Hall
Gladstone, J. E. Magdalen Hall
Gladstone, W. E. Ch. Ch. M.P.
Goldsmid, L. D. afterwards Rev.
    De Visme, Balliol
Goulburn, E. Balliol
Grant, Rev. A. New College
Gresley, R. N. Ch. Ch.

Hall, A. H. Balliol
Hamilton, Rev. W. K. Ch. Ch.
    afterwards of Merton
Hanmer, Sir John, Bart. Ch.Ch.M.P.
Hanmer, T. Brase-nose
Hansell, E. H. Magdalen
Harding, J. D. Oriel
Harrison, Rev. B. Ch. Ch.
Harrison, J. P. Ch. Ch.

Hawtayne, W. G. Balliol, after-
wards of Magdalen Hall
Herbert, Hon. S. Oriel, M.P.
Hessey, Rev. J. A. St. John's
Hewitt, Hon. J. Ch. Ch.
Highton, Rev. H. Queen's
Hill, G. St. Edmund Hall
Hobhouse, T. B. Balliol
Hodson, J. S. Merton
Hope, A. Trinity Coll. Cambridge
Hopton, R. Brase-nose
Hornby, R. A. Oriel
Hotham, G. F. Ch. Ch.
Hotham, W. F. Ch. Ch.
Hughes, Rev. H. Trinity
Humbert, L. M. St. John's
Hussey, W. Balliol

James, E. B. Queen's
Jelf, Rev. W. E. Ch. Ch.

Kempson, W. H. Ch. Ch.
Kilpin, C. J. Worcester
King, H. Wadham
Kinlock, A. St. Mary Hall
Knatchbull, C. H. Trinity

Lake, W. C. Balliol
Landon, J. F. B. Worcester
Lawrence, Rev. C. W. Brase-nose
Leach, T. Merton
Lempriere, C. St. John's
Lewis, J. Ch. Ch.
Lincoln, Earl of, Ch. Ch. M.P.
Lingen, R. R. B. Trinity
Litton, E. A. Balliol, afterwards
Fellow of Oriel
Loftus, Lord Adam, Balliol
Lonsdale, W. Oriel
Lowder, C. F. Exeter
Lowe, F. P. University, afterwards
Fellow of Magdalen
Lowe, R. University, afterwards
Fellow of Magdalen
Lyall, J. E. Balliol

Macdonald, T. Oriel
Mackintosh, D. Corpus, Cambridge

Mackintosh, R. G. New College
Mackintosh, E. W. University
Mackworth, W. H. Balliol
Maclean, D. Balliol, M.P.
Manning, Rev. H. C. Balliol, after-
wards Fellow of Merton
Mansel, H. L. St. John's
Mant, Rev. W. B. Oriel
Marjoribanks, E. Ch. Ch.
Marriott, Rev. C. Balliol, afterwards
Fellow of Oriel
Marsh, W. Oriel
Marshall, G. Ch. Ch.
Marshall, J. Ch. Ch.
Massie, E. Wadham
Matthew, Rev. H. Balliol
Maunsell, W. T. Ch. Ch.
Maurice, J. Exeter
Mayo, A. F. Oriel
Mayow, Rev. M. W. Ch. Ch.
Mellish, G. University
Merivale, H. Trinity, afterwards
Fellow of Balliol
Mills, A. Balliol
Milman, R. Exeter
Moberley, Rev. Dr. G. Balliol
Moncrieff, G. R. Balliol
Moncrieff, Rev. H. New College
Monro, E. Oriel
Moore-Stephens, J. Ch. Ch.
Morland, W. C. Ch. Ch.
Morrell, Rev. G. K. St. John's
Mortimer, Rev. G. F. W. Queen's
Mozley, R. T. Oriel

Neale, E. V. Oriel
Nesbitt, J. C. B. New College,
afterwards of Brase-nose
Newman, W. Oriel
Newton, J. Brase-nose
Northcote, G. B. Exeter
Northcote, J. S. Corpus
Northcote, S. H. Balliol

Oakes, C. H. Merton
Oldham, Rev. J. R. Oriel
Oxnam, Rev. N. Trinity, afterwards
Fellow of Exeter

Palairet, Rev. E. Queen's

Palmer, F. Ch. Ch.

Palmer, R. Trinity, afterwards Fellow of Magdalen

Palmer, W. Magdalen

Parnell, P. St. John's

Paterson, G. Wadham

Pattison, M. Oriel

Peard, J. W. Exeter

Pearson, G. C. Ch. Ch.

Pearson, J. Balliol

Peter, J. T. H. Ch. Ch. afterwards of Merton

Phillimore, G. Ch. Ch.

Phillimore, R. J. Ch. Ch.

Phillips, J. H. Worcester

Phillott, H. W. Ch. Ch.

Phin, T. Exeter

Plumptre, E. H. University

Plunkett, Hon. R. Ch. Ch.

Portal, M. Ch. Ch.

Povah, F. St. John's

Powell, J. C. Trinity

Powles, R. C. Exeter

Poynder, F. Wadham

Poynder, T. H. A. Brase-nose

Price, E. P. Lincoln

Puckle, Rev. J. Brase-nose

Puller, C. Ch. Ch.

Pusey, W. B. Oriel

Rawlinson, Rev. H. St. John's

Rawlinson, Rev. G. Trinity, afterwards of Exeter

Reeves, Rev. F. J. H. Merton

Richardson, J. Ch. Ch.

Richardson, Rev. J. Queen's

Richardson, J. J. Oriel

Rickards, G. Trinity, afterwards of Queen's

Riddell, J. C. B. Ch. Ch.

Ridley, M. W. Ch. Ch.

Ridley, W. H. Ch. Ch.

Robertson, F. W. Brase-nose

Robinson, G. Balliol

Rogers, F. Oriel

Rogers, J. E. Corpus

Ruskin, J. Ch. Ch.

Salmon, E. Exeter

Sanderson, W. St. Mary Hall

Scott, R. Ch. Ch. afterwards Fellow of Balliol

Scratton, T. Ch. Ch.

Seymour, H. Ch. Ch.

Simcox, Rev. T. G. Wadham

Simpson, E. Corpus

Sinclair, Rev. H. St. Mary Hall

Skinner, A. M. Balliol

Smith, D. Ch. Ch.

Smythe, W. B. Corpus

Smythies, C. N. Trinity

Spencer, J. St. Mary Hall

Sterling, Rev. C. J. St. Mary Hall

Stoddart, Rev. W. W. St. John's

Street, A. W. Magdalen Hall

Sugden, E. St. Alban Hall

Sulivan, H. W. Balliol

Surtees, S. V. University

Tait, Rev. A. C. Balliol

Tancred, T. Ch. Ch. afterwards Fellow of Merton

Tate, F. Balliol, afterwards of University

Taylor, W. Ch. Ch.

Thomas, G. T. St. Mary Hall

Thomas, R. J. F. Ch. Ch.

Thornton, C. Ch. Ch.

Tickell, G. Balliol

Touchet, J. H. Exeter

Townend, J. Oriel

Trench, Rev. F. Oriel

Trevor, Rev. G. Magdalen Hall

Tristram, H. B. Lincoln

Tufnell, H. Ch. Ch.

Twining, W. Balliol

Twisleton, E. B. Trinity, afterwards Fellow of Balliol

Underwood, J. Ch. Ch.

Utterton, J. S. Oriel

Vansittart, C. Oriel

Vaughan, Rev. J. Balliol

Villiers, E. E. Merton

Villiers, Lord, Ch. Ch. M.P.

Ward, G. A. Ch. Ch.

Ward, R. Oriel

Ward, Rev. W. G. Ch. Ch. afterwards of Lincoln, Fellow of Balliol

Ward, Rev. W. H. P. Oriel

Whipham, T. W. Balliol

White, W. F. Trinity

Wiggin, W. Exeter

Wilberforce, S. Oriel

Williams, R. Oriel

Wilson, Rev. R. F. Oriel

Wither, Rev. L. B. Oriel

Wood, G. Oriel

Wood, Rev. J. R. Ch. Ch.

Woodall, E. H. Exeter

Woollcombe, Rev. W. W. Exeter

Wordsworth, Rev. C. Ch. Ch.

Wortley, Hon. J. S. Merton

Wrangham, D. C. Brase-nose

Wrightson, T. B. Brase-nose

Wynn, C. W. Ch. Ch.

Yonge, C. St. Mary Hall

Young, J. Corpus, M.P.

PROCEEDINGS

OF THE

OXFORD UNION SOCIETY.

PROCEEDINGS

OF THE

OXFORD UNION SOCIETY.

THURSDAY, FEBRUARY 2, 1826.

Mr. Tufnell's Rooms, Ch. Ch.

MR. DODGSON, Ch. Ch. President, in the Chair.

MR. WORTLEY, Ch. Ch. moved:

That the present system of Mechanics' Institutions, for the Scientific Education of the Labouring Classes, is not likely to prove beneficial to the Country.

SPEAKERS.

In the Affirmative.	*In the Negative.*
Mr. Wortley, Ch. Ch.	Mr. Richardson, Oriel.
Mr. Durnford, Magdalen.	Mr. Palairet, Queen's.
	Mr. Hornby, Oriel.
	Mr. Trench, Oriel.

DIVISION.

Ayes	18
Noes	19
Majority . . .	1

THURSDAY, FEBRUARY 9, 1826.

Mr. Dewdney's Rooms, Queen's.

Mr. DODGSON, Ch. Ch. President, in the Chair.

Mr. MERIVALE, Trinity, moved:

That the misgovernment of Charles the Second was a greater evil than the usurpation of Oliver Cromwell.

SPEAKERS.

In the Affirmative.	*In the Negative.*
Mr. Merivale, Trinity.	Mr. Wood, Ch. Ch.
Mr. D. Smith, Ch. Ch.	Mr. Hobhouse, Balliol.
	Mr. Richardson, Oriel.
	Mr. Mant, Oriel.
	Mr. Gresley, Ch. Ch.

DIVISION.

Ayes 27
Noes 10
Majority . . . 17

THURSDAY, FEBRUARY 16, 1826.

Mr. Dillon's Rooms, Ch. Ch.

Mr. DODGSON, Ch. Ch. President, in the Chair.

Mr. WITHER, Oriel, moved:

That the Reign of George the Third up to the year 1811 is to be considered a disastrous period in English History.

SPEAKERS.

In the Affirmative.	*In the Negative.*
Mr. Wither, Oriel.	Mr. Richardson, Oriel.
Mr. Brown, Brase-nose.	Mr. Wrangham, Brase-nose.
Mr. Villiers, Merton.	

DIVISION.

Ayes 14
Noes 24
Majority . . . 10

THURSDAY, FEBRUARY 23, 1826.

Mr. WRANGHAM, Brase-nose, President, in the Chair.

Mr. D. Smith, Ch. Ch. moved:

That the Act for Septennial Parliaments in the Reign of George the First, was consistent with sound policy and constitutional justice.

SPEAKERS.

In the Affirmative.	In the Negative.
Mr. D. Smith, Ch. Ch.	Mr. Calvert, Ch. Ch.
Mr. Ridley, Ch. Ch.	Mr. Durnford, Magdalen.
Mr. Puller, Ch. Ch.	Mr. Wilberforce, Oriel.
Mr. Stuart Wortley, Ch. Ch.	

DIVISION.

Ayes 25
Noes 13
Majority . . . 12

THURSDAY, MARCH 2, 1826.

Mr. WRANGHAM, Brase-nose, President, in the Chair.

Mr. MACDONALD, Oriel, moved:

That the Monopoly of the East India Company is impolitic, and ought to be abolished.

SPEAKERS.

In the Affirmative.	In the Negative.
Mr. Macdonald, Oriel.	Mr. Wood, Ch. Ch.
Mr. Hobhouse, Balliol.	

DIVISION.

Ayes 27
Noes 7
Majority . . . 20

THURSDAY, MARCH 9, 1826.

MR. WRANGHAM, Brase-nose, President, in the Chair.

MR. TUFNELL, Ch. Ch. moved:

That the Abuses of a Bill against Cruelty to Animals are likely to overbalance the advantages arising from it.

SPEAKERS.

In the Affirmative.	*In the Negative.*
Mr. Tufnell, Ch. Ch.	Mr. Wrightson, Brase-nose.
Mr. Villiers, Merton.	Mr. Courtenay, Ch. Ch.
	Mr. Matthew, Balliol.

DIVISION.

Ayes 23
Noes 21
Majority . . . 2

THURSDAY, APRIL 13, 1826.

Mr. Stewart's Rooms, New College.

MR. WRANGHAM, Brase-nose, President, in the Chair.

MR. DODGSON, Ch. Ch. moved:

That it is not expedient to support Laws forbidding Usury.

SPEAKERS.

In the Affirmative.	*In the Negative.*
Mr. Dodgson, Ch. Ch.	Mr. Calvert, Ch. Ch.

DIVISION.

Ayes 27
Noes 1
Majority . . . 26

THURSDAY, APRIL 27, 1826.

Mr. Tufnell's Rooms, Ch. Ch.

Mr. DURNFORD, Magdalen, President, in the Chair.

Mr. LAWRENCE, Brase-nose, moved:

That the Abolition of Slavery is not at present desirable.

SPEAKERS.

In the Affirmative.
Mr. Lawrence, Brase-nose.
Mr. Merivale, Trinity.

Mr. VILLIERS, Merton, moved as an Amendment:

1st. That the Abolition of Slavery is desirable.
2d. That the measures proposed by the Government for the Abolition of Slavery are such as are likely to conduce to the end desired, without endangering the safety of the Colonies, and without injury to the rights of the proprietors.

SPEAKERS.

In the Affirmative.	*In the Negative.*
Mr. Villiers, Merton.	Mr. Dewdney, Queen's.
Mr. Wilberforce, Oriel.	
Mr. Macdonald, Oriel.	

The Amendment was carried without a division.

THURSDAY, MAY 4, 1826.

Mr. Macdonald's Rooms, Oriel.

Mr. HORNBY, Oriel, Secretary, in the Chair.

Mr. CRICHTON, Merton, moved:

That the system of Unpaid Magistracy is not desirable.

SPEAKERS.

In the Affirmative.	*In the Negative.*
Mr. Crichton, Merton.	Mr. Villiers, Merton.
Mr. Macdonald, Oriel.	Mr. Wrangham, Brase-nose.
Mr. Calvert, Ch. Ch.	Mr. Dewdney, Queen's.
	Mr. Wilberforce, Oriel.
	Mr. Trench, Oriel.

DIVISION.

Ayes 6
Noes 26
Majority . . . 20

F

THURSDAY, MAY 11, 1826.

New College Common Room.

MR. MERIVALE, Trinity, in the Chair.

MR. COURTENAY, Ch. Ch. moved:

That the conduct and character of John Knox were productive of the greatest benefit to his country, and are deserving of the highest admiration of posterity.

SPEAKERS.

In the Affirmative.	*In the Negative.*
Mr. Courtenay, Ch. Ch.	Mr. Wortley, Ch. Ch.
Mr. Wood, Ch. Ch.	Mr. Richardson, Oriel.
Mr. D. Smith, Ch. Ch.	Mr. Baring, Ch. Ch.
	Mr. Pearson, Balliol.

DIVISION.

Ayes 10
Noes 15
Majority . . . 5

THURSDAY, MAY 18, 1826.

Mr. Ridley's Rooms, Ch. Ch.

MR. VILLIERS, Merton, President, in the Chair.

MR. COURTENAY, Ch. Ch., as proxy for LORD ACHESON, Ch. Ch., moved:

That the law and custom of Primogeniture is advantageous.

SPEAKERS.

In the Affirmative.	*In the Negative.*
Mr. Courtenay, Ch. Ch.	Mr. Calvert, Ch. Ch.
Mr. Ridley, Ch. Ch.	Mr. Wilberforce, Oriel.
Mr. Wood, Ch. Ch.	Mr. D. Smith, Ch. Ch.
Mr. Mackworth, Balliol.	

DIVISION.

Ayes 24
Noes 9
Majority . . . 15

THURSDAY, MAY 25, 1826.

New College Common Room.

Mr. VILLIERS, Merton, President, in the Chair.

Mr. MERIVALE, Trinity, moved :

That unanimity in Juries is not necessary for the interests of Justice.

SPEAKERS.

In the Affirmative.	*In the Negative.*
Mr. Merivale, Trinity.	Mr. Macdonald, Oriel.

DIVISION.

Ayes 14
Noes 8
Majority . . . 6

THURSDAY, JUNE 1, 1826.

Mr. Dewdney's Rooms, Queen's.

Mr. VILLIERS, Merton, President, in the Chair.

Mr. WOOD, Ch. Ch. moved :

That the conduct of Mr. Burke at the two periods of the French Revolution and American War was consistent.

SPEAKERS.

In the Affirmative.	*In the Negative.*
Mr. Wood, Ch. Ch.	Mr. Macdonald, Oriel.
Mr. Calvert, Ch. Ch.	
Mr. Richardson, Oriel.	

DIVISION.

Ayes 17
Noes 7
Majority . . . 10

THURSDAY, OCTOBER 26, 1826.

MR. VILLIERS, Merton, President, in the Chair.

MR. WORDSWORTH, Ch. Ch. moved :

That the Dissolution of Monasteries by Henry the Eighth was justifiable.

SPEAKERS.

In the Affirmative.

Mr. Wordsworth, Ch. Ch.
Mr. Wrightson, Brase-nose.
Mr. Hornby, Oriel.

MR. MANT, Oriel, moved as an Amendment :

That the Dissolution of Monasteries was a justifiable measure; but that the manner in which it was accomplished, and the revenues applied, was highly culpable.

SPEAKERS.

In the Affirmative.

Mr. Mant, Oriel.
Mr. Wrangham, Brase-nose.

DIVISION.

Ayes (for the Amendment) . 23
Noes (against it) 4
             Majority . . . 19

THURSDAY, NOVEMBER 2, 1826.

MR. VILLIERS, Merton, President, in the Chair.

MR. MOBERLY, Balliol, moved :

That the conduct of Elizabeth to Mary Queen of Scots was not justifiable.

SPEAKERS.

In the Affirmative.

Mr. Wrangham, Brase-nose.
Mr. D. Smith, Ch. Ch.
Mr. Mant, Oriel.
Mr. Maclean, Balliol.
Mr. Richardson, Oriel.

In the Negative.

Mr. Calvert, Ch. Ch.
Mr. Villiers, Merton.
Mr. Wood, Ch. Ch.

DIVISION.

Ayes 18
Noes 12
         Majority . . . 6

MONDAY, NOVEMBER 13, 1826.

Mr. HORNBY, Oriel, President, in the Chair.

Mr. UNDERWOOD, Ch. Ch. moved:

That the decay of Eloquence in modern times is not to be attributed to the increase of knowledge.

SPEAKERS.

In the Affirmative.	In the Negative.
Mr. Underwood, Ch. Ch.	Mr. Macdonald, Oriel.
Mr. D. Smith, Ch. Ch.	
Mr. Chesshyre, Balliol.	
Mr. Twisleton, Trinity.	

DIVISION.

Ayes 28
Noes 2
Majority . . . 26

SATURDAY, NOVEMBER 18, 1826.

Mr. HORNBY, Oriel, President, in the Chair.

Mr. TUFNELL, Ch. Ch. moved:

That the Austrian occupation of Italy in 1821 was not justified by the circumstances of the times.

SPEAKERS.

In the Affirmative.

Mr. Tufnell, Ch. Ch.
Mr. Merivale, Trinity.

DIVISION.

Ayes 26
Noes 3
Majority . . . 23

THURSDAY, NOVEMBER 23, 1826.

MR. HORNBY, Oriel, President, in the Chair.

MR. TRENCH, Oriel, moved:

That the Legislature has an absolute power over Church Property.

SPEAKERS.

In the Affirmative.   *In the Negative.*

Mr. Trench, Oriel.   Mr. D. Smith, Ch. Ch.

                                   Mr. Pearson, Balliol.

MR. WILBERFORCE, Oriel, moved as an Amendment:

That the Property of the Church is subject to the power of the Legislature exactly in the same degree with that of its other subjects.

DIVISION.

Ayes (for the Amendment) . 16
Noes (against it) 10
              Majority . . . 6

THURSDAY, NOVEMBER 30, 1826.

MR. MACDONALD, Oriel, President, in the Chair.

MR. MACINTOSH, New College, moved:

That the Abolition of the Corn Laws would be beneficial to all classes of society.

SPEAKERS.

In the Affirmative.   *In the Negative.*

Mr. Macintosh, New Coll.   Mr. Dewdney, Queen's.
Mr. Wood, Ch. Ch.
Mr. Wilberforce, jun. Oriel.
Mr. D. Smith, Ch. Ch.

MR. WILBERFORCE, sen. moved as an Amendment:

That an alteration in the Corn Laws in the shape of a protecting duty on imported Corn, is essential to the interests of the country.

DIVISION.

Ayes (for the Amendment) . 27
Noes (against it) 2
              Majority . . . 25

THURSDAY, DECEMBER 7, 1826.

Mr. MACDONALD, Oriel, President, in the Chair.

Mr. TWISLETON, Trinity, moved:

That the Pacific System of Mr. Fox towards Revolutionary France would have been greatly beneficial to this country.

SPEAKERS.

In the Affirmative.	*In the Negative.*
Mr. Twisleton, Trinity.	Mr. Mackworth, Balliol.
Mr. Wilberforce, sen. Oriel.	Mr. Courtenay, Ch. Ch.
	Mr. Hornby, Oriel.
	Mr. Chesshyre, Balliol.

DIVISION.

Ayes 11
Noes 25
Majority . . . 14

THURSDAY, FEBRUARY 8, 1827.

Mr. Trench's Rooms, Oriel.

Mr. MACDONALD, Oriel, President, in the Chair.

Mr. CHESSHYRE, Balliol, moved:

That the present system of Large Farms is highly injurious to this country.

SPEAKERS.

In the Affirmative.	*In the Negative.*
Mr. Chesshyre, Balliol.	Mr. Twisleton, Trinity.

DIVISION.

Ayes 10
Noes 17
Majority . . . 7

THURSDAY, FEBRUARY 15, 1827.

Mr. Philips's Rooms, Oriel.

MR. MACDONALD, Oriel, President, in the Chair.

MR. PEARSON, Balliol, moved:

That the English Universities have sufficiently accommodated their system of Education to the circumstances of the existing generation.

SPEAKERS.

In the Affirmative.	*In the Negative.*
Mr. Pearson, Balliol.	Mr. Young, C. C. C.
Mr. Richardson, Oriel.	

DIVISION.

Ayes 25
Noes 25

The President gave his casting vote in favour of the Motion.

THURSDAY, FEBRUARY 22, 1827.

Mr. Ward's Rooms, Balliol.

MR. D. SMITH, Ch. Ch. President, in the Chair.

MR. MACKWORTH, Balliol, moved:

That this Country is more indebted to the exertions of Mr. Burke, than those of any other individual of his time.

SPEAKERS.

In the Affirmative.
Mr. Mackworth, Balliol.
Mr. Macdonald, Oriel.

MR. TWISLETON, Trinity, moved as an Amendment:

That lasting gratitude is due to Mr. Burke for his political exertions before the year 1790.

But, That the conduct of Mr. Burke with respect to the French Revolution, plunged this country into an unnecessary, impolitic, and unjust war.

The Amendment was lost, and the original Motion carried by a large majority.

THURSDAY, MARCH 1, 1827.

Mr. Whitmore's Rooms, Ch. Ch.

Mr. D. SMITH, Ch. Ch. President, in the Chair.

Mr. TWISLETON, Trinity, moved:

That Forgery ought not to be punished with death.

SPEAKERS.

In the Affirmative.	*In the Negative.*
Mr. Twisleton, Trinity.	Mr. Hobhouse, Balliol.
Mr. Wilberforce, Oriel.	Mr. Clark, Exeter.
	Mr. Marriott, Oriel.
	Mr. Macdonald, Oriel.

DIVISION.

Ayes 19
Noes 25
Majority . . . 6

THURSDAY, MARCH 8, 1827.

Mr. Wilberforce's Rooms, Oriel.

Mr. D. SMITH, Ch. Ch. President, in the Chair.

Mr. MERIVALE, Trinity, moved:

That the Long Parliament in 1642 was justified in taking up arms.

SPEAKERS.

In the Affirmative.	*In the Negative.*
Mr. Merivale, Trinity.	Mr. Chesshyre, Balliol.
Mr. Tufnell, Ch. Ch.	Mr. Austen, Oriel.
Mr. Marriott, Oriel.	

The Motion was carried by a large majority.

G

THURSDAY, MARCH 15, 1827.
New College Common Room.
MR. D. SMITH, Ch. Ch. President, in the Chair.

MR. MORTIMER, Queen's, moved:

That Catholic Emancipation would be highly beneficial to the interests of Great Britain in Church and State.

SPEAKERS.

In the Affirmative.	*In the Negative.*
Mr. Mortimer, Queen's.	Mr. Chesshyre, Balliol.
Mr. Trench, Oriel.	Lord Cole, Ch. Ch.
Mr. Wrightson, Brase-nose.	Mr. Macdonald, Oriel.
Mr. Pearson, Balliol.	Mr. Boyle, Oriel.
Hon. R. Plunkett, Ch. Ch.	
Lord Villiers, Ch. Ch.	
Mr. Tufnell, Ch. Ch.	
Mr. Twisleton, Trinity.	

DIVISION.
Ayes 37
Noes 36
Majority . . . 1

THURSDAY, MARCH 22, 1827.
New College Common Room.
MR. TUFNELL, Ch. Ch. President, in the Chair.

MR. WRIGHTSON, Brase-nose, moved:

That Ecclesiastics ought not to be admitted to Political power.

SPEAKERS.

In the Affirmative.	*In the Negative.*
Mr. Wrightson, Brase-nose.	Mr. Baring, Ch. Ch.

MR. CRICHTON moved as an Amendment:

That the restricted influence of a Protestant Clergy in Civil affairs, may be salutary and expedient; but that the influence of the Catholic Clergy in Secular affairs, has always been inimical to the best interests of States.

SPEAKERS.

In the Affirmative.	*In the Negative.*
Mr. Crichton, Merton.	Mr. Merivale, Trinity.
Mr. D. Smith, Ch. Ch.	Mr. Mortimer, Queen's.
Mr. Chesshyre, Balliol.	

DIVISION.
Ayes (for the Amendment) . 23
Noes (against it) 15
Majority . . . 8

THURSDAY, MARCH 27, 1827.

Mr. Stuart's Rooms, Oriel.

Mr. TUFNELL, Ch. Ch. President, in the Chair.

Mr. CROFT, Balliol, moved :

That the Retention of Hanover is disadvantageous to Great Britain.

SPEAKER.

In the Affirmative.
Mr. Croft, Balliol.

The Motion was then put, and carried without a division.

THURSDAY, MAY 10, 1827.

Mr. Dymock's Rooms, Balliol.

Mr. TUFNELL, Ch. Ch. President, in the Chair.

Mr. MOZLEY, Oriel, moved :

That the conduct of Great Britain in seizing the Danish fleet was justifiable.

SPEAKERS.

In the Affirmative. | *In the Negative.*
Mr. Mozley, Oriel. | Mr. Hobhouse, Balliol.
Mr. Marriott, Oriel. | Mr. Twisleton, Trinity.

The Motion was lost without a division.

THURSDAY, MAY 17, 1827.

Mr. Tufnell's Rooms, Ch. Ch.

Mr TUFNELL, Ch. Ch. President, in the Chair.

Mr. MARRIOTT, Oriel, moved:

That the Execution of Marshal Ney was unjustifiable.

SPEAKERS.

In the Affirmative.	*In the Negative.*
Mr. Marriott, Oriel.	Mr. Richardson, Oriel.
	Mr. Bannatyne, Balliol.

The Motion was lost without a division.

THURSDAY, MAY 24, 1827.

Mr. Hamilton's Rooms, Ch. Ch.

Mr. PEARSON, Balliol, President, in the Chair.

Mr. BOYLE, Oriel, moved:

That the conduct of the Whigs since the necessary resignation of Lord Liverpool has not been such as to entitle them to the approbation of the Country.

SPEAKERS.

In the Affirmative.	*In the Negative.*
Mr. Boyle, Oriel.	Mr. D. Smith, Ch. Ch.
Mr. Chesshyre, Balliol.	Mr. Hobhouse, Balliol.
	Mr. Richardson, Ch. Ch.
	Mr. Ridley, Ch. Ch.

DIVISION.

Ayes 43
Noes 44
Majority . . . 1

THURSDAY, MAY 31, 1827.

Mr. Clifford's Rooms, Ch. Ch.

Mr. TUFNELL, Ch. Ch. President, in the Chair.

Mr. HOBHOUSE, Balliol, moved:

That the Foreign Policy of Lord Castlereagh was disadvantageous to the Country.

SPEAKERS.

In the Affirmative.
Mr. Hobhouse, Balliol.
Mr. Wilberforce, Oriel.
Mr. Twisleton, Trinity.
Mr. Pearson, Balliol.

DIVISION.
Ayes 50
Noes 7
Majority . . . 43

THURSDAY, JUNE 7, 1827.

Mr. Underwood's Rooms, Ch. Ch.

Mr. PEARSON, Balliol, President, in the Chair.

Mr. RICHARDSON, Oriel, moved:

That Counsel for Prisoners in cases of Felony should be allowed to speak in their defence.

SPEAKERS.

In the Affirmative.　　　　*In the Negative.*
Mr. Richardson, Oriel.　　　Mr. Marriott, Oriel.
　　　　　　　　　　　　　Mr. Baring, Ch. Ch.

DIVISION.
Ayes 19
Noes 18
Majority . . . 1

THURSDAY, JUNE 14, 1827.

Mr. Wilberforce's Rooms, Oriel.

Mr. PEARSON, Balliol, President, in the Chair.

Mr. WILBERFORCE, Oriel, moved :

That Mr. Fox's East India Bill was an unconstitutional measure.

SPEAKERS.

In the Affirmative.	*In the Negative.*
Mr. Wilberforce, Oriel.	Mr. Twisleton, Trinity.
Mr. Armitage, Worcester.	Mr. Hobhouse, Balliol.
	Mr. Puller, Ch. Ch.

DIVISION.

Ayes 8
Noes 28
Majority . . . 20

THURSDAY, JUNE 21, 1827.

Mr. Pearson's Rooms, Oriel.

Mr. TWISLETON, Trinity, President, in the Chair.

Mr. HORNBY, Oriel, moved :

That the Execution of the Scotch Lords in 1745 was justifiable.

SPEAKERS.

In the Affirmative.	*In the Negative.*
Mr. Hornby, Oriel.	Mr. Chrichton, Merton.

MR. TUFNELL, Ch. Ch. moved as an Amendment :

That the measure was justifiable, but impolitic.

SPEAKERS.

In the Affirmative.	*In the Negative.*
Mr. Tufnell, Ch. Ch.	Mr. Marriott, Oriel.
Mr. D. Smith, Ch. Ch.	

The Amendment was lost without a division.

DIVISION ON THE ORIGINAL MOTION.

Ayes 29
Noes 10
Majority . . . 19

THURSDAY, OCTOBER 25, 1827.

Mr. Tufnell's Rooms, Ch. Ch.

Mr. COURTENAY, Ch. Ch., President pro tem. in the Chair.

Mr. HOBHOUSE, Balliol, moved:

That the peace of Utrecht was dishonourable to Great Britain.

SPEAKER.

In the Affirmative.
Mr. Hobhouse, Balliol.

The Motion was carried by a large majority.

THURSDAY, NOVEMBER 1, 1827.

Mr. Wiseman's Rooms, Balliol.

Mr. HOBHOUSE, Balliol, moved:

That an alteration is expedient in the Representation of the people in Parliament.

SPEAKERS.

In the Affirmative.
Mr. Hobhouse, Balliol.
Mr. Tufnell, Ch. Ch.
Mr. Evans, Jesus.

In the Negative.
Mr. Macdonald, Oriel.

Mr. GRANT, New College, moved as an Amendment:

That the course pursued by Government for preventing corruption is judicious and sufficient.

DIVISION.

Ayes (for the Amendment) 23
Noes (against it) 16
Majority . . . 7

THURSDAY, NOVEMBER 8, 1827.

Mr. Wilberforce's Rooms, Oriel.

Mr. D. SMITH, Treasurer, in the Chair.

Mr. TUFNELL, Balliol, moved :

That the sending troops to Portugal in December, 1826, was expedient and justifiable.

SPEAKERS.

In the Affirmative.
Mr. Tufnell, Balliol.
Mr. Richardson, Oriel.
Mr. Twisleton, Trinity.

The Motion was carried unanimously.

THURSDAY, NOVEMBER 15, 1827.

Mr. Hamilton's Rooms, Ch. Ch.

Mr. PULLER, Ch. Ch., President pro tem., in the Chair.

Mr. HARDING, Oriel, moved:

That the European powers would not be justified in compelling Turkey to recognise the independence of Greece.

SPEAKERS.

In the Affirmative.   *In the Negative.*

Mr. Harding, Oriel.   Mr. Hobhouse, Balliol.
Mr. Richardson, Oriel.   Mr. Wilberforce, Oriel.
Mr. Clarke, Exeter.   Mr. Pearson, Balliol.

DIVISION.

Ayes 17
Noes 36
                    ‾‾‾‾
Majority . . . 19

THURSDAY, NOVEMBER 22, 1827.

Mr. Penleaze's Rooms, Magdalen.

Mr. MERIVALE, President, in the Chair.

The Hon. R. PLUNKETT, Ch. Ch., as proxy for Mr. TUFNELL, Ch. Ch., moved:

That the effects of Buonaparte's dominion have produced no lasting benefits to Europe.

SPEAKERS.

In the Affirmative.	*In the Negative.*
Hon. R. Plunkett, Ch. Ch.	Mr. Twisleton, Trinity.
Mr. Puller, Ch. Ch.	Mr. Hobhouse, Balliol.

DIVISION.

Ayes 18
Noes 20
Majority . . . 2

THURSDAY, NOVEMBER 29, 1827.

Mr. Stewart's Rooms, Oriel.

Mr. MERIVALE, Trinity, President, in the Chair.

Mr. RICHARDSON, Oriel, as proxy for Mr. PEARSON, Oriel, moved:

That the abdication of James the Second justified the exclusion of himself and his family from the English throne.

SPEAKERS.

In the Affirmative.	*In the Negative.*
Mr. Richardson, Oriel.	Mr. Merivale, Trinity.
Mr. Pearson, Balliol.	Mr. Wilberforce, Oriel.
M r.Harding, Oriel.	

The Motion was carried by a large majority.

THURSDAY, DECEMBER 6, 1827.

Mr. Dymock's Rooms, Balliol.

Mr. MERIVALE, Trinity, President, in the Chair.

Mr. MARRIOTT, Oriel, moved :

That capital punishments are not calculated to prevent crime.

SPEAKER.

In the Affirmative.
Mr. Marriott, Oriel.

DIVISION.

Ayes 28
Noes 23
Majority . . .   5

THURSDAY, JANUARY 31, 1828.

Mr. Piggott's Rooms, Ch. Ch.

Mr. D. SMITH, Ch. Ch. Treasurer, in the Chair.

Mr. HOBHOUSE, Balliol, moved :

That it is probable that the form of Government which at present subsists in the United States of America, will be more durable than those of the ancient Republics.

SPEAKERS.

In the Affirmative.	*In the Negative.*
Mr. Hobhouse, Balliol.	Mr. Twisleton, Trinity.
Mr. Pearson, Balliol.	Mr. Grant, New College.

DIVISION.

Ayes 20
Noes 15
Majority . . .   5

THURSDAY, FEBRUARY 7, 1828.

Mr. Jefferies's Rooms, Ch. Ch.

MR. HOBHOUSE, Balliol, Secretary, in the Chair.

MR. HAMILTON, Ch. Ch. moved:

That the conduct of Sir Robert Walpole as a Minister deserves the approbation of posterity.

SPEAKERS.

In the Affirmative.	*In the Negative.*
Mr. Hamilton, Ch. Ch.	Mr. Harding, Oriel.
	Mr. Tufnell, Balliol.

The Motion was negatived without a division.

THURSDAY, FEBRUARY 14, 1828.

Mr. Hamilton's Rooms, Ch. Ch.

MR. PULLER, Ch. Ch., President pro tem., in the Chair.

MR. TWISLETON, Trinity, moved:

That the present Tory Ministry does not deserve the confidence of the Country.

SPEAKERS.

In the Affirmative.
Mr. Twisleton, Trinity.
Mr. Merivale, Trinity.

DIVISION.

Ayes 37
Noes 30
Majority . . . 7

THURSDAY, FEBRUARY 21, 1828.

Mr. Wiseman's Rooms, Balliol.

Mr. D. SMITH, Ch. Ch. President, in the Chair.

Mr. D. SMITH, Ch. Ch. moved:

That the Public Character of Mr. Canning deserved the approbation of his Country.

SPEAKERS.

In the Affirmative.	*In the Negative.*
Mr. D. Smith, Ch. Ch.	Mr. Farquhar, Ch. Ch.
Mr. Pearson, Balliol.	Mr. Marriott, Oriel.
Mr. Tufnell, Balliol.	
Mr. Twisleton, Trinity.	

DIVISION.

Ayes 50
Noes 22
Majority . . . 28

THURSDAY, FEBRUARY 28, 1828.

Mr. Smythe's Rooms, C. C. C.

Mr. PULLER, Ch. Ch. Secretary, in the Chair.

Mr. HARDING, Oriel, moved:

That Lord Russell and Algernon Sydney are rather to be respected as Patriots than condemned as Traitors.

SPEAKERS.

In the Affirmative.	*In the Negative.*
Mr. Harding, Oriel.	Mr. Neale, Oriel.

The Motion was carried without a division.

THURSDAY, MARCH 6, 1828.

Mr. Wilberforce's Rooms, Oriel.

Mr. HOBHOUSE, Balliol, Treasurer, in the Chair.

Mr. PEARSON, Oriel, moved :

That the present system of Poor Laws is injurious to the Country.

The Motion was carried unanimously.

THURSDAY, MARCH 13, 1828.

New College Common Room.

Mr. D. SMITH, Ch. Ch. President, in the Chair.

Mr. GRANT, New College, moved :

That the present system of Periodical Criticism is injurious to the interests of Literature.

The Motion was carried without a division.

THURSDAY, MARCH 20, 1828.

Marquis of Hastings's Rooms, Ch. Ch.

Mr. D. SMITH, Ch. Ch. President, in the Chair.

Mr. WILBERFORCE, Oriel, moved :

That the existing system of the Game Laws requires amendment.

SPEAKERS.

In the Affirmative.	*In the Negative.*
Mr. Wilberforce, Oriel.	Mr. Neale, Oriel.
Mr. Marriott, Oriel.	

The Motion was carried by a large majority.

THURSDAY, APRIL 24, 1828.

Mr. Hamilton's Rooms, Ch. Ch.

Mr. D. SMITH, Ch. Ch. President, in the Chair.

Mr. GRANT, New College, moved :

That the present system of Periodical Criticism is injurious to the interests of Literature.

SPEAKERS.

In the Affirmative.	*In the Negative.*
Mr. Grant, New College.	Mr. Hobhouse, Balliol.
Mr. Wilberforce, Oriel.	Mr. Povah, St. John's.
	Mr. Twisleton, Trinity.

DIVISION.

Ayes 5
Noes 22
Majority . . . 17

THURSDAY, MAY 8, 1828.

Mr. Dymock's Rooms, Balliol.

Mr. HOBHOUSE, Balliol, Treasurer, in the Chair.

Mr. HARDING, Oriel, moved :

That a Free Press is desirable.

SPEAKERS.

In the Affirmative.

Mr. Harding, Oriel.
Mr. Povah, St. John's.
Mr. Twisleton, Trinity.

The Motion was carried unanimously.

THURSDAY, MAY 15, 1828.

Mr. Hamilton's Rooms, Ch. Ch.

Mr. HOBHOUSE, Balliol, President, in the Chair.

Mr. MARRIOTT, Oriel, as proxy for Mr. RICHARDSON, Oriel, moved :

That the Catholic Claims ought to be conceded.

SPEAKERS.

In the Affirmative.	*In the Negative.*
Mr. Marriott, Oriel.	Mr. Hanmer, Ch. Ch.
Mr. D. Smith, Ch. Ch.	
Mr. Hobhouse, Balliol.	

DIVISION.

Ayes 49
Noes 28
Majority . . . 21

THURSDAY, MAY 22, 1828.

Lord Ossory's Rooms, Ch. Ch.

Mr. PEARSON, Balliol, President pro tem., in the Chair.

Mr. HAMILTON, Ch. Ch. moved:

That an Hereditary Aristocracy is beneficial to this Country.

The Motion was carried without a division.

THURSDAY, MAY 29, 1828.

Mr. Smythe's Rooms, C. C. C.

Mr. GRANT, New College, President, in the Chair.

Mr. NEALE, Oriel, as proxy for Mr. WILBERFORCE, Oriel, moved:

That the beneficial results of the French Revolution have more than counterbalanced its pernicious effects.

The Motion was carried by a large majority.

THURSDAY, JUNE 5, 1828.

Gentlemen Commoners' Common Room, C. C. C.

Mr. GRANT, New College, President, in the Chair.

Mr. WILBERFORCE, Oriel, as proxy for Mr. SEYMER, Ch. Ch. moved:

That the acquisition of Turkey by Russia would not be injurious to the interests of the European Powers.

SPEAKERS.

In the Affirmative.	In the Negative.
Mr. Tufnell, Balliol.	Mr. Marriott, sen. Oriel.
Mr. Wilberforce, Oriel.	Mr. Neale, Oriel.

DIVISION.

Ayes 7
Noes 17
Majority . . . 10

THURSDAY, JUNE 12, 1828.

Junior Common Room, New College.

Mr. GRANT, New College, President, in the Chair.

Mr. TUFNELL, Balliol, moved :

That the Impressment Laws are unnecessary.

SPEAKERS.

In the Affirmative.	*In the Negative.*
Mr. Tufnell, Balliol.	Mr. Neale, Oriel.
Mr. Wilberforce, Oriel.	Mr. Harding, Oriel.

DIVISION.

Ayes 17
Noes 12
Majority . . . 5

THURSDAY, OCTOBER 30, 1828.

Mr. Blackstone's Rooms, New Inn Hall.

Mr. HAMILTON, Ch. Ch. Secretary, in the Chair.

SIR JOHN HANMER, Ch. Ch. moved :

That a Free Trade in Corn would be in the highest degree injurious to the vital interests of Great Britain.

SPEAKERS.

In the Affirmative.	*In the Negative.*
Sir John Hanmer, Ch. Ch.	Mr. Baring, Ch. Ch.

DIVISION.

Ayes 13
Noes 24
Majority . . . 11

I

THURSDAY, NOVEMBER 6, 1828.

Baxter's Rooms.

Mr. BARING, Ch. Ch. President, in the Chair.

Mr. MARRIOTT, jun. Oriel, moved :

That Eloquence has produced greater good than evil to society.

SPEAKERS.

In the Affirmative.	*In the Negative.*
Mr. Marriott, jun. Oriel.	Mr. Neale, Oriel.

The Motion was carried without a division.

THURSDAY, NOVEMBER 13, 1828.

Baxter's Rooms.

Mr. BARING, Ch. Ch. President, in the Chair.

Mr. SMYTHE, C. C. C. moved :

That the establishment of Poor Laws would be most disadvantageous to Ireland.

The Motion was carried without a division.

THURSDAY, NOVEMBER 20, 1828.

Baxter's Rooms.

Mr. BARING, Ch. Ch. President, in the Chair.

Mr. NEALE, Oriel, moved :

That a Democratical form of Government is less likely to prove beneficial to the interests of a community than Absolute Monarchy.

SPEAKERS.

In the Affirmative.	*In the Negative.*
Mr. Neale, Oriel.	Mr. Wilson, Oriel.
	Mr. Harding, Oriel.
	Mr. Wilberforce, Oriel.

The Motion was lost without a division.

THURSDAY, NOVEMBER 27, 1828.

Baxter's Rooms.

Mr. BARING, Ch. Ch. President, in the Chair.

Mr. FARQUHAR, Ch. Ch. moved:

That the Foreign Policy of the Duke of Wellington has been most advantageous to the best interests of the Country, and strictly honourable to its character.

SPEAKERS.

In the Affirmative.	In the Negative.
Mr. Farquhar, Ch. Ch.	Mr. Phillimore, Ch. Ch.
	Mr. Marriott, sen. Oriel.
	Mr. Austen, Oriel.

DIVISION.

Ayes 19
Noes 29
Majority . . . 10

THURSDAY, DECEMBER 4, 1828.

Baxter's Rooms.

Mr. BARING, Ch. Ch. President, in the Chair.

Mr. HARDING, Oriel, moved:

That the institution and extension of Brunswick Clubs is more likely to endanger than to support the Constitution.

SPEAKERS.

In the Affirmative.	In the Negative.
Mr. Harding, Oriel.	Mr. Blackstone, Ch. Ch.
Mr. Pusey, Oriel.	Sir John Hanmer, Ch. Ch.
Mr. Marriott, sen. Oriel.	Mr. Smythe, C. C. C.
Mr. Moncrieff, New Coll.	Mr. Hughes, Trinity.

DIVISION.

Ayes 26
Noes 10
Majority . . . 16

THURSDAY, JANUARY 29, 1829.

Wyatt's Rooms.

MR. BARING, Ch. Ch. President, in the Chair.

MR. BARING, Ch. Ch. moved :

That the present system of Representation in England is corrupt, and requires a radical reform.

SPEAKERS.

In the Affirmative.	*In the Negative.*
Mr. Baring, Ch. Ch.	Mr. Blackstone, Ch. Ch.
	Mr. Wilberforce, Oriel.
	Mr. Wilson, Oriel.
	Sir John Hanmer, Ch. Ch.
	Mr. Chamberlain, Ch. Ch.

MR. ROGERS, Balliol, moved as an Amendment :

That the present system of Representation in England is corrupt in practice and imperfect in theory, and requires a constitutional reform.

DIVISION.

Ayes (for the Amendment) . 18
Noes (against it) 14
Majority . . . 4

THURSDAY, FEBRUARY 5, 1829.

Wyatt's Rooms.

MR. BARING, Ch. Ch. President, in the Chair.

MR. WILBERFORCE, Oriel, moved :

That the character of Queen Elizabeth merits the detestation of posterity.

SPEAKERS.

In the Affirmative.	*In the Negative.*
Mr. Wilberforce, Oriel.	Mr. Neale, Oriel.
	Mr. Wilson, Oriel.
	Mr. Hughes, Trinity.
	Mr. Puller, Ch. Ch.

The Motion was lost without a division.

THURSDAY, FEBRUARY 12, 1829.

Wyatt's Rooms.

MR. ACLAND, Ch. Ch. Secretary, in the Chair.

MR. FOX, Worcester, moved:

That the Execution of Charles the First was justifiable.

SPEAKERS.

In the Affirmative.	*In the Negative.*
Mr. Fox, Worcester.	Mr. Chamberlain, Ch. Ch.
	Mr. Hughes, Trinity.

The Motion was lost without a division.

THURSDAY, FEBRUARY, 19, 1829.

Wyatt's Rooms.

MR. WILBERFORCE, Oriel, President, in the Chair.

MR. MERIVALE, Balliol, moved:

That the American Constitution is better calculated than the English one to insure the liberty of the subject.

SPEAKER.

In the Affirmative.
Mr. Merivale, Balliol.

The Motion was carried without a division.

THURSDAY, FEBRUARY 26, 1829.

Wyatt's Rooms.

Mr. HARDING, Oriel, Treasurer, in the Chair.

Mr. MARRIOTT, Oriel, moved :

That the conduct of his Majesty's Government deserves the approbation and support of the nation.

SPEAKERS.

In the Affirmative.	*In the Negative.*
Mr. Marriott, Oriel.	Sir John Hanmer, Ch. Ch.
Mr. Hamilton, sen. Ch. Ch.	Mr. Farquhar, Ch. Ch.
Mr. Pusey, Oriel.	Mr. Hughes, Trinity.
Mr. Neale, Oriel.	
Mr. Austen, Oriel.	
Mr. Davison, Trinity.	

DIVISION.

Ayes 44
Noes 25
Majority . . . 19

THURSDAY, MARCH 5, 1829.

Wyatt's Rooms.

Mr. ACLAND, Ch. Ch. President, in the Chair.

Mr. BLISS, Oriel, moved :

That the substitution of a stipendiary Magistracy for the present system would be injurious to the Country.

SPEAKER.

In the Affirmative.
Mr. Bliss, Oriel.

The Motion was carried without a division.

THURSDAY, MARCH 12, 1829.

Wyatt's Rooms.

MR. ACLAND, Ch. Ch. President, in the Chair.

SIR JOHN HANMER, Ch. Ch. moved :

That the importation of Foreign Wool, and all articles of consumption which can be produced in the British Isles, ought to be discouraged.

SPEAKERS.

In the Affirmative.	*In the Negative.*
Sir John Hanmer, Ch. Ch.	Mr. Chamberlain, Ch. Ch.
	Mr. Oldham, Oriel.
	Mr. Manning, Balliol.
	Mr. Puller, Ch. Ch.
	Mr. Neale, Oriel.
	Mr. Harrison, Ch. Ch.

The Motion was lost by a large majority.

THURSDAY, MARCH 19, 1829.

Wyatt's Rooms.

MR. HARDING, Oriel, Treasurer, in the Chair.

MR. WILBERFORCE, Oriel, moved :

That those legislative enactments, by which the penalty of death is affixed to numerous and disproportionate offences, are favourable to the increase of crime.

SPEAKERS.

In the Affirmative.	*In the Negative.*
Mr. Wilberforce, Oriel.	Mr. Marriott, sen. Oriel.
Mr. Manning, Balliol.	Mr. Neale, Oriel.
Mr. Moncrieff, New Coll.	Mr. Skinner, Balliol.

DIVISION.

Ayes 41
Noes 20
Majority . . . 21

THURSDAY, MARCH 26, 1829.

Wyatt's Rooms.

Mr. WILBERFORCE, Oriel, President pro tem., in the Chair.

Mr. HARDING, Oriel, moved :

That the Execution of Lord Strafford was unjustifiable.

SPEAKERS.

In the Affirmative.	*In the Negative.*
Mr. Harding, Oriel.	Mr. Skinner, Balliol.
Sir J. Hanmer, Ch. Ch.	Mr. Wilson, Oriel.
	Mr. Hughes, Trinity.
	Mr. Marriott, sen. Oriel.
	Mr. Puller, Ch. Ch.

DIVISION.

Ayes 41
Noes 20
Majority . . . 21

THURSDAY, MAY 7, 1829.

Wyatt's Rooms.

Mr. ACLAND, Ch. Ch. President, in the Chair.

Mr. NEALE, Oriel, moved :

That the monopoly of the East India Company is injurious to this Country.

SPEAKERS.

In the Affirmative.	*In the Negative.*
Mr. Neale, Oriel.	Mr. Palmer, Ch. Ch.
Mr. Blackstone, Ch. Ch.	Sir J. Hanmer, Ch. Ch.
Mr. Moncrieff, New Coll.	Mr. Wilson, Oriel.
Mr. Wilberforce, Oriel.	
Hon. S. Herbert, Oriel.	
Mr. Acland, Ch. Ch.	

The Motion was carried by a large majority.

THURSDAY, MAY 14, 1829.

Wyatt's Rooms.

MR. HARDING, Oriel, Treasurer, in the Chair.

MR. ACLAND, Ch. Ch. moved:

That the present state of Slavery in our Colonies is one of injustice and of crime, and (however distant the period of final emancipation may be) more immediate measures ought to be taken for its abolition, than have yet been proposed to the Country.

SPEAKERS.

In the Affirmative.	*In the Negative.*
Mr. Acland, Ch. Ch.	Mr. Chamberlain, Ch. Ch.
Mr. Moncrieff, New Coll.	Mr. Vaughan, Balliol.
	Mr. Lewis, Ch. Ch.

SIR JOHN HANMER, Ch. Ch. moved as an Amendment:

That the first part of the Question be omitted.

SPEAKERS.

In the Affirmative.	*In the Negative.*
Sir J. Hanmer, Ch. Ch.	Mr. Tancred, Ch. Ch.
Mr. Manning, Balliol.	Mr. Wilberforce, Oriel.
Mr. Davison, Trinity.	

DIVISION.

On the Amendment.	On the Original Motion.
Ayes 19	Ayes 28
Noes 31	Noes 25
Majority . 12	Majority . 3

THURSDAY, MAY 21, 1829.

Wyatt's Rooms.

MR. ACLAND, sen. Ch. Ch. President, in the Chair.

MR. DAVISON, Trinity, moved:

That the Usury Laws ought to be repealed.

SPEAKERS.

In the Affirmative.	*In the Negative.*
Mr. Davison, Trinity.	Mr. Harding, Oriel.
Mr. Acland, sen. Ch. Ch.	Mr. Neale, Oriel.
Mr. Wilberforce, Oriel.	

DIVISION.

Ayes 33
Noes 17
Majority . . . 16

K

THURSDAY, MAY 28, 1829.

Wyatt's Rooms.

MR. MONCRIEFF, New College, President, in the Chair.

MR. OLDHAM, Oriel, moved :

That Septennial Parliaments are injurious to the Constitution.

SPEAKERS.

In the Affirmative.	*In the Negative.*
Mr. Oldham, Oriel.	Mr. Oakes, Merton.
	Mr. Vaughan, Balliol.
	Mr. Doyle, Ch. Ch.
	Mr. Gaskell, Ch. Ch.

The Motion was lost without a division.

THURSDAY, JUNE 4, 1829.

Wyatt's Rooms.

MR. HARDING, Oriel, Secretary, in the Chair.

MR. MONCRIEFF, New College, moved :

That the diffusion of General Knowledge amongst all Classes is attended with great benefit to the Country.

SPEAKERS.

In the Affirmative.	*In the Negative.*
Mr. Moncrieff, New Coll.	Sir J. Hanmer, Ch. Ch.
Mr. Acland, sen. Ch. Ch.	Mr. Oldham, Oriel.
Mr. Harding, Oriel.	Mr. Palmer, Ch. Ch.
Mr. Acland, jun. Ch. Ch.	

SIR J. HANMER moved as an Amendment :

That the word " appropriate" be substituted for the word " general."

The Amendment was then put, and lost ; and the original Motion carried without a division.

THURSDAY, JUNE 11, 1329.

Wyatt's Rooms.

Mr. MONCRIEFF, New College, President, in the Chair.

Mr. WILSON, Oriel, moved:

That the impolitic and reprehensible conduct of Parliament, and not any prior ill-will towards it on the part of Charles the First, caused that mutual opposition which ended in civil war.

SPEAKERS.

In the Affirmative.	*In the Negative.*
Mr. Wilson, Oriel.	Mr. Acland, sen. Ch. Ch.
Mr. Manning, Balliol.	Mr. Wilberforce, Oriel.
Mr. Acland, jun. Ch. Ch.	Mr. Neale, Oriel.

Mr. WILBERFORCE, Oriel, moved as an Amendment:

That the cause of the civil wars is to be sought for in the circumstances of the times.

The Amendment was lost without a division.

DIVISION ON THE ORIGINAL MOTION.

Ayes 28
Noes 17
Majority . . . 11

THURSDAY, JUNE 18, 1829.

Wyatt's Rooms.

Mr. MONCRIEFF, New College, President, in the Chair.

Mr. NEALE, Oriel, moved:

That the genius of Cromwell was as great as that of Buonaparte, and that his character is as deserving of admiration.

SPEAKER.

In the Affirmative.
Mr. Neale, Oriel.

The Motion was lost without a division.

THURSDAY, JUNE 25, 1829.

Wyatt's Rooms.

MR. MONCRIEFF, New College, President, in the Chair.

The HON. S. HERBERT, Oriel, moved:

That the Pacific Policy adopted towards Russia by the present Administration, ought to be persevered in.

SPEAKERS.

In the Affirmative.   *In the Negative.*
Hon. S. Herbert, Oriel.   Mr. Oldham, Oriel.
Mr. Gaskell, Ch. Ch.

The Motion was carried without a division.

THURSDAY, OCTOBER 22, 1829.

Wyatt's Rooms.

MR. MONCRIEFF, New College, President, in the Chair.

MR. GASKELL, Ch. Ch. moved:

That the conduct of Mr. Pitt, as Minister of this Country, is entitled to approbation.

SPEAKERS.

In the Affirmative.   *In the Negative.*
Mr. Gaskell, Ch. Ch.   Mr. Moncrieff, New Coll.

DIVISION.

Ayes 45
Noes 17
Majority . . . 28

THURSDAY, OCTOBER 29, 1829.

Wyatt's Rooms.

MR. MONCRIEFF, New College, President, in the Chair.

MR. DOYLE, Ch. Ch. moved :

That the conduct of the present Administration with regard to Portugal is contrary to the dignity and subversive of the best interests of the Country.

SPEAKERS.

In the Affirmative.	*In the Negative.*
Mr. Doyle, Ch. Ch.	Mr. Massie, Wadham.
Mr. Gaskell, Ch. Ch.	Mr. Manning, Balliol.
Mr. Harding, Oriel.	Mr. Vaughan, Balliol.
Mr. Austen, Oriel.	

DIVISION.

Ayes 25
Noes 21
Majority . . . 4

THURSDAY, NOVEMBER 5, 1829.

Wyatt's Rooms.

MR. MONCRIEFF, New College, President, in the Chair.

MR. ACLAND, sen. Ch. Ch. moved :

That the balance of power in the British Constitution is rather between Aristocratical Interest and Public Opinion, than between King, Lords, and Commons.

SPEAKERS.

In the Affirmative.	*In the Negative.*
Mr. Acland, sen. Ch. Ch.	Mr. Moncrieff, New Coll.
Mr. Baring, Ch. Ch.	
Mr. Wilberforce, Oriel.	

The Motion was lost without a division.

THURSDAY, NOVEMBER 12, 1829.

Wyatt's Rooms.

Mr. WILBERFORCE, Oriel, President, in the Chair.

Mr. HARDING, Oriel, moved:

That the revolt of the American Colonies was justifiable.

The Motion was carried without a division.

THURSDAY, NOVEMBER 19, 1829.

Wyatt's Rooms.

Mr. WILBERFORCE, Oriel, President, in the Chair.

Mr. ACLAND, jun. Ch. Ch. moved:

That the law requiring unanimity in Juries is prejudicial to the interests of justice.

SPEAKERS.

In the Affirmative.	*In the Negative.*
Mr. Acland, jun. Ch. Ch.	Mr. Neale, Oriel.
Mr. Manning, Balliol.	
Mr. Acland, sen. Ch. Ch.	
Mr. Moncrieff, New Coll.	

The Motion was carried without a division.

THURSDAY, NOVEMBER 26, 1829.

Wyatt's Rooms.

Mr. WILBERFORCE, Oriel, President, in the Chair.

Mr. DOYLE, Ch. Ch. moved:

That Shelley was a greater poet than Lord Byron.

SPEAKERS.

In the Affirmative.	In the Negative.
Mr. Doyle, Ch. Ch.	Mr. Manning, Balliol.
*Mr. Sunderland, Trin. Coll. Camb.	
*Mr. Hallam, Trin. Coll. Camb.	
*Mr. Milnes, Trin. Coll. Camb.	
Mr. Oldham, Oriel.	

DIVISION.

Ayes 33
Noes 90
Majority . . . 57

* Honorary Members.

THURSDAY, DECEMBER 3, 1829.

Wyatt's Rooms.

Mr. WILBERFORCE, Oriel, President, in the Chair.

Mr. GASKELL, Ch. Ch. moved:

That the terms of the late treaty between Russia and Turkey were strictly in unison with the professions of moderation made by the Emperor of Russia.

SPEAKERS.

In the Affirmative.	In the Negative.
Mr. Gaskell, Ch. Ch.	Mr. Baring, Ch. Ch.
Sir John Hanmer, Ch. Ch.	Mr. Wilson, Oriel.
Hon. S. Herbert, Oriel.	Mr. Vaughan, Balliol.
Mr. Lyall, Balliol.	Mr. Austen, Oriel.
	Mr. Acland, jun. Ch. Ch.
	Mr. Moncrieff, New Coll.
	Mr. Wilberforce, Oriel.

DIVISION.

Ayes 12
Noes 67
Majority . . . 55

THURSDAY, JANUARY 28, 1830.

Wyatt's Rooms.

Mr. WILBERFORCE, Oriel, President, in the Chair.

SIR JOHN HANMER, Ch. Ch. moved:

That the purity and independence of Parliament is better secured at present than it would be under any system of reform.

SPEAKERS.

In the Affirmative.	*In the Negative.*
Sir John Hanmer, Ch. Ch.	Mr. Oldham, Oriel.
Mr. Gaskell, Ch. Ch.	Mr. Lyall, Balliol.
	Mr. Doyle, Ch. Ch.
	Mr. Manning, Balliol.
	Mr. Moncrieff, New Coll.

Mr. MANNING moved as an Amendment:

That there is as great an infusion of popular power in the House of Commons as is consistent with the spirit of the Constitution.

SIR JOHN HANMER withdrew the original Motion.

DIVISION ON THE MOTION AS AMENDED.

Ayes 73
Noes 3
Majority . . . 70

THURSDAY, FEBRUARY 4, 1830.

Wyatt's Rooms.

Mr. WILBERFORCE, Oriel, President, in the Chair.

Mr. WILSON, Oriel, moved:

That the American Constitution is not adapted to the exigencies of a powerful state, and does not promise stability.

SPEAKERS.

In the Affirmative.	*In the Negative.*
Mr. Wilson, Oriel.	Mr. Baugh, Exeter.
Mr. Goldsmid, Balliol.	
Mr. Manning, Balliol.	

The Motion was carried without a division.

THURSDAY, FEBRUARY 11, 1830.

Wyatt's Rooms.

Mr. WILBERFORCE, Oriel, President, in the Chair.

Mr. MONCRIEFF, New College, moved :

That the conduct of Mr. Fox and his party in reference to the Treason and Sedition Bills, which were passed in the year 1795, deserved the admiration and gratitude of their Country.

SPEAKERS.

In the Affirmative.	*In the Negative.*
Mr. Moncrieff, New Coll.	Sir John Hanmer, Ch. Ch.
	Mr. Gladstone, Ch. Ch.

DIVISION.

Ayes 26
Noes 44
Majority . . . 18

THURSDAY, FEBRUARY 18, 1830.

Wyatt's Rooms.

The HON. S. HERBERT, Oriel, President, in the Chair.

Mr. WILSON, Oriel, moved :

That Cheap Justice is a National evil.

SPEAKERS.

In the Affirmative.	*In the Negative.*
Mr. Wilson, Oriel.	Mr. White, Trinity.
Mr. Moncrieff, New Coll.	Mr. Oldham, Oriel.
Mr. Hughes, Trinity.	Mr. Lyall, Balliol.
	Mr. Harding, Oriel.

DIVISION.

Ayes 37
Noes 27
Majority . . . 10

THURSDAY, FEBRUARY 25, 1830.

Wyatt's Rooms.

The HON. S. HERBERT, Oriel, President, in the Chair.

MR. VAUGHAN, Balliol, moved :

That Mr. Canning's conduct as a Minister is deserving of the highest commendation.

SPEAKER.

In the Affirmative.
Mr. Gaskell, Ch. Ch.

MR. MONCRIEFF, New College, moved as an Amendment :

That what we knew of the character and policy of Mr. Canning in 1827, justified the highest expectations from his being appointed Prime Minister.

SPEAKERS.

In the Negative.
Mr. Manning, Balliol.
Mr. Doyle, Ch. Ch.
Mr. Gladstone, Ch. Ch.

MR. HARDING moved as a second Amendment :

That Mr. Canning's conduct, from the time that he became Prime Minister, is deserving of the highest commendation.

DIVISION ON MR. MONCRIEFF'S AMENDMENT.
Ayes 1
Noes 65
Majority . . . 64

DIVISION ON MR. HARDING'S AMENDMENT.
Ayes 5
Noes 63
Majority . . . 58

DIVISION ON THE ORIGINAL MOTION.
Ayes 53
Noes 15
Majority . . . 38

THURSDAY, MARCH 4, 1830.

Wyatt's Rooms.

MR. MONCRIEFF, New Coll. Treasurer, in the Chair.

The HON. S. HERBERT, Oriel, moved:

That Amelioration in the present state of the Lower Orders depends more upon the private exertions of the Landholders, than upon any Acts of Legislation.

SPEAKERS.

In the *Affirmative.*	In the *Negative.*
Hon. S. Herbert, Oriel.	Mr. Thornton, Ch. Ch.
Marquis of Abercorn, Ch. Ch.	Mr. Oldham, Oriel.
Mr. Wilson, Oriel.	Mr. Doyle, Ch. Ch.
	Mr. Harding, Oriel.

MR. HARDING, Oriel, moved as an Amendment:

That any exertions of the Landholders must be useless, unless accompanied by a great reduction of taxation and a moderate issue of paper money.

SPEAKERS.

In the *Affirmative.*	In the *Negative.*
Mr. Harding, Oriel.	Mr. Wilberforce, Oriel.

DIVISION.

On the Amendment.	*On the Original Motion.*
Ayes . . . 4	Ayes . . . 56
Noes . . . 79	Noes . . . 34
Majority 75	Majority 22

WEDNESDAY, MARCH 10, 1830.

Wyatt's Rooms.

The HON. S. HERBERT, Oriel, President, in the Chair.

MR. WILLIAMS, Oriel, moved :

That the conduct of Great Britain in her treatment of Buonaparte was justifiable.

SPEAKERS.

In the Affirmative.	*In the Negative.*
Mr. Williams, Oriel.	Mr. Harding, Oriel.
Mr. Wilson, Oriel.	Mr. Doyle, Ch. Ch.
Hon. S. Herbert, Oriel.	

MR. MASSIE, Wadham, moved as an Amendment :

That the Banishment of Buonaparte to St. Helena was justifiable, but that the treatment of him in exile was unwarrantably severe.

DIVISION.

On the Amendment.	*On the Original Motion.*
Ayes . . . 33	Ayes . . . 62
Noes . . . 37	Noes . . . 8
Majority 4	Majority 54

THURSDAY, MARCH 18, 1830.

Wyatt's Rooms.

The HON. S. HERBERT, President, in the Chair.

MR. OLDHAM, Oriel, moved :

That our Criminal Code is a National disgrace.

SPEAKERS.

In the Affirmative.	*In the Negative.*
Mr. Oldham, Oriel.	Hon. J. Bruce, Ch. Ch.
Mr. White, Trinity.	
Mr. Wilberforce, Oriel.	
Mr. Moncrieff, New Coll.	

DIVISION.

Ayes 24
Noes 52
Majority . . . 28

THURSDAY, MARCH 25, 1830.

Wyatt's Rooms.

The HON. S. HERBERT, Oriel, President, in the Chair.

MR. MONCRIEFF, New College, as proxy for MR. LYALL, Balliol, moved :

That Leeds, Manchester, and Birmingham, ought to be represented in Parliament.

SPEAKERS.

In the Affirmative.	*In the Negative.*
Mr. Moncrieff, New Coll.	Mr. Gaskell, Ch. Ch.
Mr. Jelf, Ch. Ch.	
Mr. Wilberforce, Oriel.	

DIVISION.

Ayes 12
Noes 14
Majority . . . 2

THURSDAY, APRIL 29, 1830.

Wyatt's Rooms.

MR. MONCRIEFF, New College, Treasurer, in the Chair.

The Treasurer acquainted the House, that the noble Mover of the Question which had been chosen by the Committee (LORD C. OSBORNE), had withdrawn his name from the list of the Society. The noble Lord's Question,

That the Battle of Navarino was unjustifiable, and that its consequences have proved prejudicial to the interests of England and France, the two principal powers engaged in it,

Was then put from the Chair.

DIVISION.

Ayes 10
Noes 23
Majority . . . 13

THURSDAY, MAY 6, 1830.

Wyatt's Rooms.

The HON. S. HERBERT, Oriel, President, in the Chair.

Mʀ. HARDING, Oriel, moved:

That the Foreign Policy of the late Lord Londonderry was most disgraceful and injurious to this Country.

DIVISION.

Ayes 21
Noes 16
Majority . . . 5

THURSDAY, MAY 13, 1830.

Wyatt's Rooms.

Mʀ. MONCRIEFF, New College, Treasurer, in the Chair.

Mʀ. DOYLE, Ch. Ch. moved:

That the Expedition of Buonaparte against Russia was defensible, on the ground of policy.

DIVISION.

Ayes 6
Noes 28
Majority . . . 22

THURSDAY, MAY 20, 1830.

Wyatt's Rooms.

Mr. GASKELL, Ch. Ch. President, in the Chair.

Mr. LYALL, Balliol, moved:

That the Civil disabilities of the Jews ought to be removed.

SPEAKERS.

In the Affirmative.	*In the Negative.*
Mr. Lyall, Balliol.	Mr. Anstice, Ch. Ch.
Mr. Harding, Oriel.	Mr. Blackstone, Ch. Ch.
Mr. Acland, jun. Ch. Ch.	Mr. Gladstone, Ch. Ch.
Mr. Gaskell, Ch. Ch.	Mr. Acland, sen. Ch. Ch.
Mr. Doyle, Ch. Ch.	Mr. Oakes, Merton.
Mr. Moncrieff, New Coll.	
Mr. Peter, Ch. Ch.	

Mr. OAKES, Merton, moved as an Amendment:

That all the Civil disabilities of the Jews ought to be removed, with the exception of those which exclude them from seats in the Legislature, and from offices of influence under the Crown.

The Amendment was lost without a division.

DIVISION ON THE ORIGINAL MOTION.

Ayes 16
Noes 55
Majority . . . 39

THURSDAY, MAY 27, 1830.

Wyatt's Rooms.

Mr. GASKELL, Ch. Ch. President, in the Chair.

Mr. NEALE, Oriel, moved:

That Warren Hastings was unjustly impeached.

DIVISION.

Ayes 25
Noes 24
Majority . . . 1

THURSDAY, JUNE 3, 1830.

Wyatt's Rooms.

MR. GASKELL, Ch. Ch. President, in the Chair.

MR. MONCRIEFF, New College, moved :

That the proposal made by Mr. Brougham to establish a local Judge in each County, should be carried into effect.

DIVISION.

Ayes 18
Noes 18
. .

The numbers being even, the President gave his casting vote in favour of the Motion.

THURSDAY, JUNE 10, 1830.

Wyatt's Rooms.

MR. GASKELL, Ch. Ch. President, in the Chair.

MR. HARDING, Oriel, moved :

That the Maritime supremacy of Great Britain rests on no right save that of the strongest; but that it must be maintained at all risks, and under all circumstances.

SPEAKERS.

In the Affirmative.	*In the Negative.*
Mr. Harding, Oriel.	Mr. Acland, sen. Ch. Ch.
	Mr. Moncrieff, New Coll.

DIVISION.

Ayes 16
Noes 15
Majority . . . 1

THURSDAY, JUNE 17, 1830.

Wyatt's Rooms.

MR. GASKELL, Ch. Ch. President, in the Chair.

MR. CHAMBERLAIN, Ch. Ch. moved :

That the establishing of Colleges in London for the education of the Middle Classes, is beneficial to the interests of Society.

SPEAKERS.

In the Affirmative.	*In the Negative.*
Mr. Chamberlain, Ch. Ch.	Mr. Gladstone, Ch. Ch.
Mr. Moncrieff, New Coll.	
Mr. Acland, sen. Ch. Ch.	

DIVISION.

Ayes 19
Noes 15
Majority . . . 4

THURSDAY, OCTOBER 28, 1830.

Wyatt's Rooms.

MR. GLADSTONE, Ch. Ch. Secretary, in the Chair.

MR. GASKELL, Ch. Ch. moved :

That the Foreign Policy of the Duke of Wellington has been derogatory to the dignity, and injurious to the best interests, of the Country.

SPEAKERS.

In the Affirmative.	*In the Negative.*
Mr. Vaughan, Balliol.	Mr. Harding, Oriel.
Mr. Doyle, Ch. Ch.	
Mr. Scott, Ch. Ch.	
Mr. Wrightson, Brasen-nose.	
Mr. Gladstone, Ch. Ch.	

DIVISION.

Ayes 24
Noes 48
Majority . . 24

M

THURSDAY, NOVEMBER 4, 1830.

Wyatt's Rooms.

Mr. GASKELL, Ch. Ch. President, in the Chair.

Mr. VAUGHAN, Balliol, moved :

That the Duke of Reichstadt had a better right to the Crown of France than Charles X. before the deposition of the latter.

SPEAKERS.

In the Affirmative.	*In the Negative.*
Mr. Vaughan, Balliol.	Mr. Scott, Ch. Ch.
	Mr. Jelf, Ch. Ch.
	Mr. Denison, Balliol.

The Motion was lost without a division

THURSDAY, NOVEMBER 11, 1830.

Wyatt's Rooms.

Mr. GASKELL, Ch. Ch. President, in the Chair.

Mr GLADSTONE, Ch. Ch. moved :

That the Administration of the Duke of Wellington is undeserving of the confidence of the Country.

SPEAKERS.

In the Affirmative.	*In the Negative.*
Mr. Gladstone, Ch. Ch.	Hon. S. Herbert, Oriel.
Mr. Doyle, Ch. Ch.	Marquis of Abercorn, Ch. Ch.
Mr. Gaskell, Ch. Ch.	
Mr. Knatchbull, Trinity.	
Mr. Lyall, Balliol.	
Earl of Lincoln, Ch. Ch.	

DIVISION.

Ayes 57
Noes 56
Majority . . . 1

THURSDAY, NOVEMBER 18, 1830.

Wyatt's Rooms.

MR. GLADSTONE, Ch. Ch. President, in the Chair.

MR. DENISON, Balliol, moved :

That Free Trade is essential to the prosperity of the Country.

SPEAKERS.

In the Affirmative.	*In the Negative.*
Mr. Denison, Balliol.	Mr. Jelf, Ch. Ch.

MR. ACLAND, Ch. Ch. moved as an Amendment:

That Free Trade is based upon sound principles, although its immediate application might be attended with great difficulties.

MR. DENISON withdrew his Motion, and acquiesced in the Amendment.

DIVISION ON THE MOTION AS AMENDED.

Ayes 52
Noes 28
Majority . . . 24

THURSDAY, NOVEMBER 25, 1830.

Wyatt's Rooms.

MR. GLADSTONE, Ch. Ch. President, in the Chair.

MR. WHITE, Trinity, moved :

That the law by which Forgery is punished with Death, is unworthy of the Legislature, and ought to be repealed.

SPEAKERS.

In the Affirmative.	*In the Negative.*
Mr. White, Trinity.	Mr. Rogers, Oriel.
Mr. Wrightson, Brasen-nose.	Mr. Knatchbull, Trinity.
Mr. Rickards, Trinity.	Mr. De Salis, Oriel.
Mr. Acland, Ch. Ch.	

DIVISION.

Ayes 45
Noes 37
Majority . . . 8

THURSDAY, DECEMBER 2, 1830.

Wyatt's Rooms.

Mʀ. GLADSTONE, Ch. Ch. President, in the Chair.

Mʀ. ACLAND, sen. Ch. Ch. moved :

That the Declaration of Rights made by the National Assembly of France in 1789, was founded upon false principles.

SPEAKERS.

In the Affirmative.	*In the Negative.*
Mr. Acland, sen. Ch. Ch.	Mr. Cox, New College.
Mr. Palmer, Trinity.	Mr. Harding, Oriel.
Mr. Maurice, Exeter.	
Mr. Gaskell, Ch. Ch.	

The Motion was carried without a division.

THURSDAY, DECEMBER 9, 1830.

Wyatt's Rooms.

Mʀ. GLADSTONE, Ch. Ch. President, in the Chair.

Mʀ. RICKARDS, Trinity, moved :

That Pope has not been equalled by any Poet since his time.

SPEAKERS.

In the Affirmative.	*In the Negative.*
Mr. Rickards, Trinity.	Mr. Doyle, Ch. Ch.
	Mr. Law, King's Coll. Camb.

DIVISION.

Ayes	28
Noes	43
Majority . . .	15

THURSDAY, JANUARY 27, 1831.
Wyatt's Rooms.

Mʀ. ACLAND, Ch. Ch. Treasurer, in the Chair.

Mʀ. ALLIES, Wadham, moved :

That it behoves all lovers of their Country to unite against the spirit of Democracy, which is tending to destroy the Constitution in Church and State.

SPEAKERS.

In the Affirmative.	*In the Negative.*
Mr. Allies, Wadham.	Mr. Kempson, Ch. Ch.
Mr. Palmer, Trinity.	Mr. Tait, Balliol.
Mr. Doyle, Ch. Ch.	Mr. Cox, New College.
Mr. Anstice, Ch. Ch.	
Mr. Marriott, Balliol.	

Mʀ. ACLAND, sen. Ch. Ch. moved as an Amendment :

That evil principles are gaining ground, which can only be resisted by the adequate discharge of private duties.

DIVISION ON THE AMENDMENT.
Ayes 43
Noes 35
Majority . . . 8

THURSDAY, FEBRUARY 3, 1831.
Wyatt's Rooms.

The HON. J. BRUCE, Ch. Ch. President, in the Chair.

Mʀ. ROGERS, Oriel, moved :

That the Exclusion of the Duc de Bordeaux from the Throne of France is unjustifiable.

SPEAKERS.

In the Affirmative.	*In the Negative.*
Mr. Rogers, Oriel.	Mr. Palmer, Magdalen.
Mr. Jelf, Ch. Ch.	Mr. White, Trinity.
Mr. Palmer, Trinity.	Mr. Acland, Ch. Ch.
Hon. J. Hewitt, Ch. Ch.	Mr. Wilberforce, Oriel.
Mr. Doyle, Ch. Ch.	

DIVISION.
Ayes 56
Noes 28
Majority . . . 28

THURSDAY, FEBRUARY 10, 1821.

Wyatt's Rooms.

The HON. J. BRUCE, Ch. Ch. President, in the Chair.

MR. WARD, Oriel, moved:

That the extent to which the Liberty of the Press is now carried, is injurious to the peace and welfare of Society.

SPEAKERS.

In the Affirmative.	*In the Negative.*
Mr. Ward, Oriel.	Mr. Acland, jun. Ch. Ch.
Mr. Rickards, Trinity.	Mr. Vaughan, Ch. Ch.
Mr. Wilson, Oriel.	Mr. Anstice, Ch. Ch.
Mr. Palmer, Magdalen.	Mr. Doyle, Ch. Ch.
	Mr. Maurice, Exeter.
	Mr. Acland, sen. Ch. Ch.

DIVISION.

Ayes 35
Noes 81
Majority . . . 46

WEDNESDAY, FEBRUARY 16, 1831.

Wyatt's Rooms.

The HON. J. BRUCE, Ch. Ch. President, in the Chair.

MR. JELF, Ch. Ch. moved:

That the Catholic Relief Bill has not justified by its results the expectations which were held out by its supporters.

SPEAKERS.

In the Affirmative.	*In the Negative.*
Mr. Jelf, Ch. Ch.	Mr. White, Trinity.
Mr. Palmer, Magdalen.	Mr. Tait, Balliol.
Mr. Knatchbull, Trinity.	Mr. Gaskell, Ch. Ch.
Mr. Scott, Ch. Ch.	Mr. Anstice, Ch. Ch.
	Mr. Gladstone, Ch. Ch.
	Mr. Doyle, Ch. Ch.

DIVISION.

Ayes 40
Noes 59
Majority . . . 19

THURSDAY, FEBRUARY 24, 1831.

Wyatt's Rooms.

The HON. J. BRUCE, Ch. Ch. President, in the Chair.

MR. GASKELL, Ch. Ch. moved:

That the late Conduct of the Irish Government is entitled to approbation.

SPEAKERS.

In the Affirmative.	In the Negative.
Mr. Gaskell, Ch. Ch.	Hon. S. Herbert, Oriel.

The HON. S. HERBERT, Oriel, moved as an Amendment:

That the word " Measures" be substituted for the word "Conduct."

DIVISION ON THE AMENDMENT.

Ayes 43
Noes 33
Majority . . . 10

THURSDAY, MARCH 3, 1831.

Wyatt's Rooms.

MR. A. ACLAND, Treasurer, in the Chair.

The HON. S. HERBERT, Oriel, moved:

That a Reform in the system of Parliamentary Representation will ultimately prove destructive of the Constitution, and consequently of the Prosperity of this Country.

SPEAKERS.

In the Affirmative.	In the Negative.
Hon. S. Herbert, Oriel.	Mr. Cox, New College.
Mr. Anstice, Ch. Ch.	Mr. Gaskell, Ch. Ch.
Mr. Denison, Balliol.	Mr. Lyall, Balliol.
Mr. Wilson, Oriel.	Mr. White, Trinity.
Mr. Knatchbull, Trinity.	Mr. Palmer, Trinity.
	Mr. Maurice, Merton.

DIVISION.

Ayes 80
Noes 56
Majority . . . 24

THURSDAY, MARCH 10, 1831.

Wyatt's Rooms.

Mr. DENISON, Balliol, Secretary, in the Chair.

Mr. MASSIE, Wadham, moved:

That the present system of educating the Lower Orders is injurious to the Constitution, and demands a remedy.

SPEAKERS.

In the Affirmative.	*In the Negative.*
Mr. Massie, Wadham.	Mr. Lowe, University.
Mr. Harrison, Ch. Ch.	Mr. Palmer, Magdalen.
	Mr. Powell, Trinity.
	Mr. Lyall, Balliol.
	Mr. Anstice, Ch. Ch.
	Mr. Manning, Balliol.

Mr. ANSTICE, Ch. Ch. moved as an Amendment:

That the separation of moral from intellectual knowledge is injurious

Which he subsequently withdrew.

Mr. MANNING, Balliol, moved as an Amendment:

That the present system of educating the Lower Orders is not injurious to the Constitution.

This Amendment also was withdrawn.

DIVISION ON THE ORIGINAL MOTION.

Ayes 8
Noes 34
Majority . . . 26

THURSDAY, MARCH 17, 1831.

Wyatt's Rooms.

MR. A. ACLAND, Ch. Ch. Treasurer, in the Chair.

MR. PALMER, Trinity, moved:

That the Poor Laws are a principal cause of the present Distress.

SPEAKERS.

In the Affirmative.	*In the Negative.*
Mr. Palmer, Trinity.	Mr. Lowe, University.
Mr. Palmer, Magdalen.	Mr. Massie, Wadham.

MR. MASSIE, Wadham, moved as an Amendment:

That the abuse of the Poor Laws is the cause of great Distress among the Labouring Classes.

DIVISION ON THE AMENDMENT.

Ayes 27
Noes 11
Majority . . . 16

THURSDAY, APRIL 21, 1831.

Wyatt's Rooms.

The HON. J. BRUCE, Ch. Ch. President, in the Chair.

MR. LYALL, Balliol, moved :

That Emigration is a most effectual remedy for the Distress which prevails, among the Labouring Classes of the United Kingdom.

SPEAKERS.

In the Affirmative.	*In the Negative.*
Mr. Lyall, Balliol.	Hon. J. Hewitt, Ch. Ch.
	Mr. Knatchbull, Trinity.

MR. KNATCHBULL, Trinity, moved as an Amendment:

That the Distress which at present exists requires some more immediate and permanent remedy than any which can be expected to result from Emigration.

DIVISION ON THE AMENDMENT.

Ayes 31
Noes 11
Majority . . . 20

N

THURSDAY, APRIL 28, 1831.

Wyatt's Rooms.

The HON. J. BRUCE, Ch. Ch. President, in the Chair.

MR. JELF, Ch. Ch. moved:

That the Conduct of the Manchester Magistrates in 1819 was deserving of approbation.

SPEAKER.

In the Affirmative.
Mr. Jelf, Ch. Ch.

The Motion was carried without a division.

THURSDAY, MAY 5, 1831.

Wyatt's Rooms.

MR. LYALL, Balliol, President pro tem., in the Chair.

MR. RICKARDS, Trinity, moved:

That the system of Tithes is injurious and inconvenient, and that a just commutation is highly to be desired by the best friends of the Church.

SPEAKERS.

In the Affirmative.	*In the Negative.*
Mr. Rickards. Trinity.	Mr. Ward, Oriel.
Mr. Moncrieff, New Coll.	Hon. J. Hewitt, Ch. Ch.
	Mr. Palmer, Magdalen.

The Motion was carried without a division.

MONDAY, MAY 16, 1831.

Wyatt's Rooms.

Mr. LYALL, Balliol, President, in the Chair.

Mr. KNATCHBULL, Trinity, moved :

That the present Ministry is incompetent to carry on the Government of the Country.

SPEAKERS.

In the Affirmative.	*In the Negative.*
Mr. Knatchbull, Trinity.	Mr. White, Trinity.
Mr. Palmer, Magdalen.	Mr. Lowe, University.
Mr. Doyle, Ch. Ch.	Mr. Massie, Wadham.
Hon. S. Herbert, Oriel.	Mr. Cox, New College.
Mr. Anstice, Ch. Ch.	Mr. Tait, Balliol.

Adjourned at half-past eleven.

TUESDAY, MAY 17, 1831.

Wyatt's Rooms.

Mr. LYALL, Balliol, President, in the Chair.

ADJOURNED DEBATE.

SPEAKERS.

In the Affirmative.	*In the Negative.*
Mr. Palmer, Trinity.	Mr. Thomas, St. Mary Hall.
Mr. Jelf, Ch. Ch.	Mr. Oakes, Merton.
Earl of Lincoln, Ch. Ch.	Mr. Reeves, Merton.
Mr. Gladstone, Ch. Ch.	Mr. Gaskell, Ch. Ch.

Mr. GLADSTONE, Ch. Ch. moved as a Rider to the Motion :

That the Ministry has unwisely introduced, and most unscrupulously forwarded, a measure which threatens not only to change the form of our Government, but ultimately to break up the very foundations of social order, as well as materially to forward the views of those who are pursuing this project throughout the civilized world.

Adjourned till Thursday, May 19th.

THURSDAY, MAY 19, 1831.

Wyatt's Rooms.

Mr. LYALL, Balliol, President, in the Chair.

ADJOURNED DEBATE.

SPEAKERS.

In the Affirmative.	*In the Negative.*
Mr. Rickards, Trinity.	Mr. Moncrieff, New Coll.
Mr. Harrison, Ch. Ch.	Mr. Acland, jun. Ch. Ch.
Mr. Alston, Ch. Ch.	Mr. Lyall, Balliol.
Hon. J. Bruce, Ch. Ch.	

DIVISION.

Ayes 94
Noes 38
Majority . . . 56

THURSDAY, MAY 26, 1831.

Wyatt's Rooms.

Mr. LYALL, Balliol, President, in the Chair.

Mr. REEVES, Merton, moved :

That the Charter of the East India Company ought to be Renewed.

SPEAKER.

In the Affirmative.
Mr. Reeves, Merton.

DIVISION.

Ayes 29
Noes 11
Majority . . . 18

THURSDAY, JUNE 2, 1831.

Wyatt's Rooms.

MR. GASKELL, Ch. Ch. President pro tem., in the Chair.

MR. MONCRIEFF, New College, moved:

That the Slaves in our West India Colonies ought to be Emancipated without delay, and that all due precaution should be taken which is consistent with that measure.

SPEAKERS.

In the Affirmative.	*In the Negative.*
Mr. Moncrieff, New Coll.	Mr. Goldsmid, Balliol.
Mr. Dupuis, King's Coll. Camb.	Mr. Ward, Oriel.
	Mr. Lowe, University.
	Mr. Gladstone, Ch. Ch.

MR. WARD, Oriel, moved as an Amendment:

That since it is the Policy of the British Government that all its subjects should be free, means should be taken to render the state of society in the West Indies fit to receive the Emancipation of the Slaves; and encouragement should be given to the Planters to ameliorate the present condition of the Slaves.

This Amendment was withdrawn.

MR. GLADSTONE, Ch. Ch. moved as an Amendment:

That Legislative enactments ought to be made, and if necessary to be enforced:

1st, For better guarding the personal and civil rights of the Negroes in our West India Colonies.

2d, For establishing compulsory Manumission.

3d, For securing universally the receiving a Christian education, under the Clergy and Teachers, independent of the Planters; a measure of which total but gradual Emancipation will be the natural consequence, as it was of a similar procedure in the first ages of Christianity.

DIVISION ON THE AMENDMENT.

Ayes 31
Noes 11
Majority . . . 20

THURSDAY, JUNE 9, 1831.

Wyatt's Rooms.

MR. LYALL, Balliol, President, in the Chair.

MR. JELF, Ch. Ch. moved:

That the French Revolution in 1830 has caused the most pernicious effects to the whole of Europe.

SPEAKERS.

In the Affirmative.	*In the Negative.*
Mr. Jelf, Ch. Ch.	Mr. Lowe, University.
Mr. Anstice, Ch. Ch.	Mr. Dupuis, King's Coll. Camb.
	Mr. Moncrieff, New College.
	Mr. Thomas, St. Mary Hall.

DIVISION.

Ayes 29
Noes 21
Majority . . . 8

THURSDAY, OCTOBER 20, 1831.

Wyatt's Rooms.

MR. OAKES, Merton, Treasurer, in the Chair.

MR. A. ACLAND, Ch. Ch. as proxy for MR. MASSIE, Wadham, moved:

That to punish sheep-stealing with death is a greater crime than to steal sheep.

MR. WHITE, Trinity, moved as an Amendment:

That our criminal code is in many instances unnecessarily severe, and that a speedy repeal of many portions of it is desirable.

MR. LOWE, University, proposed as an Amendment:

That to punish sheep-stealing with death is inexpedient.

MR. WHITE withdrew his Amendment, and MR. LOWE'S Amendment, as well as the original Motion, was opposed by MR. VAUGHAN, Ch. Ch. and MR. KNATCHBULL, Trinity.

MR. LOWE'S Amendment was then put, and lost without a division. The original Motion was then put, and negatived without a division.

THURSDAY, OCTOBER 27, 1831.

Wyatt's Rooms.

Mʀ. OAKES, Merton, Treasurer, in the Chair.

Mʀ. REEVES, Merton, moved :

That though some legislative interference for the relief of Ireland is highly desirable, any system founded on the principle of the English Poor Laws would be injurious to that Country.

SPEAKERS.

In the Affirmative.	*In the Negative.*
Mr. Reeves, Merton.	Mr. Lowe, University.
Mr. Doyle, Ch. Ch.	Hon. J. Hewitt, Ch. Ch.
Mr. White, Trinity.	

Mʀ. GOLDSMID, Balliol, moved as an Amendment :

That the words, " as they are at present administered," be inserted after the words " English Poor Laws."

The Motion, as amended, was carried without a division.

THURSDAY, NOVEMBER 3, 1831.

Wyatt's Rooms.

Mʀ. GASKELL, Ch. Ch. President, in the Chair.

Mʀ. HANMER, Brasen-nose, moved :

That the doctrine of the Divine Right of Kings tends to undermine the liberties of the People.

SPEAKERS.

In the Affirmative.	*In the Negative.*
Mr. Hanmer, Brasen-nose.	Mr. Palmer, Magd.
	Mr. Acland, sen. Ch. Ch.

Mr. HANMER replied.—The House then divided: the numbers being,

DIVISION.

Ayes 8
Noes 82
Majority . . . 74

THURSDAY, NOVEMBER 10, 1831.
Wyatt's Rooms.

The EARL OF LINCOLN, Ch. Ch. President, in the Chair.

MR. LOWE, University, moved:

That the King ought to create new Peers to pass the Reform Bill.

SPEAKERS.

In the Affirmative.	*In the Negative.*
Mr. Lowe, University.	Mr. Doyle, Ch. Ch.
Mr. Massie, Wadham.	Mr. Oakes, Merton.
Mr. Bingham, New Coll.	Mr. Knatchbull, Trinity.
	Mr. Mayow, Ch. Ch.
	Mr. Tait, Balliol.
	Mr. Cox, New Coll.
	Mr. Sugden, St. Alban Hall.
	Hon. S. Herbert, Oriel
	Mr. Gaskell, Ch. Ch.

MR. MASSIE, moved as an Amendment:

That the King will be justified in exerting, at the present juncture, his prerogative of creating Peers.

MR. LOWE replied.—The House then divided on the Amendment.

DIVISION.

Ayes 5
Noes 92
Majority . . . 87

MR. LOWE then withdrew his Motion.

THURSDAY, NOVEMBER 17, 1831.
Wyatt's Rooms.

MR. OAKES, Merton, Treasurer, in the Chair.

MR. MASSIE, Wadham, moved:

That Triennial Parliaments ought to be restored.

SPEAKERS.

In the Affirmative.	*In the Negative.*
Mr. Massie, Wadham.	Mr. Gaskell, Ch. Ch.
Mr. Cox, New College.	Mr. Cardwell, Balliol.

MR. MASSIE replied.—The House then divided.

DIVISION.

Ayes 8
Noes 61
Majority . . . 53

THURSDAY, NOVEMBER 24, 1831.

Wyatt's Rooms.

The EARL of LINCOLN, Ch. Ch. President, in the Chair.

Mr. SCOTT, Ch. Ch. as proxy for Mr. DOYLE, Ch. Ch. moved:

That the recognition of the Birmingham Political Union by Lord Althorp and Lord John Russell was highly imprudent and unconstitutional.

SPEAKERS.

In the Affirmative.	*In the Negative.*
Mr. Scott, Ch. Ch.	Mr. Lowe, University.
Mr. Jelf, Ch. Ch.	Mr. Touchet, Exeter.
Mr. Sugden, St. Alban Hall.	

Mr. KNATCHBULL, Trinity, moved as an Amendment:

That the words, " by Lord Althorp and Lord John Russell" be omitted, and the word " ministerial" be inserted before the word " recognition."

SPEAKERS.

In the Affirmative.
Hon. J. Hewitt, Ch. Ch.
Mr. Rickards, Trinity.
Mr. Acland, All Souls. [a]

Mr. MASSIE, Wadham, moved as an Amendment:

That the Proclamation for the suppression of Political Unions was called for by the danger which they threatened to the interests of the Country.

The House then divided on Mr. KNATCHBULL's Amendment.

DIVISION.

Ayes 67
Noes 12
Majority . . . 55

[a] Late of Christ Church.

THURSDAY, DECEMBER 1, 1831.

Wyatt's Rooms.

The EARL OF LINCOLN, Ch. Ch. President, in the Chair.

MR. WARD, Oriel, moved:

That the same Court which has received the Ambassadors of Louis Philippe, ought in consistency to receive those of Don Miguel.

SPEAKERS.

In the Affirmative.	*In the Negative.*
Mr. Ward, Oriel.	Mr. Cox, New College.

DIVISION.

Ayes 26
Noes 24
Majority . . 2

MONDAY, DECEMBER 5, 1831.

Wyatt's Rooms.

The EARL OF LINCOLN, Ch. Ch. President, in the Chair.

MR. WATSON TAYLOR, Ch. Ch. as proxy for MR. ALSTON, Ch. Ch. moved:

That the new Game Bill, as far as it legalizes the sale of Game, is likely to prove injurious, and to increase poaching.

DIVISION.

Ayes 17
Noes 25
Majority . . . 8

THURSDAY, FEBRUARY 2, 1832.

Wyatt's Rooms.

The EARL OF LINCOLN, Ch. Ch. President, in the Chair.

MR. JELF, Ch. Ch. moved:

That the Repeal of the law of primogeniture would tend to embarrass the Community, without ultimately benefitting any class of Society.

The Motion was carried *nem. con.*

THURSDAY, FEBRUARY 9, 1832.

Wyatt's Rooms.

The EARL OF LINCOLN, Ch. Ch. President, in the Chair.

MR. MAYOW, Ch. Ch. as proxy for MR. COLE, Ch. Ch. moved:

That the conduct of the British Government towards Poland and Belgium is inconsistent and unjust.

SPEAKERS.

In the Affirmative.	*In the Negative.*
Mr. Mayow, Ch. Ch.	Mr. Lowe, University.
Mr. Lyall, Balliol.	Mr. Tait, Balliol.

MR. COX, New College, moved as an Amendment:

That mutual confidence between France and England might have guaranteed the independence of Poland, without endangering the peace of Europe.

MR. MAYOW, Ch. Ch. replied.

The Amendment was put, and lost without a division.

DIVISION ON THE ORIGINAL MOTION.

Ayes 26
Noes 12
Majority . . . 14

THURSDAY, FEBRUARY 16, 1832.

Wyatt's Rooms.

The EARL OF LINCOLN, Ch. Ch. President, in the Chair.

MR. PALMER, Trinity, moved:

That the policy of Lord Castlereagh was consistent with sound justice, and beneficial to the Country.

SPEAKERS.

In the Affirmative.	*In the Negative.*
Mr. Palmer, Trinity.	Mr. White, Trinity.
Mr. Jelf, Ch. Ch.	Mr. Lowe, University.
Mr. Neal, Oriel.	Mr. Cox, New College.
	Mr. Lyall, Balliol.

MR. PALMER replied.

DIVISION.

Ayes 45
Noes 33
Majority . . . 12

THURSDAY, FEBRUARY 23, 1832.

Wyatt's Rooms.

The EARL OF LINCOLN, Ch. Ch. President, in the Chair.

MR. BERRY, Brasen-nose, moved:

That the weak and vacillating conduct of the Ministry has mainly tended to produce the present distressed state of Ireland.

. SPEAKER.

In the Affirmative.
Mr. Berry, Brasen-nose.

MR. WARD, Ch. Ch. moved as an Amendment:

That whatever may be the main causes which have produced the present alarming condition of Ireland, the weak and vacillating conduct of Lord Grey's Government has in no small degree aggravated the existing evils.

MR. CARDWELL, Balliol, moved as an Amendment:

That the evils which for the last thirty years have afflicted Ireland, have not been ameliorated by the measures of late pursued towards it.

MR. MAYOW, Ch. Ch. supported MR. WARD's Amendment.

MR. BERRY replied, and professed himself willing to adopt MR. WARD's Amendment.

DIVISION ON MR. CARDWELL'S AMENDMENT.

Ayes 18
Noes 42
Majority . . . 24

Mr. WARD's Amendment was then carried without a division.

THURSDAY, FEBRUARY 29, 1832.

Wyatt's Rooms.

The EARL OF LINCOLN, Ch. Ch. President, in the Chair.

MR. ALSTON, Ch. Ch. moved:

That the public character of Napoleon is entitled to our highest approbation.

SPEAKER.

In the Affirmative.
Mr. Alston, Ch. Ch.

MR. LOWE, University, moved as an Amendment:

That the talents of Napoleon extort from us that Admiration, which can never be due to his character.

SPEAKERS.

In the Negative.
Mr. Reeves, Merton.
Mr. Hussey, Balliol.

DIVISION.
Ayes (for the Amendment) . 54
Noes (against it) 8
Majority . . . 46

THURSDAY, MARCH 8, 1832.

Wyatt's Rooms.

Mr. RICKARDS, Trinity, President, in the Chair.

Mr. BARNES, Ch. Ch. moved:

That the continued opposition at the present time to the Reform Bill is both useful and laudable.

SPEAKER.

In the Affirmative.
Mr. Barnes, Ch. Ch.

Mr. RICKARDS, Trinity, moved an Amendment, which at the suggestion of Mr. ACLAND, All Souls, was withdrawn.

Mr. DE VISME, Balliol[b], moved an Amendment, which was also withdrawn.

Mr. MAURICE, Merton, moved an Amendment, which was also withdrawn.

Mr. REEVES, Merton, moved an Amendment, which was also withdrawn.

SPEAKERS.

In the Affirmative.	*In the Negative.*
Mr. Acland, All Souls.	Mr. Lowe, University.
Mr. Surtees, University.	Mr. Lyall, Balliol.

Mr. BARNES, Ch. Ch. replied.

DIVISION.

Ayes 54
Noes 15
Majority . . . 39

[b] Late Mr. Goldsmid, Balliol.

THURSDAY, MARCH 15, 1832.

Wyatt's Rooms.

MR. RICKARDS, Trinity, President, in the Chair.

MR. CARDWELL, Balliol, moved:

That the restrictions on the Corn Trade have been injurious to the Country.

Rejected without a division.

THURSDAY, MARCH 22, 1832.

Wyatt's Rooms.

MR. REEVES, Merton, Treasurer, in the Chair.

MR. TAIT, Balliol, as proxy for MR. ACLAND, Ch. Ch. moved:

That the public character of George IV, has been unjustly depreciated since his death.

DIVISION.
Ayes 33
Noes 14
Majority . . . 19

THURSDAY, MARCH 29, 1832.

Wyatt's Rooms.

MR. RICKARDS, Trinity, President, in the Chair.

MR. SIMCOX, Wadham, moved :

That the conduct of the American Colonies in revolting from England was not justifiable.

SPEAKERS.

In the Affirmative.	*In the Negative.*
Mr. Simcox, Wadham.	Mr. Hussey, Balliol.
Mr. Mayow, Ch. Ch.	Mr. Palmer, Trinity.
	Mr. Massie, Wadham.
	Mr. Marriott, Balliol.
	Mr. Allies, Wadham.
	Mr. De Visme, Balliol.

MR. SIMCOX replied.

DIVISION.

Ayes 6
Noes 23
Majority . . . 17

THURSDAY, MAY 10, 1832.

Wyatt's Rooms.

MR. RICKARDS, Trinity, President, in the Chair.

MR. LOWE, University, moved :

That all taxes on knowledge ought to be removed.

SPEAKERS.

In the Affirmative.	*In the Negative.*
Mr. Lowe, University.	Mr. Chapman, Exeter.

The Motion was lost without a division.

THURSDAY, MAY 17, 1832.

Wyatt's Rooms.

Mr. RICKARDS, Trinity, President, in the Chair.

Mr. WARD, Ch. Ch. moved :

That an Absolute Monarchy is a more desirable form of Government than the Constitution proposed by the Reform Bill of Lord John Russell.

SPEAKERS.

In the Affirmative.	*In the Negative.*
Mr. Ward, Ch. Ch.	Mr. Lowe, University.
Mr. Jelf, Ch. Ch.	Mr. Cole, Ch. Ch.
Mr. Palmer, Trinity.	* Mr. Lucas, of the Historical
Mr. Chapman, Exeter.	Society, Dublin.
	Mr. Massie, Wadham.

Mr. COLE, Ch. Ch. moved as an Amendment :

That a pure and unadulterated Monarchy is better than a pure unadulterated Democracy.

Mr. WARD, Ch. Ch. replied.

The Amendment was lost without a division.

DIVISION ON THE ORIGINAL MOTION.
Ayes 27
Noes 33
Majority . . . 6

THURSDAY, MAY 24, 1832.

Wyatt's Rooms.

Mr. RICKARDS, Trinity, President, in the Chair.

Mr. PALMER, Trinity, moved :

That the suppression of Political Unions is necessary for the safety of the State.

The Motion was put and carried without a division.

* Honorary Member.

P

THURSDAY, MAY 31, 1832.

Wyatt's Rooms.

Mr. PALMER, Trinity, President, in the Chair.

Mr. DE VISME, Balliol, moved:

That a creation of Peers for the purpose of carrying the Reform Bill would be an unconstitutional exercise of the Prerogative of the Crown.

SPEAKERS.

In the Affirmative.	*In the Negative.*
Mr. De Visme, Balliol.	Mr. Woollcombe, Exeter.
Hon. J. Bruce, Ch. Ch.	Mr. Hanmer, Brasen-nose.
Mr. Hussey, Balliol.	Mr. Massie, Wadham.
The President.	
Mr. Marriott, Balliol.	

Mr. HUSSEY, Balliol, moved an Amendment, which was withdrawn at the suggestion of the President.

Mr. DE VISME replied.

DIVISION.

Ayes 44
Noes 8
Majority . . . 36

THURSDAY, JUNE 7, 1832.

Wyatt's Rooms.

Mr. REEVES, Merton, Treasurer, in the Chair.

Mr. TAIT, Balliol, moved:

That the Political Character of Mr. Pitt is entitled to the highest approbation.

SPEAKERS.

In the Affirmative.
Mr. Tait, Balliol.
Mr. Ward, Ch. Ch.

Mr. Tait replied to some observations of the latter Gentleman, when the Motion was carried without a division.

THURSDAY, JUNE 14, 1832.

Wyatt's Rooms.

MR. PALMER, Trinity, President, in the Chair.

MR. WARD, Ch. Ch. moved :

That a Censorship, unconnected with the Ministry for the time being, on the daily and weekly Press, would be of great advantage at the present time.

DIVISION.

Ayes 25
Noes 27
Majority . . . 2

THURSDAY, JUNE 21, 1832.

Wyatt's Rooms.

MR. PALMER, Trinity, President, in the Chair.

MR. MASSIE, Wadham, moved :

That the Banishment of Napoleon to St. Helena was justifiable, but his treatment in exile unnecessarily severe.

SPEAKERS.

In the Affirmative.
Mr. Massie, Wadham.

MR. ALSTON, Ch. Ch. moved as an Amendment :

That the severity of treatment adopted towards Napoleon while at St. Helena, was only exceeded in unworthiness by his exile to that place.

AGAINST MOTION AND AMENDMENT.

Mr. Rickards, Trinity.
Mr. Doyle, Ch. Ch.
The President.

The Amendment was lost without a division. The House divided on the original Motion.

DIVISION.

Ayes 4
Noes 33
Majority . . . 29

THURSDAY, JUNE 28, 1832.

Wyatt's Rooms.

Mʀ. PALMER, Trinity, President, in the Chair.

Mʀ. HUSSEY, Balliol, moved :

That the recent attempt of the Duke of Wellington to form an Administration, with the view of carrying a modified measure of Reform, was justifiable.

SPEAKERS.

In the Affirmative.	*In the Negative.*
Mr. Hussey, Balliol.	Mr. Mayow, Ch. Ch.
	Mr. Chapman, Exeter.

Mʀ. MAYOW, Ch. Ch. moved as an Amendment :

That the motives which influenced the Duke of Wellington in his attempt to form an Administration with the view of carrying a modified measure of Reform were such as to demand our highest admiration ; but that the failure of that attempt was beneficial to the Country.

DIVISION.

On the Amendment.	*On the Original Motion.*
Ayes 10	Ayes 13
Noes 19	Noes 15
Majority . 9	Majority . 2

THURSDAY, OCTOBER 25, 1832.

Wyatt's Rooms.

Mʀ. PALMER, Trinity, President, in the Chair.

Mʀ. DE VISME, Balliol, (as proxy for Mr. ALSTON, Ch. Ch.) moved :

That the prompt and decisive conduct of the French Government, during the late disturbances in Paris, has been highly praiseworthy.

Mʀ. WARD, Ch. Ch. moved as an Amendment :

That the prompt and decisive conduct of the French Government, during the disturbances occasioned in Paris by the funeral of General Lamarque, was highly praiseworthy.

The Amendment was carried without a division.

THURSDAY, NOVEMBER 1, 1832.

Wyatt's Rooms.

MR. WARD, Ch. Ch. Treasurer, in the Chair.

MR. PUCKLE, Brasen-nose, moved :

That a Measure of Church Reform, embracing the leading features of Lord Henley's plan, would be highly advantageous to the Country.

SPEAKERS.

In the Negative.

Mr. Cardwell, Balliol.
Mr. Doyle, Ch. Ch.
Mr. Cotton, Ch. Ch.
Mr. Domville, Ch. Ch.
Mr. Ward, Ch. Ch.

MR. CARDWELL, Balliol, moved as an Amendment :

That no Measure of Church Reform would deserve the approbation of the Legislature, which did not ensure,

1st. Greater power vested in the Bishops ;

2d. The entire abolition of Pluralities ;

3d. The abolition of all Sinecures consistently with a due observance of the rights of property.

This Amendment was withdrawn.

MR. DOYLE, Ch. Ch. moved a second Amendment :

That the Question of Church Reform is far too difficult and extensive to be hastily decided upon ; and that the Specific Reform proposed by Lord Henley does not seem calculated to meet the difficulties which are on all hands acknowledged.

MR. PUCKLE then replied, when the second Amendment was agreed to without a division.

THURSDAY, NOVEMBER 8, 1832.

Wyatt's Rooms.

MR. CARDWELL, Balliol, Secretary, in the Chair.

MR. WARD, Ch. Ch. moved:

That there being at present no hope of the establishment of any permanent Tory Ministry, the Conservative party will best consult the interest of the Country by firmly supporting the present Government.

SPEAKERS.

In the Affirmative.	*In the Negative.*
Mr. Ward, Ch. Ch.	Mr. J. Adams, Ch. Ch.
Mr. Tait, Balliol.	Mr. Stoddart, St. John's.
Mr. Mayow, Ch. Ch.	

MR. DE VISME, Balliol, moved as an Amendment:

That it is desirable that the Tory and Whig parties should form a coalition against their common enemies.

MR. MAYOW, MR. TAIT. MR. MASSIE, explained.

MR. J. ADAMS, Ch. Ch. and MR. STODDART, St. John's, explained.

MR. WARD, Ch. Ch. replied, and professed himself willing to adopt MR. DE VISME's Amendment.

DIVISION.

Ayes (for the Amendment) . 42
Noes (against it) 8
                    Majority . . . 34

THURSDAY, NOVEMBER 15, 1832.

Wyatt's Rooms.

MR. WARD, Ch. Ch. President, in the Chair.

MR. DE VISME, Balliol, moved:

That the conduct of the present Ministry as regards the King of Holland has been unjustifiable.

SPEAKERS.

In the Affirmative.	*In the Negative.*
Mr. De Visme, Balliol.	*Mr. Leigh, Trinity College, Cambridge.
Mr. Stoddart, St. John's.	Mr. Tait, Balliol.
Mr. Chapman, Exeter.	Mr. Bayntun, Balliol.
Mr. Palmer, Trinity.	
Mr. Oxnam, Exeter.ᶜ	
Mr. Brancker, Wadham.	
Mr. Ward, Ch. Ch.	

MR. BRANDRETH, Ch. Ch. moved as an Amendment:

That sufficient information has not been laid before the public to enable us to draw any inference against Ministers.

> Mr. Brandreth, Ch. Ch.
> Mr. Cardwell, Balliol.
> Mr. Massie, Wadham.

Mr. LOWE, University, moved as an Amendment:

That the conduct of the present Ministry as regards the King of Holland neither was nor is justifiable.

MESSRS. DE VISME, LOWE, LEIGH, and CARDWELL, explained.

MR. LOWE's Amendment was lost without a division.

MR. BRANDRETH's Amendment was put, when the House divided.

DIVISION.

Ayes 12
Noes 48
Majority . . . 36

THE ORIGINAL QUESTION WAS THEN PUT.

Ayes 48
Noes 12
Majority . . . 36

ᶜ Late of Trinity.　　　* Honorary Member.

THURSDAY, NOVEMBER 22, 1832.

Wyatt's Rooms.

MR. WARD, Ch. Ch. President, in the Chair.

MR. ALSTON, Ch. Ch. moved :

That the complete abolition of Slavery should be immediately enforced.

SPEAKERS.

In the Affirmative.	*In the Negative.*
*Mr. Leigh, Trinity College, Cambridge.	Mr. Ward, Ch. Ch.
	Mr. Cox, New College.
	Mr. Jelf, Ch. Ch.
	Mr. Hussey, Balliol.
	Mr. Chapman, Exeter.

MR. COX, New College, proposed as an Amendment:

That it is expedient that Government should recommend to the Colonial Legislatures to adopt such measures as they shall judge best calculated for the mitigation and ultimate abolition of Slavery, without compromising the interest of the Mother Country, the Colonist, or the Slaves themselves.

Mr. CHAPMAN, Exeter, moved as an Amendment:

That those vassals of our West India Colonies who are commonly and improperly designated Slaves ought not to be emancipated until a proper education has enabled them to appreciate the blessing of true liberty.

MR. ALSTON, Ch. Ch. replied.

MR. COX's Amendment was then put from the Chair.

DIVISION.

Ayes 21
Noes 17
Majority . . . 4

* Honorary Member.

THURSDAY, DECEMBER 6, 1832.

Wyatt's Rooms.

Mr. WARD, Ch. Ch. President, in the Chair.

Mr. MAYOW, Ch. Ch. moved:

That the war with France, in which Mr. Pitt engaged England, was essential not only to the dignity but to the security of the Country.

SPEAKERS.

In the Affirmative.	*In the Negative.*
Mr. Mayow, Ch. Ch.	Mr. Cox, New College.
Mr. Stoddart, St. John's.	Mr. Cardwell, Balliol.
Mr. Palmer, Trinity.	Mr. Massie, Wadham.
Mr. Ward, Ch. Ch.	Mr. Lowe, University.

Mr. MAYOW, Ch. Ch. replied.

DIVISION.

Ayes 35
Noes 15
Majority . . . 20

SATURDAY, DECEMBER 8, 1832.

Wyatt's Rooms.

Mr. WARD, Ch. Ch. President, in the Chair.

Mr. COTTON, Ch. Ch. moved:

That a gradual but complete change is absolutely necessary in our present system of Secondary Punishment.

SPEAKERS.

In the Affirmative.

Mr. Cotton, Ch. Ch.
Mr. Ward, Ch. Ch.

The Motion was carried *nem. con.*

Q

WEDNESDAY, JANUARY 23, 1833.

Wyatt's Rooms.

Mr. WARD, Ch. Ch. President, in the Chair.

Mr. PUCKLE, Brasen-nose, moved:

That the repeal of the law, by which Forgery was punishable by death, was alike called for by justice, humanity, and expediency.

SPEAKERS.

In the Affirmative.	*In the Negative.*
Mr. Puckle, Brasen-nose.	Mr. Ward, Ch. Ch.
Mr. Twining, Balliol.	Mr. Palmer, Trinity.

DIVISION.

Ayes 11
Noes 15
Majority . . . 4

THURSDAY, JANUARY 31, 1833.

Wyatt's Rooms.

Mr. WARD, Ch. Ch. President, in the Chair.

Mr. TAIT, Balliol, moved:

That it is highly to be desired that the blessings of Education, secular as well as religious, should be as widely as possible diffused through the Community.

SPEAKERS.

In the Affirmative.	*In the Negative.*
Mr. Tait, Balliol.	Mr. Tickell, Balliol.
Mr. Cotton, Ch. Ch.	
Mr. Cardwell, Balliol.	
Mr. Ward, Ch. Ch.	
Mr. Puckle, Brasen-nose.	

Mr. TAIT, Balliol, replied, and the Question was carried without a division.

THURSDAY, FEBRUARY 7, 1833.

Wyatt's Rooms.

Mr. WARD, Ch. Ch. President, in the Chair.

Mr. CARDWELL, Balliol, moved :

That no change is expedient in the Laws which regulate the Daily and Weekly Press.

SPEAKERS.
In the Affirmative.
Mr. Cardwell, Balliol.
Mr. Cotton, Ch. Ch.

In the Negative.
Mr. Palmer, Trinity.
Mr. Ward, Ch. Ch.
Mr. Mayow, Ch. Ch.

Mr. COTTON, Ch. Ch. moved as an Amendment :

That although no change is expedient in the Laws which regulate the Press, it is highly desirable that the Sunday Newspapers should gradually disappear, by no penal enactments, but by the discountenance of individuals.

Mr. COTTON, Ch. Ch. and Mr. MAYOW, Ch. Ch. explained.

Mr. PALMER, Trinity, and Mr. WARD, Ch. Ch. explained.

Mr. CARDWELL, Balliol, replied.

Mr. COTTON's Amendment was then put, and lost without a division.

DIVISION ON THE ORIGINAL MOTION.
Ayes 19
Noes 39
Majority . . . 20

THURSDAY, FEBRUARY 14, 1833.

Wyatt's Rooms.

Mr. CARDWELL, Balliol, President, in the Chair.

Mr. WARD, Ch. Ch. moved:

That the suspension of the Habeas Corpus Act and of Trial by Jury would be a most salutary measure in the present alarming condition of Ireland.

SPEAKERS.

In the Affirmative.	*In the Negative.*
Mr. Ward, Ch. Ch.	Mr. Thomas, Ch. Ch.
Mr. Surtees, University.	Mr. Lowe, University.
Mr. Mayow, Ch. Ch.	
Mr. Cardwell, Balliol.	
Mr. Hansell, Magd. Coll.	
Mr. Palmer, Trinity.	
Mr. Massie, Wadham.	

Mr. MASSIE, Wadham, moved as an Amendment:

That owing to the mal-administration of former Governments, Ireland has been brought to a state which demands measures strong indeed, but deeply deplorable.

Mr. THOMAS, Ch. Ch. moved as an Amendment:

That if the Grievances, under which the Irish now labour, were promptly redressed by the Government, there would be no occasion for the suspension of the Habeas Corpus Act and Trial by Jury: and that therefore those Grievances ought to be redressed, and the Habeas Corpus Act and Trial by Jury not suspended.

Mr. WARD, Ch. Ch. replied.

THE HOUSE DIVIDED ON MR. MASSIE'S AMENDMENT.

Ayes 13
Noes 56
Majority . . . 43

THE HOUSE DIVIDED ON MR. THOMAS'S AMENDMENT.

Ayes 15
Noes 50
Majority . . . 35

DIVISION ON THE ORIGINAL MOTION.

Ayes 51
Noes 14
Majority . . . 37

THURSDAY, FEBRUARY 21, 1833.

Wyatt's Rooms.

Mr. CARDWELL, Balliol, President, in the Chair.

Mr. PUCKLE, Brasen-nose, moved:

That the prospects of Great Britain were never more brilliant than at the present time.

SPEAKERS.

In the Affirmative.	*In the Negative.*
Mr. Puckle, Brasen-nose.	Mr. Hussey, Balliol.
Mr. Allen, Balliol.	Mr. Leach, Merton.
Mr. Cardwell, Balliol.	Mr. Ward, Ch. Ch.
	Mr. Lowe, University.

Mr. LEACH, Merton, proposed as an Amendment:

That our prospects are in a more brilliant state than under the Duke of Wellington's Administration.

Adjourned to Saturday.

SATURDAY, FEBRUARY 23, 1833.

Wyatt's Rooms.

Mr. CARDWELL, Balliol, President, in the Chair.

ADJOURNED DEBATE.

SPEAKERS.

In the Affirmative.	*In the Negative.*
Mr. Massie, Wadham.	Mr. Brancker, Wadham.
Mr. Fowle, Wadham.	Mr. Barne, Exeter.
Mr. Thomas, Ch. Ch.	Mr. Chapman, Exeter.
Mr. Richardson, Queen's.	Mr. Oxnam, Exeter.
Mr. Davies, Brasen-nose.	
Mr. Tait, Balliol.	

Mr. WARD, Ch. Ch. and Mr. LOWE, University, explained.

The Amendment was lost without a division.

DIVISION ON THE ORIGINAL MOTION.

Ayes 6
Noes 47
Majority . . . 41

WEDNESDAY, FEBRUARY 27, 1833.

Wyatt's Rooms.

MR. CARDWELL, Balliol, President, in the Chair.

MR. COTHER, Ch. Ch. moved:

That Vote by Ballot is an unnecessary expedient, unlikely to effect the objects which are professedly designed by its supporters.

SPEAKERS.

In the Affirmative.	*In the Negative.*
Mr. Cother, Ch. Ch.	Mr. Davies, Brasen-nose.
Mr. Massie, Wadham.	Mr. Twining, Balliol.
Mr. Cardwell, Balliol.	Mr. Lowe, University.
Mr. Mayow, Ch. Ch.	
Mr. Maunsell, Ch. Ch.	
Mr. Ward, Ch. Ch.	

MR. WARD, Ch. Ch. moved as an Amendment:

That it is not expedient that the votes in the election of Members to serve in Parliament should be taken by the Ballot.

Mr. COTHER, Ch. Ch. replied, and expressed himself willing to accede to the Amendment.

DIVISION.

Ayes (for the Amendment) . 57
Noes (against it) 5
Majority . . . 52

THURSDAY, MARCH 7, 1833.

Wyatt's Rooms.

MR. WARD, Ch. Ch. Treasurer, in the Chair.

MR. BRUXNER, Ch. Ch. moved:

That the Emperor Nicholas has, for the most part, shewn great wisdom and moderation in the Government of his Empire.

SPEAKERS.

In the Affirmative.	*In the Negative.*
Mr. Bruxner, Ch. Ch.	Mr. Hawtayne, Balliol.
	Mr. Lowe, University.

DIVISION.

Ayes 13
Noes 43
Majority . . . 30

THURSDAY, MARCH 14, 1833.

Wyatt's Rooms.

MR. CARDWELL, Balliol, President, in the Chair.

MR. MAYOW, Ch. Ch. moved

That the ' six Acts' of Lord Castlereagh were highly conducive to the Peace and Tranquillity of the Country, without any too great infringement on the Liberty of the Subject.

SPEAKERS.

In the Affirmative.	*In the Negative.*
Mr. Mayow, Ch. Ch.	Mr. Davies, Brasen-nose.
Mr. R. Ward, Oriel.	Mr. Massie, Wadham.
Mr. Maunsell, Ch. Ch.	Mr. Thomas, Ch. Ch.
Mr. Harding, Oriel.	
Mr. Barne, Exeter.	
Mr. Allen, Balliol.	

MR. HARDING, Oriel, moved as an Amendment:

That all the words after ' Tranquillity of the Country,' be omitted.

MESSRS. DAVIES, MASSIE, and **HARDING** explained.

MR. MAYOW agreed to **MR. HARDING's** Amendment, which was carried without a division.

THURSDAY, MARCH 21, 1833.

Wyatt's Rooms.

Mr. CARDWELL, Balliol, President, in the Chair.

Mr. BARNE, Exeter, moved:

That a cordial Union between Great Britain and France would be highly conducive to the Welfare of both Countries, as well as to the Happiness and Peace of Europe.

SPEAKERS.

In the Affirmative.	*In the Negative.*
Mr. Barne, Exeter.	Mr. Thomas, Ch. Ch.
Mr. Clarke, Balliol.	Mr. Capes, Balliol.
Mr. Cardwell, Balliol.	Mr. Hussey, Balliol.
Mr. Tait, Balliol.	Mr. R. Ward, Oriel.
Mr. Massie, Wadham.	Mr. Ward, Ch. Ch.
	Mr. Maunsell, Ch. Ch.
	Mr. Tickell, Balliol.
	Mr. Harding, Oriel.
	Mr. Mayow, Ch. Ch.

Mr. ALLEN, Balliol, moved as an Amendment:

That a Cordial Union between Great Britain and France would be highly conducive to the Political Welfare of Europe.

Mr. BARNE replied.

Mr. ALLEN's Amendment was lost without a division.

DIVISION ON THE ORIGINAL MOTION.

Ayes 6
Noes 48
Majority . . . 42

THURSDAY, APRIL 25, 1833.

Wyatt's Rooms.

Mr. WARD, Ch. Ch. Treasurer, in the Chair.

Mr. THOMAS, Ch. Ch. moved:

That an Hereditary Aristocracy is an evil.

SPEAKERS.

In the Affirmative.	*In the Negative.*
Mr. Thomas, Ch. Ch.	Mr. Cotton, Ch. Ch.
	Mr. J. Adams, Ch. Ch.
	Mr. Maunsell, Ch. Ch.
	Mr. Simpson, C. C. C.
	Mr. Barne, Exeter.
	Mr. Denison, Balliol.
	Mr. Ward, Ch. Ch.

Mr. THOMAS, Ch. Ch. replied.

DIVISION.

Ayes 1
Noes 96
Majority . . . 95

THURSDAY, MAY 2, 1833.

Wyatt's Rooms.

Mr. CARDWELL, Balliol, President, in the Chair.

Mr. WARD, Ch. Ch. moved:

That Charles the Xth's Ordinances of July, 1830, were in themselves wise and necessary measures; but that the great error of the French Ministry at that period was the not having at hand a sufficient Military Force to support them.

SPEAKERS.

In the Affirmative.	*In the Negative.*
Mr. Ward, Ch. Ch.	Mr. Cardwell, Balliol.
Mr. Mayow, Ch. Ch.	Mr. Fowle, Wadham.
	Mr. Hawtayne, Balliol.

Mr. WARD, Ch. Ch. replied: Mr. CARDWELL, Balliol, and Mr. HAWTAYNE, Balliol, explained.

DIVISION.

Ayes 35
Noes 17
Majority . . . 18

R

THURSDAY, MAY 9, 1833.

Wyatt's Rooms.

MR. CARDWELL, Balliol, President, in the Chair.

MR. TICKELL, Balliol, moved :

That the conduct of the Ministry since the passing of the Reform Bill has not been such as to deserve the confidence of the Country.

SPEAKERS.

In the Affirmative.	*In the Negative.*
Mr. Tickell, Balliol.	Mr. Hall, Balliol.
Mr. Simpson, C. C. C.	Mr. Davies, Brasen-nose.
Mr. Capes, Balliol.	Mr. Tait, Balliol.
Mr. Thomas, Ch. Ch.	
Mr. Mayow, Ch. Ch.	
Mr. Palmer, Trinity.	

MR. CAPES, Balliol, moved as an Amendment :

That the words ' since their coming into office' be substituted for ' since the passing of the Reform Bill.' This Amendment was withdrawn.

Adjourned till Saturday.

SATURDAY, MAY 11, 1833.

Wyatt's Rooms.

ADJOURNED DEBATE.

Mr. TAIT, Balliol, President, in the Chair.

Mr. MAYOW and Mr. SIMPSON explained.

Mr. PALMER, Trinity, moved as a Rider:

That it is equally inconsistent with the true policy of Conservatives to offer any opposition to the Ministry from factious motives, and to give them any support which requires the smallest sacrifice of political principle.

SPEAKERS.

In the Affirmative.	*In the Negative.*
Mr. Barne, Exeter.	Mr. Pearson, Ch. Ch.
Mr. Twining, Balliol.	Mr. Woollcombe, Exeter.
Mr. Rickards, Trinity.	
Mr. Ward, Ch. Ch. who opposed the Rider.	

Mr. PALMER, Trinity, explained, and amended his Rider as follows:

That the true policy of Conservatives is not to oppose the present Ministry, or support them as a party, but to vote according to their honest opinions upon all important questions; looking rather to the final triumph of true principles, than to the appearance of short and unsubstantial present advantage.

Mr. R. Ward, Oriel.	Mr. Awdry, Exeter.
Mr. Peard, Exeter.	Mr. Cardwell, Balliol.
Mr. Oxnam, Exeter.	

Mr. TICKELL replied.

DIVISION.

Ayes 63
Noes 19
Majority . . . 44

The Rider was carried without a division.

THURSDAY, MAY 16, 1833.

Wyatt's Rooms.

MR. TAIT, Balliol, President, in the Chair.

MR. TWINING, Balliol, moved :

That the Emancipation of the Jews is desirable.

SPEAKERS.

In the Affirmative.	*In the Negative.*
Mr. Twining, Balliol.	Mr. Peard, Exeter.
Mr. Massie, Wadham.	Mr. Tait, Balliol.
Mr. Thomas, Ch. Ch.	Mr. Rickards, Trinity.
Mr. Davis, Brasen-nose.	Mr. Cardwell, Balliol.
Mr. Cotton, Ch. Ch.	Mr. Marriott, Oriel.

MR. WARD, Ch. Ch. moved as an Amendment:

That although there are some privileges which should still be withholden from the Jews, yet it is highly expedient that they should be admitted to many from which they are now excluded, and, among others, to seats in the Legislature.

MR. TAIT, Balliol, moved as an Amendment:

That the Jews ought to be freed from the restrictions under which they labour, with the exception of those which exclude them from the Judicial situation and the Legislature.

MR. PEARD, MR. WARD, MR. TWINING, MR. MASSIE, MR. TAIT, MR. COTTON, explained. MR. TWINING agreed to MR. WARD's Amendment.

DIVISION ON MR. WARD'S AMENDMENT.

Ayes 18
Noes 42
Majority . . . 24

The House then divided on MR. TAIT's Amendment.

DIVISION.

Ayes 42
Noes 18
Majority . . . 24

THURSDAY, MAY 23, 1833.

Wyatt's Rooms.

Mr. TAIT, Balliol, President, in the Chair.

Mr. LYALL, Balliol, moved :

That the general line of conduct pursued by Sir Robert Peel, since the passing of the Reform Measure, has been in the highest degree creditable to him, and beneficial to the Country.

SPEAKERS.

In the Affirmative.
Mr. Lyall, Balliol.
Mr. Cardwell, Balliol.
Mr. Ward, Ch. Ch.

Mr. WARD, Ch. Ch. moved as an Amendment:

That the conduct of Sir Robert Peel, since the passing of the Reform Bill, particularly in the disinterested support which he has given to the present Ministry, is a noble instance of wisdom and patriotism.

Mr. LYALL, Balliol, agreed to the Amendment, which was carried without a division.

THURSDAY, MAY 30, 1833.

Wyatt's Rooms.

MR. TAIT, Balliol, President, in the Chair.

MR. FOWLE, Wadham, moved:

That the Property now enjoyed by the Established Churches in this Kingdom belongs of right to the State, and may be applied by the Legislature to any purposes it shall think fit.

SPEAKERS.

In the Affirmative.	*In the Negative.*
Mr. Fowle, Wadham.	Mr. Denison, Balliol.
	Mr. Phillips, Worcester.
	Mr. Surtees, University.
	Mr. Barne, Exeter.
	Mr. Maunsell, Ch. Ch.

MR. DENISON, Balliol, moved as an Amendment:

That the Property of the Established Church belongs of right to the Church, and that any attempts on the part of the Legislature to diminish the Revenue of the Established Church would be inexpedient and unjust.

MR. FOWLE, Wadham, replied.

DIVISION ON THE AMENDMENT.

Ayes 57
Noes 1
Majority . . . 56

THURSDAY, JUNE 6, 1833.

Wyatt's Rooms.

MR. TAIT, Balliol, President, in the Chair.

MR. MASSIE, Wadham, moved:

That Byron was a better poet than Milton.

SPEAKERS.

In the Affirmative.	*In the Negative.*
Mr. Massie, Wadham.	Mr. Thomas, Ch. Ch.
Mr. Capes, Balliol.	Mr. Sinclair, St. Mary Hall.
	Mr. Lyall, Balliol.
	Mr. De Visme, Balliol.

MR. MASSIE replied.

DIVISION.

Ayes 16
Noes 40
Majority . . . 24

THURSDAY, JUNE 13, 1833.

Wyatt's Rooms.

MR. TAIT, Balliol, President, in the Chair.

MR. WOOLLCOMBE, Exeter, moved :

That the Reign of George the Third up to the year 1811 is to be considered as a disastrous period in English history.

SPEAKERS.

In the Affirmative.	*In the Negative.*
Mr. Woollcombe, Exeter.	Mr. Sinclair, St. Mary Hall.
Mr. Cardwell, Balliol.	Mr. Chapman, Exeter.
	Mr. Ward, Ch. Ch.

MR. CARDWELL, Balliol, moved as an Amendment :

That the Foreign Policy of England during the Reign of George the Third was in the highest degree disastrous, and more particularly in reference to the American and French wars.

MR. WOOLLCOMBE, Exeter, replied, and objected to the Amendment, which was then put.

DIVISION ON THE AMENDMENT.

Ayes 9
Noes 43
Majority . . . 34

THE HOUSE DIVIDED ON THE ORIGINAL MOTION.

Ayes 12
Noes 42
Majority . . . 30

SATURDAY, OCTOBER 19, 1833.

Wyatt's Rooms.

MR. TAIT, Balliol, President, in the Chair.

MR. HUSSEY, Balliol, moved:

That Mr. Stanley's plan for the Abolition of Slavery in our West India Colonies is unjust and inexpedient.

SPEAKERS.

In the Affirmative.	*In the Negative.*
Mr. Hussey, Balliol.	Mr. Awdry, Exeter.
Mr. Ward, Ch. Ch.	Mr. Hanmer, Brasen-nose.
Mr. Barne, Exeter.	Mr. Cardwell, Balliol.

MR. WARD, Ch. Ch. moved as an Amendment:

That the word ' unjust' be omitted.

MR. HUSSEY acquiesced in the Amendment, which was then put.

DIVISION ON THE AMENDMENT.

Ayes 29
Noes 10
Majority . . . 19

SATURDAY, OCTOBER 26, 1833.

Wyatt's Rooms.

MR. WARD, Ch. Ch. Treasurer, in the Chair.

MR. PEARSON, Ch. Ch. as proxy for MR. PUCKLE, Brasen-nose, moved:

That the union of Conciliatory and Coercive Measures which has been pursued towards Ireland, has been in the highest degree beneficial.

SPEAKERS.

In the Affirmative.	*In the Negative.*
Mr. Pearson, Ch. Ch.	Mr. Thomas, Ch. Ch.
Mr. Massie, Wadham.	Mr. Ward, Ch. Ch.
Mr. Cardwell, Balliol.	Mr. Sinclair, St. Mary Hall.
Mr. Hanmer, Brasen-nose.	
Mr. Puckle, Brasen-nose.	

DIVISION.

Ayes 16
Noes 44
Majority . . . 28

THURSDAY, OCTOBER 31, 1833.

Wyatt's Rooms.

Mr. WARD, Ch. Ch. Treasurer, in the Chair.

Mr. PEARSON, Ch. Ch. moved:

That in the event of a general movement in Europe, the ascendancy of popular principles is to be ardently desired.

SPEAKERS.

In the Affirmative.	In the Negative.
Mr. Pearson, Ch. Ch.	Mr. R. Ward, Oriel.
Mr. Twining, Balliol.	Mr. Chapman, Exeter.
Mr. Lowe, University.	Mr. Doyle, Ch. Ch.
Mr. Awdry, Exeter.	Mr. Sinclair, St. Mary Hall.
Mr. Cardwell, Balliol.	Mr. Palmer, Trinity.

Mr. PEARSON replied.

DIVISION.

Ayes 21
Noes 61
Majority . . . 40

THURSDAY, NOVEMBER 7, 1833.

Wyatt's Rooms.

Mr. MASSIE, Wadham, President, in the Chair.

Mr. BARNE, Exeter, moved:

That Mr. Sadler's Bill for the regulation of the Factories was a desirable measure.

SPEAKERS.

In the Affirmative.

Mr. Barne, Exeter.
Mr. Capes, Balliol.
Mr. Simpson, C. C. C.
Mr. Thomas, Ch. Ch.

Mr. F. P. LOWE moved as an Amendment:

That the conduct of Ministers with regard to Mr. Sadler's Bill was most unjust.

Mr. BARNE, Exeter, in reply, acquiesced in Mr. LOWE's Amendment, which was accordingly carried *nem. con.*

s

MONDAY, NOVEMBER 18, 1833.

Wyatt's Rooms.

MR. MASSIE, Wadham, President, in the Chair.

MR. FOWLE, Wadham, moved:

That Donna Maria has a legitimate right to the throne of Portugal.

SPEAKERS.

In the Affirmative.	*In the Negative.*
Mr. Fowle, Wadham.	Mr. Simpson, C. C. C.
	Mr. Brancker, Wadham.

MR. FOWLE, Wadham, replied.

DIVISION.

Ayes 16
Noes 8
Majority . . . 8

THURSDAY, NOVEMBER 21, 1833.

Wyatt's Rooms.

MR. MASSIE, Wadham, President, in the Chair.

MR. BRANCKER, Wadham, moved:

That the appointment of the Commission for investigating into Municipal Corporations involves an unjustifiable attack upon private property.

SPEAKERS.

In the Affirmative.	*In the Negative.*
Mr. Brancker, Wadham.	Mr. Twining, Balliol.
Mr. Thomas, Ch. Ch.	Mr. Hanmer, Brasen-nose.
Mr. Simpson, C. C. C.	*Mr. Leigh, Trin. Camb.
Mr. A. R. Campbell, Balliol.	Mr. Lowe, University.
*Mr. Burke, Peter Coll. Camb.	Mr. Connell, Balliol.

MR. BRANCKER replied.

DIVISION.

Ayes 25
Noes 18
Majority . . . 7

* Honorary Members.

SATURDAY, NOVEMBER 23, 1833.

Wyatt's Rooms.

MR. MASSIE, Wadham, President, in the Chair.

MR. BRUXNER, Ch. Ch. moved:

That Buonaparte was a greater man than Cæsar.

SPEAKERS.

In the Affirmative.	*In the Negative.*
Mr. Bruxner, Ch. Ch.	Mr. Hopton, Brasen-nose.
Mr. Connell, Balliol.	Mr. Thomas, Ch. Ch.
Mr. Lowe, University.	Mr. Marriott, Oriel.
	Mr. Entwistle, Oriel.
	Mr. Simpson, C. C. C.
	Mr. Massie, Wadham.

MR. BRUXNER replied.

DIVISION.

Ayes 14
Noes 27
Majority . . . 13

THURSDAY, DECEMBER 5, 1833.

Wyatt's Rooms.

MR. LOWE, University, Librarian, in the Chair.

MR. THOMAS, Ch. Ch. moved:

That the Civilization of Europe is at present in its infancy.

SPEAKERS.

In the Affirmative.	*In the Negative.*
Mr. Thomas, Ch. Ch.	Mr. Hopton, Brasen-nose.
Mr. Twining, Balliol.	Mr. Brancker, Wadham.
Mr. Connell, Balliol.	Mr. Rickards, Trinity.
	Mr. Lowe, University.
	Mr. Dalton, Wadham.

MR. FOWLE, Wadham, moved as an Amendment:

That the Civilization of Europe may be yet more extended.

MR. THOMAS, Ch. Ch. replied, and professed himself willing to adopt this Amendment, which was carried without a division.

THURSDAY, JANUARY 23, 1834.

Wyatt's Rooms.

Mr. MASSIE, Wadham, President, in the Chair.

Mr. WOODALL, Exeter, moved :

That Painting realizes its subject to the mind more vividly than Poetry.

SPEAKERS.

In the Affirmative.	*In the Negative.*
Mr. Woodall, Exeter.	Mr. Hawtayne, Balliol.

Mr. WOODALL replied.

The Motion was lost without a division.

THURSDAY, JANUARY 30, 1834.

Wyatt's Rooms.

Mr. PEARSON, Ch. Ch. Treasurer, in the Chair.

Mr. LOWE, University, moved :

That the measures taken for the suppression of the Rebellion in 1745, were disgraceful to the Government of that period.

SPEAKERS.

In the Affirmative.	*In the Negative.*
Mr. Lowe, University.	Mr. Cardwell, Balliol.
Mr. Cotton, Ch. Ch.	Mr. Sinclair, St. Mary Hall.
Mr. Campbell, Balliol.	Mr. Ward, Ch. Ch.
Mr. Tait, Balliol.	

Mr. LOWE replied.

DIVISION.

Ayes 35
Noes 36
Majority . . 1

WEDNESDAY, FEBRUARY 5, 1834.

Wyatt's Rooms.

MR. PEARSON, Ch. Ch. Treasurer, in the Chair.

MR. MARJORIBANKS, Ch. Ch. moved :

That the present system of appointing County Magistrates by the Lord Lieutenants is attended with the highest advantages.

SPEAKERS.

In the Affirmative.	*In the Negative.*
Mr. Marjoribanks, Ch. Ch.	Mr. Rawlinson, St. John's.
Mr. Connell, Balliol.	
Mr. Riddell, Ch. Ch.	
Mr. Cardwell, Balliol.	

MR. MARJORIBANKS replied.

The Motion was carried without a division.

THURSDAY, FEBRUARY 13, 1834.

Wyatt's Rooms.

MR. MARRIOTT, Oriel, President, in the Chair.

MR. HUSSEY, Balliol, moved :

That Popular Education ought not to be placed under the direct superintendence of the Government.

SPEAKERS.

In the Affirmative.	*In the Negative.*
Mr. Hussey, Balliol.	Mr. Downie, Trinity.
Mr. Cardwell, Balliol.	Mr. Browne, C. C. C.
Mr. Cotton, Ch. Ch.	Mr. Ward, Ch. Ch.
Mr. Massie, Wadham.	Mr. Sinclair, St. Mary Hall.
	Mr. Rickards, Trinity.

MR. CARDWELL, Balliol, having obtained leave of the Mover of the Question, proposed as an Amendment:

That it is the duty of Government to provide by every possible means for the extension of general Education; but that any system of Education can only be carried practically into effect by active individual exertion, and not by the direct interference of Government.

MR. HUSSEY replied.

DIVISION ON THE AMENDMENT.

Ayes 40
Noes 38
Majority . . . 2

THURSDAY, FEBRUARY 20, 1834.

Wyatt's Rooms.

Mr. MARRIOTT, Oriel, President, in the Chair.

Mr. CARDWELL, Balliol, moved:

That Emigration and Free Trade afford the only prospect of relief from our present financial embarrassment.

SPEAKERS.

In the Affirmative.	In the Negative.
Mr. Cardwell, Balliol.	Mr. R. Ward, Oriel.
Mr. Thomas, Ch. Ch.	Mr. Rickards, Trinity.
Mr. Marriott, Oriel.	Mr. Simpson, C. C. C.
	Mr. Sinclair, St. Mary Hall.
	Mr. Connell, Balliol.
	Mr. Trench, Oriel.

Mr. CARDWELL replied.

DIVISION.

Ayes 22
Noes 53
Majority . . . 31

THURSDAY, FEBRUARY 27, 1834.

Wyatt's Rooms.

Mr. MARRIOTT, Oriel, President, in the Chair.

Mr. FABER, Balliol, moved:

That the Reign of Charles the Second was a less disastrous period of English history than the Commonwealth.

SPEAKERS.

In the Affirmative.

Mr. Faber, Balliol.
Mr. Hopton, Brasen-nose.
Mr. Cardwell, Balliol.
Mr. Thomas, Ch. Ch.
Mr. Campbell, Balliol.
Mr. Allen, Balliol.

The Motion was carried without a division.

THURSDAY, MARCH 6, 1834.

Wyatt's Rooms.

MR. MARRIOTT, Oriel, President, in the Chair.

MR. R. WARD, Oriel, moved:

That Cheap Law would be a national evil.

SPEAKERS.

In the Affirmative.	*In the Negative.*
Mr. R. Ward, Oriel.	Mr. Barne, Exeter.
Mr. Mellish, University.	Mr. Ward, Ch. Ch.
Mr. Lowe, University.	Mr. Cardwell, Balliol.
Mr. Marriott, Oriel.	Mr. Hopton, Brasen-nose.
Mr. Rickards, Trinity.	

MR. WARD, Oriel, replied.

DIVISION.

Ayes 39
Noes 20
Majority . . . 19

THURSDAY, MARCH 13, 1834.

Wyatt's Rooms.

MR. RICKARDS, Trinity, Librarian, in the Chair.

MR. PUCKLE, Brasen-nose, moved:

That the chief security for the stability of the American Government consists in the less popular constitution of its Upper House.

SPEAKERS.

In the Affirmative.	*In the Negative.*
Mr. Puckle, Brasen-nose.	Mr. Ward, Ch. Ch.
Mr. Dewar, Exeter.	Mr. Barne, Exeter.
Mr. Hopton, Brasen-nose.	
Mr. R. Ward, Oriel.	

MR. PUCKLE replied.

DIVISION.

Ayes 17
Noes 9
Majority . . . 8

THURSDAY, APRIL 17, 1834.

Wyatt's Rooms.

Mr. MARRIOTT, Oriel, President, in the Chair.

Mr. ENTWISTLE, Oriel, moved :

That the introduction of Poor Laws into Ireland would be a measure highly beneficial to that Country.

SPEAKER.

In the Affirmative.
Mr. Entwistle, Oriel.

DIVISION.

Ayes 21
Noes 25
Majority . . . 4

THURSDAY, APRIL 24, 1834.

Wyatt's Rooms.

Mr. MARRIOTT, Oriel, President, in the Chair.

Mr. CAMPBELL, Balliol, moved :

That the conduct of the present Ministry during the agitation of the Reform Question as regards the Political Unions, is in the highest degree reprehensible.

SPEAKERS.

In the Affirmative.	*In the Negative.*
Mr. Campbell, Balliol.	Mr. Richardson, St. John's.
Mr. Dewar, Exeter.	Mr. Whipham, Balliol.
Mr. Robinson, Balliol.	*Mr. Cardwell, Balliol.
Mr. C. Marriott, Oriel.	
Rev. W. W. Stoddart, St. John's.	
Mr. Rickards, Trinity.	
Mr. Connell, Balliol.	

Mr. CAMPBELL, Balliol, replied, when the Motion was carried without a division.

* Mr. Cardwell, Balliol, did not give a vote.

SATURDAY, MAY 3, 1834.

Wyatt's Rooms.

MR. MARRIOTT, Oriel, President, in the Chair.

MR. WARD, Lincoln [a], as proxy for MR. CORNISH, Ch. Ch. moved :

That the foreign Policy of the Duke of Wellington was calculated to promote the honour and the best interests of the Country; and that the system pursued by the present Ministry has been destructive of both.

SPEAKERS.

In the Affirmative.	*In the Negative.*
Mr. Ward, Lincoln.	Mr. Sterling, St. Mary Hall.
Mr. Sinclair, St. Mary Hall.	Mr. Cardwell, Balliol.
Mr. Dewar, Exeter.	
Mr. Simpson, C. C. C.	

MR. WARD replied.

DIVISION.

Ayes 43
Noes 8
Majority . . . 35

THURSDAY, MAY 8, 1834.

Wyatt's Rooms.

MR. SINCLAIR, St. Mary Hall, President, in the Chair.

MR. FOWLE, Wadham, moved:

That it is expedient to repeal the Septennial Act.

SPEAKERS.

In the Affirmative.	*In the Negative.*
Mr. Fowle, Wadham.	Mr. Faber, Balliol.
	Mr. Sinclair, St. Mary Hall.

MR. FOWLE, Wadham, replied, when the Motion was put, and rejected without a division.

[a] Late of Ch. Ch.

T

THURSDAY, MAY 15, 1834.

Wyatt's Rooms.

Mr. SINCLAIR, St. Mary Hall, President, in the Chair.

Mr. HUSSEY, Balliol, moved :

That the proposed removal of the Civil Disabilities of the Jews is highly to be deprecated.

SPEAKERS.

In the Affirmative.	*In the Negative.*
Mr. Hussey, Balliol.	Mr. Dewar, Exeter.
Rev. W. W. Stoddart, St. John's.	Mr. Sinclair, St. Mary Hall.

Mr. SPENCER, St. Mary Hall, moved as an Amendment :

That the Civil Disabilities of the Jews, with the exception of those which prohibit them from possessing a share in the Legislation or Executive Government, ought to be removed.

Mr. HUSSEY, Balliol, replied against the Amendment.

The Amendment having been put, and rejected without a division; there appeared for the original Motion,

Ayes 32
Noes 12
Majority . . . 20

THURSDAY, MAY 22, 1834.

Wyatt's Rooms.

MR. SINCLAIR, St. Mary Hall, President, in the Chair.

MR. FABER, Balliol, moved:

That Wordsworth is in every respect a superior poet to Lord Byron.

SPEAKERS.

In the Affirmative.	*In the Negative.*
Mr. Faber, Balliol.	Mr. Capes, Balliol.
Mr. Marriott, Oriel.	Mr. Sinclair, St. Mary Hall.
Mr. Rickards, Trinity.	
Mr. Spencer, St. Mary Hall	

MR. FABER, Balliol, replied.

DIVISION.

Ayes 14
Noes 34
Majority . . . 20

FRIDAY, MAY 30, 1834.

Wyatt's Rooms.

MR. SINCLAIR, St. Mary Hall, President, in the Chair.

MR. FABER, Balliol, as proxy for MR. MARJORIBANKS, Ch. Ch. moved, but without speaking on the Question:

That the character of Lord Castlereagh, as a statesman, is more deserving the gratitude and admiration of his Countrymen than that of Mr. Canning.

DIVISION.

Ayes 11
Noes 14
Majority . . . 3

FRIDAY, JUNE 6, 1834.

Wyatt's Rooms.

MR. SINCLAIR, St. Mary Hall, President, in the Chair.

MR. CARDWELL, Balliol, moved:

That the late separation between the members of Earl Grey's Administration is deeply to be deplored: and that no Ministry can hope to carry on the Government of the Country, which is not framed as well upon a principle of extensive practical Reform, as of preserving the established rights of property.

SPEAKERS.

In the Affirmative.	*In the Negative.*
Mr. Cardwell, Balliol.	Mr. Trevor, Magd. Hall.
Mr. Lowe, University.	Mr. Spencer, St. Mary Hall.
Mr. Capes, Balliol.	

MR. TREVOR, Magdalen Hall, moved as an Amendment:

That the late separation between the members of Earl Grey's Administration is greatly to be rejoiced at, as at once vindicating the honesty of the Statesmen who have seceded, and unmasking the unprincipled designs of their colleagues, and thereby it may be hoped tending to elevate the standard of political morality; and so hastening the downfal of a Government, less distinguished for any measure of sound practical Reform, than for reckless and repeated assaults on the sacred rights of property.

Adjourned to Saturday.

SATURDAY, JUNE 7, 1834.

Wyatt's Rooms.

ADJOURNED DEBATE.

MR. SINCLAIR, St. Mary Hall, President, in the Chair.

SPEAKERS.

In the Affirmative.	*In the Negative.*
Mr. Armstrong, Lincoln.	Mr. Faber, Balliol.
Mr. Tait, Balliol.	Mr. Mellish, University.
	Mr. Young, St. Mary Hall.
	Mr. Rickards, Trinity.
	Mr. Sinclair, St. Mary Hall.

MR. TREVOR's Amendment was then put.

DIVISION.

Ayes 13
Noes 17
Majority . . . 4

DIVISION ON THE ORIGINAL MOTION.

Ayes 13
Noes 22
Majority . . . 9

THURSDAY, OCTOBER 23, 1834.

Wyatt's Rooms.

In the absence of the President, MR. COTTON, Ch. Ch. in the Chair.

MR. ADAMS, Ch. Ch. moved:

That the authority of Governments does not emanate from the People.

SPEAKERS.

In the Affirmative.	*In the Negative.*
Mr. Adams, Ch. Ch.	Mr. Cornish, Ch. Ch.
	Mr. Trevor, Magdalen Hall.

DIVISION.

Ayes 12
Noes 16
Majority . . . 4

THURSDAY, OCTOBER 30, 1834.
Wyatt's Rooms.

Mr. CAPES, Balliol, Treasurer, in the Chair.

Mr. RAWLINSON, St. John's, moved:

That the measure of Reform has proved highly beneficial to the Country.

SPEAKERS.

In the Affirmative.	In the Negative.
Mr. Rawlinson, St. John's.	Rev. W. W. Stoddart, St. John's.
Mr. Lowe, University.	Mr. Connell, Balliol.
	Mr. Trevor, Magd. Hall.

Mr. RAWLINSON replied.

DIVISION.
Ayes 7
Noes 40
Majority . . . 33

THURSDAY, NOVEMBER 6, 1834.
Wyatt's Rooms.

Mr. ADAMS, Ch. Ch. President, in the Chair.

Mr. CAPES, Balliol, moved:

That the prospects of the Established Church have been, and are, steadily and continually improving.

SPEAKERS.

In the Affirmative.	In the Negative.
Mr. Capes, Balliol.	Mr. Hopton, Brasen-nose.
Mr. Monro, Oriel.	Mr. Butterworth, Exeter.
Mr. Trevor, Magd. Hall.	Mr. Marsh, Oriel.

Mr. SIMPSON, C. C. C. moved as an Amendment:

That the eyes of the Educated part of the Country are gradually opening to the benefits of the Established Church.

Mr. CAPES, Balliol, replied.

DIVISION ON THE AMENDMENT.
Ayes 1
Noes 130
Majority . . 129

DIVISION ON THE ORIGINAL MOTION.
Ayes 52
Noes 60
Majority . . . 8

THURSDAY, NOVEMBER 13, 1834.

Wyatt's Rooms.

Mr. CAPES, Balliol, Treasurer, in the Chair.

Mr. CONNELL, Balliol, moved:

That the Stage always has been, and is at this present time, prejudicial to Morality.

SPEAKER.

In the Affirmative.
Mr. Connell, Balliol.

DIVISION.

Ayes 7
Noes 16
Majority . . . 9

THURSDAY, NOVEMBER 20, 1834.

Wyatt's Rooms.

Mr. J. ADAMS, Ch. Ch. President, in the Chair.

Mr. TREVOR, Magdalen Hall, moved:

That the Policy of Lord Grey's Administration was opposed to the first principles of sound practical Reform.

SPEAKERS.

In the Affirmative.	*In the Negative.*
Mr. Trevor, Magdalen Hall.	Mr. Cardwell, Balliol.

Mr. WARD, Lincoln, moved as an Amendment:

That the Errors of Lord Grey's Administration have not proceeded from too little concession to the wishes of the people.

SPEAKER ON THE AMENDMENT.

In the Affirmative.
Mr. Ward, Lincoln.

Mr. TREVOR and Mr. CARDWELL said a few words, and Mr. WARD consented to withdraw his Amendment.

Mr. TREVOR, Magdalen Hall, obtained leave to substitute in the place of the original Motion, the following one:

That the Policy of Lord Grey's Administration was not calculated to redress the grievances nor to promote the welfare of the people.

Mr. TREVOR spoke in reply, in favour of his amended Motion.

The original Motion was carried without a division.

THURSDAY, NOVEMBER 27, 1834.

Wyatt's Rooms.

MR. J. ADAMS, Ch. Ch. President, in the Chair.

MR. MORRELL, St. John's, moved :

That an intimate connexion on the part of England with France is prejudicial to the best interests of the Country.

SPEAKERS.

In the Affirmative.	*In the Negative.*
Mr. Morrell, St. John's.	Mr. Rawlinson, St. John's.
Mr. Trevor, Magdalen Hall.	Mr. Cardwell, Balliol.
Mr. Cornish, Ch. Ch.	
Mr. Capes, Balliol.	

MR. MORRELL replied.

DIVISION.

Ayes 52
Noes 11
Majority . . . 41

THURSDAY, DECEMBER 4, 1834.

Wyatt's Rooms.

MR. J. ADAMS, Ch. Ch. President, in the Chair.

MR. CORNISH, Ch. Ch. moved :

That the conduct of the Majority of the House of Lords during the last Session of Parliament was highly noble and patriotic; and that the formation of a strong Government by that party under the Duke of Wellington, is an event to be hailed with satisfaction by every well-wisher to the Country.

SPEAKERS.

In the Affirmative.	*In the Negative.*
Mr. Cornish, Ch. Ch.	Mr. Hussey, Balliol.
Mr. Simpson, C. C. C.	Mr. Capes, Balliol.
Mr. Marsh, Oriel.	Mr. Cardwell, Balliol.
Mr. Connell, Balliol.	
Mr. Trevor, Magdalen Hall.	

MR. CORNISH replied.

DIVISION.

Ayes 36
Noes 10
Majority . . . 26

MONDAY, DECEMBER 8, 1834.

Wyatt's Rooms.

MR. J. ADAMS, Ch. Ch. President, in the Chair.

MR. ARMSTRONG, Lincoln, moved :

That the European Powers have not sufficiently interfered with Russia in her late conduct towards Poland.

SPEAKERS.

In the Affirmative.	In the Negative.
Mr. Armstrong, Lincoln.	Mr. Trevor, Magdalen Hall.
Mr. Marsh, Oriel.	Mr. Connell, Balliol.
Mr. Monro, Oriel.	

MR. ARMSTRONG replied.

DIVISION.

Ayes 15
Noes 7
Majority . . . 8

THURSDAY, JANUARY 29, 1835.

Wyatt's Rooms.

MR. J. ADAMS, Ch. Ch. President, in the Chair.

MR. MARSH, Oriel, moved :

That the interests of England have not been sufficiently consulted in her Continental Wars.

SPEAKERS.

In the Affirmative.	In the Negative.
Mr. Marsh, Oriel.	Mr. Hawtayne, Balliol.
	Mr. Cornish, Ch. Ch.
	Mr. Poynder, Brasen-nose.
	Mr. Ward, Balliol.

MR. MARSH replied.

The Motion was lost without a division.

U

SATURDAY, FEBRUARY 7, 1835.

Wyatt's Rooms.

Mr. J. ADAMS, Ch. Ch. President, in the Chair.

Mr. HUSSEY, Balliol, moved:

That the hopelessness and absurdity of attempting to construct a Cabinet upon Tory principles have been satisfactorily demonstrated; and that no Administration can hope to carry on the government of the Country except upon the principles of extensive practical Reform.

SPEAKERS.

In the Affirmative.	*In the Negative.*
Mr. Hussey, Balliol.	Mr. Cornish, Ch. Ch.
	Mr. Giles, Magdalen Hall.
	Mr. Barne, Exeter.
	Mr. Sinclair, St. Mary Hall.

Mr. WARD, Balliol, moved as an Amendment:

That while no Administration can hope to carry on the government of the Country except upon the principles of extensive practical Reform; the adoption of that line of conduct under existing circumstances is by no means unjustifiable with reference to the former professions of the Tory party.

SPEAKERS ON THE AMENDMENT.

In the Affirmative.	*In the Negative.*
Mr. Ward, Balliol.	Mr. Cardwell, Balliol.
Mr. Capes, Balliol.	Mr. Sinclair, St. Mary Hall.
Mr. Tait, Balliol.	

Mr. CORNISH, Ch. Ch. moved as an Amendment:

That no Administration which does not in accordance with true Tory principles, while it proceeds sincerely to redress real grievances, oppose itself most strenuously to the principle of agitation, and to all concessions to mere popular clamour, will deserve the confidence of their Sovereign, or satisfy the real wishes of the Nation.

Mr. HUSSEY replied.

Mr. WARD's Amendment was then put, and carried.

DIVISION.

Ayes 54
Noes 26
Majority . . . 28

THURSDAY, FEBRUARY 12, 1835.

Wyatt's Rooms.

Mʀ. HUSSEY, Balliol, Treasurer, in the Chair.

Mʀ. CAPES, Balliol, as proxy for Mʀ. WARD, Balliol, moved:

That of all methods for promoting the substantial education of the people, the diffusion of desultory and entertaining information is the least efficient.

SPEAKERS.

In the Affirmative.	*In the Negative.*
Mr. Capes, Balliol.	Mr. Litton, Balliol.
Mr. Hussey, Balliol.	
Mr. Hawtayne, Balliol.	

Mʀ. CAPES replied.

The Motion was lost without a division.

THURSDAY, FEBRUARY 19, 1835.

Wyatt's Rooms.

Mʀ. WARD, Balliol, President, in the Chair.

Mʀ. CORNISH, Ch. Ch. moved:

That the policy of Lord Castlereagh, both foreign and domestic, deserves our highest admiration.

SPEAKERS.

In the Affirmative.	*In the Negative.*
Mr. Cornish, Ch. Ch.	Mr. Hussey, Balliol.
Mr. Morrell, St. John's.	Mr. Marsh, Oriel.
The President.	

Mʀ. CORNISH replied.

DIVISION.

Ayes 45
Noes 11
Majority . . . 34

SATURDAY, FEBRUARY 28, 1835.

Wyatt's Rooms.

Mr. WARD, Balliol, President, in the Chair.

Mr. PEARSON, Ch. Ch. moved:

That the Chivalrous Spirit of the Middle Ages most powerfully promoted the Moral and Civil Reformation of Europe.

SPEAKERS.

In the Affirmative.	*In the Negative.*
Mr. Pearson, Ch. Ch.	Mr. Hussey, Balliol.
Mr. Whipham, Balliol.	The President.
Mr. Litton, Balliol.	Mr. Capes, Balliol.

Mr. PEARSON replied.

DIVISION.

Ayes 46
Noes 25
Majority . . . 21

THURSDAY, MARCH 5, 1835.

Wyatt's Rooms.

Mr. WARD, Balliol, President, in the Chair.

Mr. MONRO, Oriel, moved:

That the conduct of Queen Elizabeth to Mary Queen of Scots merits the extreme reprobation of posterity.

SPEAKERS.

In the Affirmative.	*In the Negative.*
Mr. Monro, Oriel.	Mr. Burney, Magdalen.

Mr. BURNEY, Magdalen, moved as an Amendment:

That while the conduct of Elizabeth to a certain extent is highly reprehensible, yet from the state of feeling at that time, there was much to justify harsh measures towards Mary.

Mr. MONRO replied.

DIVISION ON THE AMENDMENT.

Ayes 16
Noes 58
Majority . . . 42

The original Motion was carried without a division.

THURSDAY, MARCH 12, 1835.

Wyatt's Rooms.

Mr. WARD, Balliol, President, in the Chair.

Mr. HUSSEY, Balliol, as proxy for Mr. CAPES, Balliol, moved:

That the conduct of the opposition to Sir Robert Peel's Ministry since the meeting of Parliament has been factious and unjustifiable in the extreme.

SPEAKERS.

In the Affirmative.	*In the Negative.*
Mr. Hussey, Balliol.	Mr. Cardwell, Balliol.
Mr. Mellish, University.	
The President.	
Mr. Whipham, Balliol.	
Mr. Sinclair, St. Mary Hall.	

Mr. HUSSEY replied. Mr. CARDWELL explained.

DIVISION.

Ayes 79
Noes 11
Majority . . . 68

THURSDAY, MARCH 19, 1835.

Wyatt's Rooms.

Mr. WARD, Balliol, President, in the Chair.

Mr. BRUXNER, Ch. Ch. moved:

That the decisions of the Congress of Vienna were not in unison with the principles of a sound and equitable policy.

SPEAKERS.

In the Affirmative.	*In the Negative.*
Mr. Bruxner, Ch. Ch.	Mr. Cornish, Ch. Ch.
Mr. Hussey, Balliol.	

Mr. BRUXNER replied.

DIVISION.

Ayes 19
Noes 14
Majority . . . 5

SATURDAY, MARCH 28, 1835.

Wyatt's Rooms.

The President being the Mover of the Question, MR. HUSSEY, Balliol, Treasurer, in the Chair.

MR. WARD, Balliol, moved:

That a legislative provision for the Roman Catholic Priesthood in Ireland would be a most beneficial measure.

SPEAKERS.

In the Affirmative.	*In the Negative.*
Mr. Ward, Balliol.	Mr. Marsh, Oriel.
Mr. Tait, Balliol.	Mr. Morrell, St. John's.
Mr. Sterling, St. Mary Hall.	Mr. Litton, Balliol.
	Mr. Mellish, University.
	Mr. Monro, Oriel.
	Mr. Cardwell, Balliol.

MR. WARD replied.

DIVISION.

Ayes 35
Noes 74
Majority . . . 39

THURSDAY, MAY 7, 1835.

Wyatt's Rooms.

MR. WARD, Balliol, President, in the Chair.

MR. G. L. BROWNE, St. John's, moved:

That the causes of the Great Civil War are to be sought for not so much in the licentiousness of the People, as in the arbitrary and disingenuous conduct of Charles the First.

SPEAKERS.

In the Affirmative.	*In the Negative.*
Mr. Browne, St. John's.	Mr. Trevor, Magdalen Hall.
Mr. Hussey, Balliol.	

MR. TREVOR moved as an Amendment:

That the causes of the Great Civil War are not to be sought for in the licentiousness of the People, nor in the arbitrary and disingenuous conduct of Charles the First.

MR. BROWNE replied.

The Amendment was then put, and lost without a division.

DIVISION ON THE ORIGINAL MOTION.

Ayes 11
Noes 43
Majority . . . 32

THURSDAY, MAY 14, 1835.

Wyatt's Rooms.

Mr. WARD, Balliol, President, in the Chair.

Mr. MORRELL, St. John's, moved :

That Cheap Law is a National Evil.

SPEAKER.

In the Affirmative.
Mr. Morrell, St. John's.

DIVISION.

Ayes 49
Noes 26
Majority . . . 23

THURSDAY, MAY 21, 1835.

Wyatt's Rooms.

Mr. WARD, Balliol, President, in the Chair.

Mr. HUSSEY, Balliol, moved :

That in the present state of Parties, it is the duty of the Conservatives in Parliament to give their disinterested support to Lord Melbourne's Administration, wherever they can do so without a sacrifice of principle.

SPEAKERS.

In the Affirmative.   *In the Negative.*
Mr. Hussey, Balliol.   Mr. Mellish, University.
The President.   Mr. Trevor, Magdalen Hall.
                                         Lord Adam Loftus, Balliol.

Mr. HUSSEY replied.

DIVISION.

Ayes 53
Noes 45
Majority . . . 8

THURSDAY, MAY 28, 1835.

Wyatt's Rooms.

MR. CAPES, Balliol, President, in the Chair.

MR. TREVOR, Magdalen Hall, moved :

That the Resolution moved by Lord John Russell on the 7th of April last, relative to the property of the Established Church in Ireland, is unconstitutional, illegal, and immoral.

SPEAKERS.

In the Affirmative.	*In the Negative.*
Mr. Trevor, Magdalen Hall.	The President.
	Mr. Cripps, New College.
	Mr. Cardwell, Balliol.

THE PRESIDENT moved as an Amendment :

That while the Legislature has an equal right to public and private property, any interference with either, except in the greatest extremities, is in the highest degree dangerous; and that Lord John Russell's Resolution on the 7th of April, directly tends to the subversion of public safety, and of Christian truth.

MR. TREVOR objected to the Amendment, as inapplicable to the present Motion.

THE LIBRARIAN (Mr. Ward, Balliol, from the Chair) decided in favour of the Amendment.

MR. CARDWELL, Balliol, gave notice of a second Amendment :

That the property of the Irish Church rests upon the same foundation with all trust property; and that further, no alteration is expedient in the regulation of this property, which is not conducive to the promotion of the Protestant religion in Ireland.

Adjourned.

THURSDAY, JUNE 25, 1835.

Wyatt's Rooms.

ADJOURNED DEBATE.

The adjourned Debate on Mr. Trevor's Motion was then commenced by Mr. Cornish, Ch. Ch. who was in possession of the House, who moved that the Debate do proceed without speaking on the Question.

SPEAKER.

In the Affirmative.
Mr. Burney, Magdalen.

MR. TREVOR replied.

Both the Amendments were then put, and lost without a division.

The original Motion was then put, and carried with one dissentient voice.

THURSDAY, OCTOBER 22, 1835.

Wyatt's Rooms.

MR. CAPES, Balliol, President, in the Chair.

MR. WARD, Balliol, moved :

That the conduct of the Agricultural and Ultra-Tory party since the year 1828 is worthy of the highest reprobation.

SPEAKERS.

In the Affirmative.	*In the Negative.*
Mr. Ward, Balliol.	Mr. Trevor, Magdalen Hall.
Mr. Cripps, New College.	Mr. Highton, Queen's.
Mr. Giles, Magdalen Hall.	Mr. Phinn, Exeter.
	Mr. Poynder, Wadham.
	Mr. Mellish, University.

MR. WARD replied.

DIVISION.
Ayes 12
Noes 33
Majority . . . 21

x

THURSDAY, OCTOBER 29, 1835.

Wyatt's Rooms.

MR. CAPES, Balliol, President, in the Chair.

MR. CORNISH, Ch. Ch. moved :

That the stability of the Government of Louis Philippe is of the highest importance to the peace and welfare of Europe.

SPEAKERS.

In the Affirmative.	In the Negative.
Mr. Cornish, Ch. Ch.	Mr. Phinn, Exeter.
Mr. Morrell, St. John's.	
Mr. Brancker, Wadham.	
Mr. Salmon, Exeter.	
Mr. Cardwell, Balliol.	
Mr. Trevor, Magdalen Hall.	

MR. CORNISH replied. The Motion was then put, and carried without a division.

THURSDAY, NOVEMBER 5, 1835.

Wyatt's Rooms.

MR. CAPES, Balliol, President, in the Chair.

MR. TREVOR, Magdalen Hall, moved:

That the safety and happiness of the United Kingdom demand the immediate introduction of a judicious Poor-Law into Ireland.

SPEAKERS.

In the Affirmative.	In the Negative.
Mr. Trevor, Magd. Hall.	Mr. Phinn, Exeter.
Mr. Mellish, University.	Mr. Cripps, New Coll.
	Mr. Cardwell, Balliol.

MR. CRIPPS moved as an Amendment :

Provided that such Act extend no further than to the care of orphans, and the relief of the old and infirm.

Adjourned.

SATURDAY, NOVEMBER 7, 1835.

Wyatt's Rooms.

ADJOURNED DEBATE.

MR. CARDWELL, Balliol, President, in the Chair.

SPEAKERS.

In the Affirmative.
Mr. Giles, Magdalen Hall.
Mr. Salmon, Exeter.
Mr. Highton, Queen's.

MR. TREVOR replied.

The Motion was then put, and carried without a division.

THE PRESIDENT proposed, that Mr. Cripps's Amendment should be put as a Rider, which was agreed to; the Rider was then put, and lost without a division.

THURSDAY, NOVEMBER 12, 1835.

Wyatt's Rooms.

MR. CARDWELL, Balliol, President, in the Chair.

MR. MELLISH, University, moved:

That the suspension of the Foreign Enlistment Act in favour of the Queen of Spain was injurious to the honour and true interests of this Country.

SPEAKERS.

In the Affirmative.	*In the Negative.*
Mr. Mellish, University.	Mr. Cripps, New Coll.
Mr. Nesbitt, Brasen-nose.	
Mr. Phinn, Exeter.	
The President.	

MR. MELLISH replied.

The Motion was carried without a division.

THURSDAY, NOVEMBER 19, 1835.

Wyatt's Rooms.

MR. CARDWELL, Balliol, President, in the Chair.

MR. BROWNE, St. John's, moved :

That the influence exercised by the Conservative Associations is pernicious.

SPEAKERS.

In the Affirmative.	In the Negative.
Mr. Browne, St. John's.	Mr. Monro, Oriel.
Mr. Cripps, New Coll.	Mr. Morrell, St. John's.
Mr. Burrows, St. John's.	Mr. Barne, Exeter.
	Mr. Brancker, Wadham.
	Mr. Highton, Queen's.
	The President.

MR. BROWNE replied.

MR. BUDDICOM, Brasen-nose, made an observation on part of Mr. Cripps's speech.

DIVISION.

Ayes 24
Noes 78
Majority . . . 54

THURSDAY, NOVEMBER 26, 1835.

Wyatt's Rooms.

MR. MELLISH, University, Treasurer, in the Chair.

MR. HESSEY, St. John's, moved :

That the late unflinching resistance of the House of Lords to popular innovations has entitled it to the gratitude of the Country.

SPEAKERS.

In the Affirmative.	In the Negative.
Mr. Hessey, St. John's.	Mr. Moncreiff, Balliol.
Mr. Ridley, Ch. Ch.	Mr. Phinn, Exeter.
Mr. Mellish, University.	
Mr. Trevor, Magdalen Hall.	

MR. PHINN, Exeter, moved as an Amendment:

That after the words " of the House of Lords," be inserted " with the exception of the Irish Church Bill."

MR. HESSEY replied.

Mr. Phinn's Amendment was then put, and lost without a division.

The original Motion was carried without a division.

THURSDAY, DECEMBER 3, 1835.

Wyatt's Rooms.

The President being the Mover of the Question,

The Librarian (MR. BRANCKER, Wadham) took the Chair.

MR. CARDWELL, Balliol, moved:

That Restrictions upon the Freedom of Commerce are indefensible in theory, and injurious in practice.

SPEAKERS.

In the Affirmative.	*In the Negative.*
Mr. Cardwell, Balliol.	Mr. Phinn, Exeter.
Mr. Cripps, New Coll.	Mr. Highton, Queen's.
	Mr. Giles, Magdalen Hall.

MR. HIGHTON, Queen's, moved as an Amendment:

That some Restrictions on the unlimited freedom of Commerce are useful and necessary.

On MR. CARDWELL rising to reply, and the Librarian taking the Chair,

MR. CARDWELL put a question to the Librarian as to the legality of the Amendment.

The Librarian, then in the Chair, decided that the Amendment could not be put to the vote.

MR. CARDWELL replied.

DIVISION.

Ayes 16
Noes 15
Majority . . . 1

THURSDAY, DECEMBER 10, 1835.

Wyatt's Rooms.

MR. BRANCKER, Wadham, Librarian, in the Chair.

MR. MONRO, sen. Oriel, moved:

That Mr. Pitt's conduct with respect to his foreign policy was highly conducive to the best interests of this Country.

SPEAKERS.

In the Affirmative.	*In the Negative.*
Mr. Monro, sen. Oriel.	Mr. Marsh, Oriel.
Mr. Morrell, St. John's.	Mr. Moncreiff, Balliol.

MR. MONRO replied.

The Motion was then put, and carried without a division.

THURSDAY, JANUARY 28, 1836.

Wyatt's Rooms.

MR. CARDWELL, Balliol, President, in the Chair.

MR. SALMON, Exeter, moved:

That the Orange Societies in Ireland have been prejudicial to the peace and prosperity of that Country.

SPEAKERS.

In the Affirmative.	*In the Negative.*
Mr. Salmon, Exeter.	Mr. Phillott, Ch. Ch.
Mr. Phinn, Exeter.	Mr. Marsh, Oriel.

MR. POYNDER, Wadham, moved as an Amendment:

That the present proceedings of Papists in Ireland render Orange Societies justifiable.

Against the Amendment.
Mr. Mellish, University.
The President.

MR. SALMON replied. The Amendment was then put.

DIVISION.

Ayes 22
Noes 16
Majority . . . 6

THURSDAY, FEBRUARY 4, 1836.

Wyatt's Rooms.

MR. CARDWELL, President, in the Chair.

MR. PHINN, Exeter, moved:

That Lord Stanley as a Statesman is entitled to our respect and admiration.

SPEAKERS.

In the Affirmative.	*In the Negative.*
Mr. Phinn, Exeter.	Mr. Cornish, Ch. Ch.
Mr. Mellish, University.	Mr. Monro, Oriel.

MR. RIDLEY, Ch. Ch. moved as an Amendment:

That Lord Stanley's conduct in separating himself from the Whig-Radical party is highly honourable, and deserving of admiration.

Against the Amendment.
Mr. Cripps, New Coll.

MR. HIGHTON, Queen's, moved a second Amendment:

That while this House feel the highest respect and admiration for the honesty and sincerity which they conceive to have influenced Lord Stanley's political conduct; yet that they consider that he made a most fatal mistake in supporting so democratic a measure as the Reform Bill.

MR. PHINN replied.

The first Amendment was then put.

DIVISION.

Ayes 23
Noes 17
Majority . . . 6

THURSDAY, FEBRUARY 11, 1836.

Wyatt's Rooms.

MR. CARDWELL, Balliol, President, in the Chair.

MR. CRIPPS, New College, moved :

That an Administration, formed upon the principles of Earl Grey's Cabinet, would be best calculated to meet the present exigencies of the Country.

SPEAKERS.

In the Affirmative.	*In the Negative.*
Mr. Cripps, New Coll.	Mr. Morrell, St. John's.
Mr. Moncreiff, Balliol.	Mr. Price, Lincoln.
The President.	Mr. Poynder, Wadham.
	Mr. Hadden, Brasen-nose.
	Mr. Phinn, Exeter.
	Rev. G. Trevor, Magd. Hall.

MR. CRIPPS replied.

DIVISION.

Ayes 61
Noes 19
Majority . . . 42

THURSDAY, FEBRUARY 18, 1836.

Wyatt's Rooms.

Mr. BRANCKER, Wadham, President, in the Chair.

Mr. MONCREIFF, Balliol, moved:

That an interference on the part of Earl Grey's Government on behalf of the Poles in the late struggle with Russia, would have best preserved the honour and protected the interests of this Country.

SPEAKERS.

In the Affirmative.	*In the Negative.*
Mr. Moncreiff, Balliol.	Mr. Mellish, University.
Mr. Harrison, Ch. Ch.	Mr. Cripps, New Coll.
Mr. Browne, St. John's.	Mr. Cornish, Ch. Ch.
Mr. Burrows, St. John's.	Mr. Poynder, Brasen-nose.
	Mr. Phinn, Exeter.

Mr. BROWNE, St. John's, moved as a Rider:

And that at the present time the British Government is even more called upon to interfere for the restoration of Polish Independence.

Mr. MONCREIFF replied.

The Motion was then put.

DIVISION.

Ayes 27
Noes 23
Majority . . . 4

The Rider was then put, and negatived without a division.

Y

THURSDAY, FEBRUARY 25, 1836.

Wyatt's Rooms.

MR. BRANCKER, Wadham, President, in the Chair.

MR. RIDLEY, Ch. Ch. moved :

That in the present state of affairs, Sir R. Peel's speedy return to Office is absolutely necessary.

SPEAKERS.

In the Affirmative.	*In the Negative.*
Mr. Ridley, Ch. Ch.	Mr. Phillott, Ch. Ch.
Mr. Price, Lincoln.	Mr. Fowler, Pembroke.
Mr. Buckley, Brasen-nose.	Mr. Phinn, Exeter.
Mr. Cornish, Ch. Ch.	Mr. Cripps, New Coll.
	Mr. Hodson, Merton.
	Mr. Poynder, Brasen-nose.

MR. FOWLER, Pembroke, moved as an Amendment :

That it is highly expedient that the principle of government with which Sir R. Peel is identified as a statesman should speedily be invested with power.

MR. RIDLEY replied.

The Amendment was then put, and negatived without a division.

The original Motion was then put.

DIVISION.

Ayes 52
Noes 29
Majority . . . 23

THURSDAY, MARCH 3, 1836.

Wyatt's Rooms.

MR. BRANCKER, Wadham, President, in the Chair.

MR. CAMPBELL, Exeter, moved :

That Education in this Country ought to be established on a National plan.

SPEAKERS.

In the Affirmative.	*In the Negative.*
Mr. Campbell, Exeter.	Mr. King, Wadham.
Mr. Fooks, Exeter.	Mr. Mills, Balliol.
Mr. Harrison, Ch. Ch.	

MR. CAMPBELL, Exeter, replied.

DIVISION.

Ayes 13
Noes 16
Majority . . . 3

THURSDAY, MARCH 10, 1836.

Wyatt's Rooms.

MR. CORNISH, Ch. Ch. Librarian, in the Chair.

MR. BRANCKER, Wadham, moved:

That the Resolution of the House of Commons, " That any surplus revenue of the present Church Establishment in Ireland, not required for the support or spiritual care of its members, be applied to the moral and religious education of all classes of the people, without any distinction of religious persuasion," is both unjust in itself, and calculated to destroy the very existence of the Protestant religion in Ireland.

SPEAKERS.

In the Affirmative.	*In the Negative.*
Mr. Brancker, Wadham.	Mr. Cripps, New Coll.
Mr. Cornish, Ch. Ch.	Mr. Moncreiff, Balliol.
Mr. Newman, Oriel.	
Mr. Hodson, Merton.	
Mr. Poynder, Wadham.	
Mr. Mellish, University.	

MR. CRIPPS, New College, moved as an Amendment:

That should any surplus revenue remain after the wants of the Protestant Church in Ireland have been amply provided for, it would be expedient to apply such revenue to the education of all classes without distinction of religious persuasion; but that any coalition with the Irish Radical party for the purpose of carrying such a measure, is disgraceful to its advocates, and injurious to the Protestant interests of Great Britain.

MR. BRANCKER, Wadham, replied.

DIVISION.

Ayes 41
Noes 8
Majority . . . 33

The Amendment, having been previously put, was negatived without a division.

THURSDAY, MARCH 17, 1836.

Wyatt's Rooms.

MR. BRANCKER, Wadham, President, in the Chair.

MR. GILES, Magdalen Hall, moved :

That the repeal of the so-called Taxes on Knowledge would be injurious to the Country.

SPEAKERS.

In the Affirmative.	*In the Negative.*
Mr. Giles, Magd. Hall.	Mr. Pattison, Oriel.
Mr. Ridley, Ch. Ch.	Mr. Fooks, Exeter.
Mr. Fowler, Pembroke.	
Mr. Campbell, Exeter.	
Mr. Harrison, Ch. Ch.	
Mr. Andrew, Exeter.	

MR. GILES, Magdalen Hall, replied.

DIVISION.

Ayes 33
Noes 5
Majority . . . 28

THURSDAY, APRIL 21, 1836.

Wyatt's Rooms.

MR. BRANCKER, Wadham, President, in the Chair.

MR. CORNISH, Ch. Ch. moved :

That the Foreign Policy of Lord Palmerston has been disastrous and disgraceful to the Country.

SPEAKERS.

In the Affirmative.	*In the Negative.*
Mr. Cornish, Ch. Ch.	Mr. Phinn, Exeter.
Mr. Mellish, University.	Mr. Cardwell, Balliol.
The President.	

MR. CORNISH, Ch. Ch. replied.

DIVISION.

Ayes 38
Noes 5
Majority . . . 33

THURSDAY, APRIL 28, 1836.

Wyatt's Rooms.

Mr. BRANCKER, Wadham, President, in the Chair.

Mr. HODSON, Merton, moved :

That the measure of the Duke of Wellington's Administration for removing the Civil Disabilities of the Roman Catholics was in itself dangerous and unjustifiable, and has proved highly prejudicial to the welfare of the Country.

SPEAKERS.

In the Affirmative.	*In the Negative.*
Mr. Hodson, Merton.	Mr. Moncreiff, Balliol.
Mr. Ridley, Ch. Ch.	Mr. Mellish, University.
Mr. Bernard, Exeter.	
Mr. Courtenay, Exeter.	
Mr. Giles, Magdalen Hall.	

Mr. RIDLEY, Ch. Ch. moved as a Rider :

That the words, " and disgraceful to the Ministry who carried it," be inserted after the word, " unjustifiable."

Adjourned to Saturday.

SATURDAY, APRIL 30, 1836.

Wyatt's Rooms.

ADJOURNED DEBATE.

MR. BRANCKER, Wadham, President, in the Chair.

SPEAKERS.

In the Affirmative.	*In the Negative.*
Mr. Rogers, Corpus.	Mr. Phinn, Exeter.
	Mr. Cripps, New College.

MR. ROGERS, Corpus, moved as an Amendment:

That the gradual development of Ultra Liberalism since 1829, is to be attributed to the worthlessness of the Whig Governments since that period, rather than to be considered as a consequence of the Catholic Relief Bill, which though unsound in principle, might in the hands of honest Ministers have been rendered innocuous in effect.

SPEAKERS ON THE ORIGINAL MOTION.

In the Affirmative.	*In the Negative.*
Mr. Campbell, Exeter.	
Mr. Fowler, Pembroke.	
Mr. Burney, Magdalen.	
Mr. Phillott, Ch. Ch.	

The President rose to object to the Amendment that had been moved; and also to declare the Rider to be informal.

MR. RIDLEY, Ch. Ch. then withdrew the Rider: and MR. CORNISH, Ch. Ch. moved the following Rider:

That the Ministry with whom it originated most shamefully betrayed the confidence of their supporters, and exhibited a degree of inconsistency almost unparalleled in history.

In favour of the Rider.
Mr. Lonsdale, Oriel.

MR. HODSON, Merton, replied.

DIVISION ON THE ORIGINAL MOTION.

Ayes	43
Noes	12
Majority	31

DIVISION ON THE RIDER.

Ayes	30
Noes	21
Majority	9

THURSDAY, MAY 5, 1836.

Wyatt's Rooms.

Mr. BRANCKER, Wadham, President, in the Chair.

Mr. MONCREIFF, Balliol, moved:

That the present system of Government Education in Ireland is entitled to the unreserved confidence and support of every well-wisher to the Irish people.

SPEAKERS.

In the Affirmative.	*In the Negative.*
Mr. Moncreiff, Balliol.	Mr. Ridley, Ch. Ch.
Mr. Salmon, Exeter.	Mr. Newman, Oriel.
Mr. Phinn, Exeter.	Mr. Marsh, Oriel.
Mr. Cripps, New College.	The President.

Mr. MONCREIFF, Balliol, replied.

DIVISION.

Ayes 22
Noes 32
Majority . . . 10

THURSDAY, MAY 12, 1836.

Wyatt's Rooms.

Mr. CORNISH, Ch. Ch. President, in the Chair.

Mr. CRIPPS, New College, moved:

That the attempt to abolish Local Government by the overthrow of the Municipal Corporations in Ireland, is an unprincipled and destructive measure, exhibiting in its advocates a total disregard of the ancient rights and existing institutions of the Country.

SPEAKERS.

In the Affirmative.	*In the Negative.*
Mr. Cripps, New College.	Mr. Phinn, Exeter.
Mr. Brancker, Wadham.	Mr. Cardwell, Balliol.
Mr. Moncreiff, Balliol[a].	

Mr. CRIPPS replied.

DIVISION.

Ayes 22
Noes 25
Majority . . . 3

[a] Mr. Moncreiff, Balliol, did not vote.

THURSDAY, MAY 19, 1836.

Wyatt's Rooms.

MR. CORNISH, Ch. Ch. President, in the Chair.

MR. MARSH, Oriel, moved:

That the insertion of Anonymous Articles in Reviews and public Journals is injurious in itself, while it adds nothing to the freedom of opinion.

SPEAKERS.

In the Affirmative.	*In the Negative.*
Mr. Marsh, Oriel.	Mr. Pattison, Oriel.
Mr. Phinn, Exeter.	Mr. Hill, Edmund Hall.
	Mr. Moncreiff, Balliol.
	Mr. Street, Magdalen Hall.

MR. MARSH, Oriel, replied.

DIVISION.

Ayes 12
Noes 37
Majority . . . 25

THURSDAY, MAY 26, 1836.

Wyatt's Rooms.

MR. CORNISH, Ch. Ch. President, in the Chair.

MR. PHILLOTT, Ch. Ch. moved:

That the Policy pursued by the Government of this Country towards her North American Colonies has been injurious to the interests of the Empire.

SPEAKERS.

In the Affirmative.	*In the Negative.*
Mr. Phillott, Ch. Ch.	Mr. Phinn, Exeter.
Mr. Campbell, Exeter.	

MR. PHILLOTT, Ch. Ch. replied.

DIVISION.

Ayes 23
Noes 15
Majority . . . 8

THURSDAY, JUNE 2, 1836.

Wyatt's Rooms.

Mr. CORNISH, Ch. Ch. President, in the Chair.

Mr. SALMON, Exeter, moved:

That Lord Brougham's public character deserves our highest admiration and respect.

SPEAKERS.

In the Affirmative.	In the Negative.
Mr. Salmon, Exeter.	Mr. Fagan, Oriel.
Mr. Phinn, Exeter.	Mr. Mellish, University.
Mr. Moncreiff, Balliol.	Mr. Fooks, Exeter.

Mr. KING, Wadham, moved as an Amendment, without speaking on it:

That while we admire the past talents of Lord Brougham, we cannot but regret the use to which he has applied them.

Mr. SALMON, Exeter, replied.

DIVISION ON THE AMENDMENT.

Ayes 40
Noes 18
Majority . . 22

The original Motion was consequently not put.

THURSDAY, JUNE 9, 1836.

Wyatt's Rooms.

Mr. CORNISH, Ch. Ch. President, in the Chair.

Mr. FOWLER, Pembroke, moved:

That the present Ministry are undeserving of the confidence of the Country.

SPEAKERS.

In the Affirmative.	In the Negative.
Mr. Fowler, Pembroke.	Mr. Phinn, Exeter.
Mr. Hussey, Balliol.	
Mr. Street, Magdalen Hall.	
Mr. Mellish, University.	
Mr. Cardwell, Balliol.	

Mr. HUSSEY, Balliol, moved the following Rider:

That our want of confidence is occasioned by their cowardice in shrinking from the obvious duty of destroying the present Church Establishment in Ireland, and of adapting generally the institutions of the Country to the inevitable progress of Democracy.

In favour of the Amendment.

Mr. Hussey, Balliol.

Adjourned.

z

SATURDAY, JUNE 11, 1836.

Wyatt's Rooms.

ADJOURNED DEBATE.

Mr. CORNISH, Ch. Ch. President, in the Chair.

SPEAKERS.

In the Affirmative.	*In the Negative.*
Mr. Hodson, Merton.	Mr. Fowle, Wadham.
The President.	Mr. Cripps, New College.
Mr. Campbell, Exeter.	Mr. Moncreiff, Balliol.
	Mr. Salmon, Exeter.

Mr. FOWLER, Pembroke, replied.

Mr. CORNISH, Ch. Ch. moved the following Rider:

That our want of confidence is grounded as well on the degrading alliance with O'Connell, as on the miserable experience which the English people have had of genuine Whig policy, the supporters of which have consulted the interests of a faction at the expense of a nation, have preferred tortuous paths to an honest and straightforward course, availing themselves of temporary expedients, instead of relying on fixed principles, and have ever been found the ready tools for measures, the disastrous consequences of which they were not sagacious enough to foresee, or too unprincipled to regard.

DIVISION ON THE ORIGINAL MOTION.

Ayes 48
Noes 9
Majority . . . 39

The first Rider was then put, and lost without a division.

The second Rider was then put.

DIVISION.

Ayes 39
Noes 12
Majority . . . 27

THURSDAY, OCTOBER 20, 1836.

Wyatt's Rooms.

MR. CORNISH, Ch. Ch. President, in the Chair.

MR. BERNARD, Exeter, moved :

That the French Revolution of 1830 has been productive of the most pernicious effects upon the state and prospects of that Nation.

SPEAKERS.

In the Affirmative.	*In the Negative.*
Mr. Bernard, Exeter.	Mr. Fooks, Exeter.
Mr. Hessey, St. John's.	Mr. Phinn, Exeter.

MR. FOOKS, Exeter, moved the following Amendment :

That in consequence of the unconstitutional government of Louis-Philippe, the French Revolution of 1830 has failed in producing many of the beneficial effects which its advocates had naturally anticipated.

MR. BERNARD, Exeter, replied.

DIVISION ON THE AMENDMENT.

Ayes 3
Noes 19
Majority . . . 16

The original Motion was then carried without a division.

THURSDAY, OCTOBER 27, 1836.

Wyatt's Rooms.

MR. CORNISH, Ch. Ch. President, in the Chair.

In the absence of MR. RIDLEY, Ch. Ch. MR. FOWLER, Pembroke, moved :

That the evils of American Society are to be traced to the pernicious form of government existing in that Country.

SPEAKERS.

In the Affirmative.	*In the Negative.*
Mr. Fowler, Pembroke.	Mr. Moncreiff, Balliol.
Mr. Ridley, Ch. Ch.	Mr. Phinn, Exeter.
Mr. Donaldson, Trinity Coll. Cambridge.	
Mr. Forsyth, Trin. Coll. Camb.	
Mr. Mellish, University.	

MR. CARDWELL, Balliol, moved as an Amendment :

That no remedy can be expected for the evils of American Society, without an entire change in the form of government in that Country.

DIVISION ON THE AMENDMENT.

Ayes 56
Noes 16
Majority . . . 40

THURSDAY, NOVEMBER 3, 1836.

Wyatt's Rooms.

MR. MARSH, Oriel, Librarian, in the Chair.

MR. FOOKS, Exeter, moved :

That Lord Stanley's Act for the Emancipation of the Slaves in our West Indian Colonies was correct in point of principle, and has fully satisfied all the expectations of its supporters.

SPEAKERS.

In the Affirmative.	*In the Negative.*
Mr. Fooks, Exeter.	Mr. Campbell, Exeter.
Mr. Moncreiff, Balliol.	Mr. Hodson, Merton.
Mr. Monro, Oriel.	
Mr. Ridley, Ch. Ch.	
Mr. Utterton, Oriel.	
Mr. Newman, Oriel.	

MR. HESSEY, St. John's, moved as an Amendment :

That Lord Stanley's Act being correct in principle, it is the earnest hope of this House that its results will be satisfactory to its supporters.

In favour of the Amendment.
Mr. Buckley, Brasen-nose.

MR. FOOKS, Exeter, replied.

DIVISION ON THE AMENDMENT.

Ayes 19
Noes 15
Majority . . . 4

THURSDAY, NOVEMBER 10, 1836.

Wyatt's Rooms.

MR. MARSH, Oriel, President, in the Chair.

MR. MONCREIFF, Balliol, moved:

That the political principles of Mr. Fox are in accordance with the spirit of the British Constitution; and are calculated to promote the happiness of the Nation.

SPEAKERS.

In the Affirmative.	*In the Negative.*
Mr. Moncreiff, Balliol.	Mr. Campbell, Exeter.
Mr. Phinn, Exeter.	Mr. Monro, Oriel.

MR. MONCREIFF, Balliol, replied.

DIVISION.

Ayes 8
Noes 41
Majority . . . 33

THURSDAY, NOVEMBER 17, 1836.

Wyatt's Rooms.

MR. MARSH, Oriel, President, in the Chair.

MR. CRIPPS, New College, moved:

That the character of Napoleon is deserving the admiration of posterity.

SPEAKERS.

In the Affirmative.	*In the Negative.*
Mr. Cripps, New Coll.	Mr. Browne, St. John's.
	Mr. Litton, Oriel.

MR. BROWNE, St. John's, moved as an Amendment:

That the talents of Napoleon extort from us that admiration which can never be due to either his Moral or Political character.

MR. CRIPPS, New Coll. replied. The Amendment was then put.

DIVISION.

Ayes 53
Noes 9
Majority . . . 44

THURSDAY, NOVEMBER 24, 1836.
Wyatt's Rooms.

Mr. MELLISH, University, Librarian, in the Chair.

Mr. PHILLOTT, Ch. Ch. moved:

That the disgraceful alliance which exists between the Government and the Radical party, fully justifies their former supporters in separating from them.

SPEAKERS.

In the Affirmative.	*In the Negative.*
Mr. Phillott, Ch. Ch.	Mr. Moncreiff, Balliol.
Mr. Monro, Oriel.	Mr. Phinn, Exeter.
Mr. Cardwell, Balliol.	
Mr. Cripps, New College.	

Mr. PHILLOTT, Ch. Ch. replied. The Question was then put.

DIVISION.

Ayes 67
Noes 7
Majority . . . 60

THURSDAY, DECEMBER 1, 1836.
Wyatt's Rooms.

Mr. MARSH, Oriel, President, in the Chair.

Mr. FAGAN, Oriel, moved:

That while it must be allowed that the present Poor-Law System has relieved the rate-payers from an oppressive burden, and imposed some just restraints on the able-bodied and idle; yet it treats the poorer classes with such unnatural severity, that its consequences cannot be regarded without dismay.

SPEAKERS.

In the Affirmative.	*In the Negative.*
Mr. Fagan, Oriel.	Mr. Courtenay, Exeter.
Mr. Cosserat, Exeter.	Mr. Fooks, Exeter.

Mr. COSSERAT, Exeter, moved as a Rider,

And that the conduct of his Majesty's Ministers, in bringing forward this Measure, is utterly inconsistent with the liberal Principles which they profess to hold.

Against the Rider.

Mr. Phinn, Exeter.

DIVISION ON THE ORIGINAL MOTION.

Ayes 25
Noes 20
Majority . . . 5

THURSDAY, DECEMBER 8, 1836.

Wyatt's Rooms.

MR. MONCREIFF, Balliol, Treasurer, in the Chair.

In the absence of MR. HESSEY, St. John's, MR. BROWNE, St. John's, moved:

That the United States were justified in asserting their independence.

SPEAKERS.

In the Affirmative.
Mr. Browne, St. John's.
Mr. Ridley, Ch. Ch.
Mr. Cripps, New College.

DIVISION.

Ayes 16
Noes 36
Majority . . . 20

THURSDAY, DECEMBER 15, 1836.

Wyatt's Rooms.

MR. MARSH, Oriel, President, in the Chair.

MR. MONCREIFF, Balliol, moved:

That Lord Byron's poetical merits have been greatly overrated.

SPEAKERS.

In the Affirmative.	*In the Negative.*
Mr. Moncreiff, Balliol.	Mr. Fooks, Exeter.

MR. MONCREIFF, Balliol, replied.

DIVISION.

Ayes 13
Noes 23
Majority . . . 10

THURSDAY, JANUARY 26, 1837.

Wyatt's Rooms.

MR. MELLISH, University, Librarian, in the Chair.

MR. BERNARD, Exeter, moved:

That it is desirable for the interests of Spain and of Europe that the present struggle in the Peninsula terminate in favour of Don Carlos.

SPEAKERS.

In the Affirmative.	*In the Negative.*
Mr. Bernard, Exeter.	Mr. Moncreiff, Balliol.
Mr. Campbell, Exeter.	Mr. Cripps, New College.

MR. BERNARD, Exeter, replied.

DIVISION.

Ayes 16
Noes 8
Majority . . . 8

THURSDAY, FEBRUARY 2, 1837.

Wyatt's Rooms.

MR. MARSH, Oriel, President, in the Chair.

MR. HESSEY, St. John's, moved:

That Constantine's policy in removing the seat of the empire from Rome to Constantinople was judicious.

SPEAKERS.

In the Affirmative.	*In the Negative.*
Mr. Hessey, St. John's.	Mr. Christie, Oriel.
Mr. Moncreiff, Balliol.	Mr. Cripps, New College.

MR. HESSEY, St. John's, replied.

DIVISION.

Ayes 8
Noes 16
Majority . . . 8

A a

THURSDAY, FEBRUARY 9, 1837.

Wyatt's Rooms.

Mr. HESSEY, St. John's, Treasurer, in the Chair.

Mr. MONCREIFF, Balliol, moved :

That the recent political agitation by the Conservative Party throughout the Country has been productive of the greatest evil, and cannot be justified on the principle of self-defence.

SPEAKERS.

In the Affirmative.	*In the Negative.*
Mr. Moncreiff, Balliol.	Mr. Tate, Balliol.
Mr. Fooks, Exeter.	Mr. Poynder, Wadham.
	Mr. Chadwick, Hon. M.A. Worcester.
	Mr. Mellish, University.
	Mr. G. Wood, Oriel.
	Mr. Fowler, Pembroke.

Mr. POYNDER, Wadham, moved as an Amendment :

That such demonstrations of Conservative feelings as have been general throughout the Country during the last recess of Parliament, need not to be justified on the ground of expediency or of self-defence, but that inasmuch as they are not opposed to the spirit of the British Constitution, they are justifiable *per se.*

SPEAKERS.

For the Amendment.	*Against the Amendment.*
Mr. Campbell, Exeter.	Mr. Mellish, University.
	Mr. Hodson, Merton.

Mr. MONCREIFF replied.

DIVISION ON THE AMENDMENT.

Ayes 10
Noes 22
Majority . . . 12

DIVISION ON THE ORIGINAL MOTION.

Ayes 2
Noes 34
Majority . . . 32

THURSDAY, FEBRUARY 16, 1837.

Wyatt's Rooms.

MR. CRIPPS, New College, President, in the Chair.

MR. MONRO, Oriel, moved :

That it is necessary for the Peace and Prosperity of Ireland, that a national system of Poor-Laws should be established in that Country.

SPEAKERS.

In the Affirmative.	*In the Negative.*
Mr. Monro, Oriel.	Mr. Hessey, St. John's.
Mr. Ridley, Ch. Ch.	The President.
Mr. Browne, St. John's.	
Mr. Utterton, Oriel.	
Mr. Giles, Magdalen Hall.	
Mr. Campbell, Exeter.	

MR. HESSEY, St. John's, moved as an Amendment:

That the introduction of a Poor-Law might be made beneficial to Ireland, but that the present time is not a suitable one for its Proposal.

MR. MONRO, Oriel, replied.

The Amendment was then put, and lost without a division. The original Motion was then put, and carried without a division.

THURSDAY, FEBRUARY 23, 1837.

Wyatt's Rooms.

Mr. CRIPPS, New College, President, in the Chair.

Mr. TATE, Balliol, moved:

That the Execution of King Charles the Martyr is to be esteemed an act of atrocious and sacrilegious Murder.

SPEAKERS.

In the Affirmative.	*In the Negative.*
Mr. Tate, Balliol.	The President.
Mr. Harrison, Ch. Ch.	Mr. Fooks, Exeter.
Mr. Newman, Oriel.	Mr. Moncreiff, Balliol.
Mr. Fowler, Pembroke.	
Mr. Northcote, Balliol.	
Mr. Fortescue, Wadham.	
Mr. Campbell, Exeter.	

Mr. JACKSON, Trinity, moved as an Amendment:

That it must be admitted, that the Murder of King Charles I. cannot be justified, and that he was a Martyr to Episcopacy.

Mr. TATE, Balliol, replied.

The Amendment was then put, and lost without a division.

DIVISION ON THE ORIGINAL MOTION.

Ayes 45
Noes 4
Majority . . . 41

THURSDAY, MARCH 2, 1837.

Wyatt's Rooms.

MR. CRIPPS, New College, President, in the Chair.

MR. PHILLOTT, Ch. Ch. moved:

That Napoleon's expedition to Russia was based upon principles of sound Policy, inasmuch as to its failure may be attributed all the evils that have since arisen to Europe from the aggressions of that Country.

SPEAKERS.

In the Affirmative.	In the Negative.
Mr. Phillott, Ch. Ch.	Mr. Campbell, Exeter.
The President.	
Mr. Moncreiff, Balliol.	

MR. PHILLOTT, Ch. Ch. replied.

DIVISION.

Ayes 7
Noes 27
Majority . . . 20

THURSDAY, MARCH 9, 1837.

Wyatt's Rooms.

MR. CRIPPS, New College, President, in the Chair.

MR. ANDERSON, St. John's, moved:

That the conduct of the present Government towards Ireland is contrary to the best interests of that Country.

SPEAKERS.

In the Affirmative.	In the Negative.
Mr. Anderson, St. John's.	Mr. Browne, St. John's.
Mr. Fowler, Pembroke.	Mr. Moncreiff, Balliol.
Mr. Ridley, Ch. Ch.	
Mr. Morland, Ch. Ch.	

MR. ANDERSON, St. John's, replied.

The Question was then put, and carried without a division.

THURSDAY, MARCH 16, 1837.
Wyatt's Rooms.

Mr. MONCREIFF, Balliol, Librarian, in the Chair.

Mr. CAMPBELL, Exeter, moved:

That the conduct of the Radicals in Canada and of their friends in this Country has been unconstitutional and disloyal.

SPEAKER.

In the Affirmative.
Mr. Campbell, Exeter.

The Question was then put, and carried without a division.

THURSDAY, APRIL 13, 1837.
Wyatt's Rooms.

Mr. MONCREIFF, Balliol, Librarian, in the Chair.

Mr. BRODIE, Balliol, moved:

That it is the duty of the Legislature to endeavour, by the Political Education of the People, to render the inevitable extension of the Suffrage desirable and safe.

SPEAKERS.

In the Affirmative.	*In the Negative.*
Mr. Brodie, Balliol.	Mr. Northcote, Balliol.
Mr. Lake, Balliol.	Mr. Courtenay, Exeter.
	Mr. Tate, Balliol.
	Mr. Campbell, Exeter.

Mr. COURTENAY, Exeter, moved as an Amendment:

That it is the duty of the Legislature to provide for the Religious Instruction of the people, according to the Principles of the Established Church.

Mr. TATE, Balliol, moved a second Amendment:

That the Extension of the Suffrage is not inevitable; and that, even if it were, the Political Education of the People is any thing rather than the means of rendering such extension either desirable or safe.

Mr. BRODIE, Balliol, replied:

The House then proceeded to vote on Mr. Tate's Amendment, the President having decided that the first Amendment was irrelevant.

DIVISION ON MR. TATE'S AMENDMENT.

Ayes 28
Noes 8
Majority . . . 20

THURSDAY, APRIL 20, 1837.

Wyatt's Rooms.

MR. CRIPPS, New College, President, in the Chair.

MR. TATE, Balliol, moved:

That the Orange Institution, as it existed in Ireland, was strictly legal, and necessary for the maintenance of the Protestant Religion in that Country.

SPEAKER.

In the Affirmative.
Mr. Tate, Balliol.

DIVISION.
Ayes 77
Noes 12
Majority . . . 65

THURSDAY, APRIL 27, 1837.

Wyatt's Rooms.

MR. CRIPPS, New College, President, in the Chair.

MR. CAMPBELL, Exeter, moved:

That the Foreign Policy of the present Government with regard to the Peninsula has been unwise, dishonourable, and productive of the worst possible effects.

SPEAKERS.

In the Affirmative.	*In the Negative.*
Mr. Campbell, Exeter.	Mr. Sulivan, Balliol.

MR. CAMPBELL, Exeter, replied:

DIVISION.
Ayes 34
Noes 10
Majority . . . 24

THURSDAY, MAY 4, 1837.

Wyatt's Rooms.

Mr. MONCREIFF, Balliol, President, in the Chair.

Mr. CRIPPS, New College, moved:

That the scheme for the abolition of Church-Rates brought forward by Mr. Spring Rice, fully justifies every member of the Established Church in withdrawing his support from the present Ministry.

SPEAKERS.

In the Affirmative.	*In the Negative.*
Mr. Cripps, New Coll.	Mr. Phinn, Exeter.
Mr. Poynder, Wadham.	Mr. G. L. Browne, St. John's.

Mr. BROWNE, St. John's, moved as an Amendment:

That it is the duty of every Government to make such an alteration in the present law of Church-Rates, as shall ensure the establishment of the Protestant Church, but relieve the scruples of the conscientious Dissenter.

SPEAKERS.

In the Affirmative.	*In the Negative.*
Mr. Newton, Brasen-nose.	Mr. Moncreiff, Balliol.
Mr. Fooks, Exeter.	

Mr. MONCREIFF, Balliol, moved a second Amendment:

That the Church-Rates' Bill contains no principle necessarily hostile to the interests of the Established Church; but that to render it either justifiable or expedient, Ministers are bound to declare their readiness to provide from national sources whatever funds may at any time be found necessary.

Mr. CRIPPS, New College, then replied:

The first Amendment was then put, and lost, as also the second.

The original Motion was then put.

DIVISION.

Ayes 28
Noes 7
Majority . . . 21

THURSDAY, MAY 11, 1837.

Wyatt's Rooms.

MR. MONCREIFF, Balliol, President, in the Chair.

MR. LAKE, Balliol, moved :

That the excesses of the French Revolution are to be attributed not so much to any inherent evils in a popular Government, as to the effects produced on the mind of the people by the unnatural delay of change, and to the long abuse of their power by the King, the Clergy, and the Aristocracy.

SPEAKERS.

In the Affirmative.	*In the Negative.*
Mr. Lake, Balliol.	Mr. Tate, Balliol.
Mr. Phinn, Exeter.	Mr. Campbell, Exeter.
Mr. Fagan, Oriel.	
Mr. Lonsdale, Oriel.	

MR. LAKE, Balliol, replied.

DIVISION.

Ayes 17
Noes 20
Majority . . . 3

THURSDAY, MAY 18, 1837.

Wyatt's Rooms.

MR. MONCREIFF, Balliol, President, in the Chair.

MR. FOWLER, Pembroke, moved:

That those Statesmen who refuse to make their principles conform to the spirit of the Reform Bill, are unfit to be at present called to take a part in the Government.

SPEAKER.

In the Affirmative.
Mr. Fowler, Pembroke.

DIVISION.

Ayes 7
Noes 7
Majority . . . 0

The President gave his casting vote in favour of the Motion.

THURSDAY, MAY 25, 1837.

Wyatt's Rooms.

Mr. MONCREIFF, Balliol, President, in the Chair.

Mr. FAGAN, Oriel, moved :

That that doctrine which represents the King merely as the Chief Magistrate of the people, is in direct opposition to the spirit of the British Constitution.

SPEAKERS.

In the Affirmative.	*In the Negative.*
Mr. Fagan, Oriel.	Mr. Milman, Exeter.
Mr. Fowler, Pembroke.	Mr. Salmon, Exeter.
	The President.

Mr. SALMON, Exeter, explained expressions to which Mr. FOWLER had alluded.

Mr. FAGAN, Oriel, replied.

The Motion was then put, and carried without a division.

THURSDAY, JUNE 1, 1837.

Wyatt's Rooms.

Mr. MONCREIFF, Balliol, President, in the Chair.

Mr. MONCREIFF, Balliol, moved :

That the evils of Ireland are chiefly to be attributed to the misgovernment of its rulers ; and especially to their having placed the Established Church in a position alike hurtful to its own interests, and unsuitable to its situation as the Church of the Minority.

SPEAKERS.

In the Affirmative.	*In the Negative.*
Mr. Moncreiff, Balliol.	Mr. Campbell, Exeter.

Mr. MONCREIFF, Balliol, replied.

The Motion was then put, and lost without a division.

THURSDAY, OCTOBER 19, 1837.

Masonic Hall.

Mr. HESSEY, St. John's, Treasurer, in the Chair.

Mr. MONCREIFF, Balliol, as proxy for Mr. LAKE, Balliol, moved:

That the great defects which exist in the political views of the principal parties in the State fully justify us, while we refuse our sympathy to the complete triumph of either of them, in holding opinions which on some points are Whig, on others Tory, and on others Radical.

SPEAKERS.

In the Affirmative.	*In the Negative.*
Mr. Moncreiff, Balliol.	Mr. Tate, Balliol.
	Mr. Brodie, Balliol.
	Mr. Poynder, Wadham.

Mr. TATE, Balliol, moved as an Amendment:

That we regard the principles of the Tories as the only definite and reasonable ones; and that we do therefore rejoice in the prospect of their ultimate and immediate triumph.

DIVISION.

Ayes 16
Noes 9
Majority . . . 7

THURSDAY, OCTOBER 26, 1837.

Masonic Hall.

Mr. MONCREIFF, Balliol, President, in the Chair.

Mr. HESSEY, St. John's, moved:

That the Crusades exercised a beneficial influence on Europe.

SPEAKERS.

In the Affirmative.	*In the Negative.*
Mr. Hessey, St. John's.	Mr. Sulivan, Balliol.

Mr. HESSEY, St. John's, replied.

DIVISION.

Ayes 35
Noes 5
Majority . . . 30

THURSDAY, NOVEMBER 2, 1837.

Masonic Hall.

MR. MONCREIFF, Balliol, President, in the Chair.

MR. POYNDER, Wadham, moved :

That while National Education, if conducted on solid principles, must be hailed as a valuable boon, it is to be feared that any scheme of that nature proposed by the present Ministry would fail of producing a desirable effect.

SPEAKERS.

In the Affirmative.	*In the Negative.*
Mr. Poynder, Wadham.	Mr. Moncreiff, Balliol.
Mr. Campbell, Exeter.	

MR. POYNDER, Wadham, replied.

The Question was then put, and carried without a division.

THURSDAY, NOVEMBER 9, 1837.

Masonic Hall.

MR. HESSEY, St. John's, President, in the Chair.

MR. TATE, Balliol, moved :

That the Roman Catholic Relief Bill has been as ruinous in its effects, as it is dangerous in principle, and ought immediately to be repealed.

SPEAKERS.

In the Affirmative.	*In the Negative.*
Mr. Tate, Balliol.	Mr. Arnold, Magd. Hall.
Mr. Northcote, Balliol.	Mr. Moncreiff, Balliol.
Mr. Fowler, Pembroke.	Mr. Emeris, University.

MR. TATE, Balliol, replied.

DIVISION.

Ayes 36
Noes 7
Majority . . . 29

THURSDAY, NOVEMBER 16, 1837.

Masonic Hall.

MR. HESSEY, St. John's, President, in the Chair.

MR. NORTHCOTE, Balliol, moved:

That the Feudal System was admirably adapted to the age in which it prevailed, and as such deserves our highest approbation.

SPEAKER.

In the Affirmative.
Mr. Northcote, Balliol.

DIVISION.
Ayes 21
Noes 4
Majority . . . 17

THURSDAY, NOVEMBER 23, 1837.

Masonic Hall.

MR. HESSEY, St. John's, President, in the Chair.

MR. NEWMAN, Oriel, moved:

That in matters of taste, the Literature of the Middle Ages is a better model for imitation in the present day than Classical antiquity.

SPEAKERS.

In the Affirmative.   *In the Negative.*
Mr. Newman, Oriel.   Mr. Moncreiff, Balliol.

MR. NEWMAN, Oriel, replied.

DIVISION.
Ayes 35
Noes 25
Majority . . . 10

SATURDAY, DECEMBER 2, 1837.

Wyatt's Rooms.

MR. HESSEY, St. John's, President, in the Chair.

MR. LAKE, Balliol, moved:

That the character of the Puritans, however defaced by individual faults and extravagances, is more deserving of admiration, both in principle and action, than that of the Cavaliers,

SPEAKERS.

In the Affirmative.	*In the Negative.*
Mr. Lake, Balliol.	Mr. Tate, Balliol.
Mr. Moncreiff, Balliol.	Mr. Newman, Oriel.
	Mr. King, Wadham.
	Mr. Newton, Brasen-nose.
	Mr. Courtenay, Exeter.

MR. LAKE, Balliol, replied.

DIVISION.

Ayes 13
Noes 32
Majority . . . 19

THURSDAY, DECEMBER 7, 1837.

Wyatt's Rooms.

MR. HESSEY, St. John's, President, in the Chair,

MR. CAMPBELL, Exeter, moved:

That the Athenian Government, from the time of Pericles, was conducted on principles most injurious to society, and affords a practical illustration of the evil influence of Democracy.

SPEAKERS.

In the Affirmative.	*In the Negative.*
Mr. Campbell, Exeter.	Mr. Lake, Balliol.
Mr. Northcote, Balliol.	Mr. Moncreiff, Balliol.

MR. CAMPBELL, Exeter, replied.

DIVISION.

Ayes 14
Noes 7
Majority . . . 7

THURSDAY, FEBRUARY 1, 1838.

Wyatt's Rooms.

REV. J. A. HESSEY, St. John's, President, in the Chair.

MR. TATE, Balliol, moved :

That the proceedings of the Convention on the retreat of James II. were unjustifiable.

SPEAKERS.

In the Affirmative.	*In the Negative.*
Mr. Tate, Balliol.	Mr. Lake, Balliol.
Mr. Hodson, Merton.	Mr. Moncreiff, Balliol.
Mr. Northcote, Balliol.	
Mr. Robertson, Brasen-nose.	

MR. HODSON, Merton, moved the following Rider :

And that what is called the ' glorious Revolution' of 1688, was an act of the most flagrant Usurpation on the part of the Prince of Orange, and of Rebellion upon that of the nation at large.

MR. TATE replied.

DIVISION ON THE ORIGINAL MOTION.

Ayes 19
Noes 10
Majority . . . 9

DIVISION ON THE RIDER.

Ayes 12
Noes 10
Majority . . . 2

THURSDAY, FEBRUARY 8, 1838.

Wyatt's Rooms.

REV. J. A. HESSEY, St. John's, President, in the Chair.

MR. GOULBURN, Balliol, moved :

That the Law of Primogeniture is productive of the best effects, and that its repeal would have a tendency to destroy a valuable part of our Constitution.

SPEAKERS.

In the Affirmative.	*In the Negative.*
Mr. Goulburn, Balliol.	Mr. Moncreiff, Balliol.
Mr. Lonsdale, Oriel.	

MR. GOULBURN, Balliol, replied.

The Question being put by the President, was carried *nem. con.*

THURSDAY, FEBRUARY 15, 1838.

Wyatt's Rooms.

REV. J. A. HESSEY, St. John's, President, in the Chair.

MR. PHILLOTT, Ch. Ch. moved :

That the public character of the late Lord Eldon demands universal respect and admiration.

SPEAKER.

In the Affirmative.
Mr. Phillott, Ch. Ch.

The Question being put to the vote, was carried *nem. con.*

THURSDAY, FEBRUARY 22, 1838.

Wyatt's Rooms.

Mr. RIDLEY, Ch. Ch. President, in the Chair.

Mr. NORTHCOTE, Balliol, moved :

That the resistance offered by the Americans to the British Government in 1765 and the following years was unjustifiable, and deserves the highest reprobation.

SPEAKER.

In the Affirmative.
Mr. Northcote, Balliol.

The Question was carried without a division.

THURSDAY, MARCH 1, 1838.

Wyatt's Rooms.

Mr. RIDLEY, Ch. Ch. President, in the Chair.

Mr. HODSON, Merton, moved :

That the recommendations of the Ecclesiastical Commission are most strongly to be reprobated, as a specimen of the sacrifice of Principle to Expediency (so called), by a Conservative Administration.

SPEAKERS.

In the Affirmative.
Mr. Hodson, Merton.
The President.

DIVISION.

Ayes 37
Noes 7
Majority . . . 30

SATURDAY, MARCH 10, 1838.
Wyatt's Rooms.

MR. RIDLEY, Ch. Ch. President, in the Chair.

MR. SULIVAN, Balliol, moved :

That the permanent establishment of Queen Isabella is essential to the interests both of Spain and of the rest of Europe.

SPEAKERS.

In the Affirmative.	*In the Negative.*
Mr. Sulivan, Balliol.	Mr. Tripp, Worcester.
Mr. Lonsdale, Oriel.	Mr. Courtenay, Exeter.
	Mr. Hodson, Merton.

MR. SULIVAN replied.

DIVISION.

Ayes 20
Noes 48
Majority . . . 28

THURSDAY, MARCH 15, 1838.
Wyatt's Rooms.

MR. RIDLEY, Ch. Ch. President, in the Chair.

MR. COURTENAY, Exeter, moved :

That the suppression of Religious Houses by Henry VIII. was unjust both in principle and in manner of execution, and injurious in its consequences.

SPEAKERS.

In the Affirmative.	*In the Negative.*
Mr. Courtenay, Exeter.	Mr. Lonsdale, Oriel.
Mr. Highton, Queen's.	
Mr. Tripp, Worcester.	

MR. LONSDALE, Oriel, moved as an Amendment :

That the suppression of Religious Houses by Henry VIII. although unjust in execution, has been productive of beneficial consequences to the Country.

MR. COURTENAY replied.

DIVISION ON THE AMENDMENT.

Ayes 41
Noes 46
Majority . . . 5

DIVISION ON THE ORIGINAL MOTION.

Ayes 46
Noes 43
Majority . . . 3

THURSDAY, MARCH 22, 1838.

Wyatt's Rooms.

Rev. W. C. COTTON, Ch. Ch. Librarian, in the Chair.

Mr. LONSDALE, Oriel, moved:

That the conduct of the King of Hanover, in abrogating the Constitution given by William IV. to the people of Hanover, is deserving of the highest reprobation.

SPEAKERS.

In the Affirmative.	*In the Negative.*
Mr. Lonsdale, Oriel.	Mr. Tate, University.

Mr. LONSDALE replied.

DIVISION.

Ayes 19
Noes 63
Majority . . . 44

THURSDAY, MARCH 29, 1838.

Wyatt's Rooms.

Mr. RIDLEY, Ch. Ch. President, in the Chair.

Mr. HIGHTON, Queen's, moved:

That the present system of transportation is deserving of strong condemnation.

SPEAKERS.

In the Affirmative.	*In the Negative.*
Mr. Highton, Queen's.	Mr. Marsh, Oriel.
The President.	

Mr. HIGHTON replied.

DIVISION.

Ayes 20
Noes 12
Majority . . . 8

THURSDAY, MAY 3, 1838.

Wyatt's Rooms.

Mr. RIDLEY, Ch. Ch. President, in the Chair.

Mr. BUCKLEY, Brasen-nose, moved:

That the national prosperity of this Country is to be attributed rather to Commerce than to Agriculture.

SPEAKERS.

In the Affirmative.	*In the Negative.*
Mr. Buckley, Brasen-nose.	Mr. Tate, University.
Mr. Lake, Balliol.	

Mr. BUCKLEY, Brasen-nose, replied.

DIVISION.

Ayes 11
Noes 13
Majority . . . 2

THURSDAY, MAY 10, 1838.

Wyatt's Rooms.

Rev. W. C. COTTON, Ch. Ch. Librarian, in the Chair.

Mr. TATE, University, moved:

That the policy pursued by Lord Melbourne's Cabinet towards the United Church of England and Ireland has been a uniform succession of heavy blows, and deep discouragements to Protestantism in the Realm.

SPEAKER.

In the Affirmative.
Mr. Tate, University.

The Question was carried without a division.

THURSDAY, MAY 17, 1838.

Wyatt's Rooms.

Mr. HIGHTON, Queen's, Treasurer, in the Chair.

Mr. W. H. RIDLEY, Ch. Ch. moved:

That the present facilities of acquiring knowledge through the medium of the Press are, on the whole, productive of more harm than benefit.

SPEAKERS.

In the Affirmative.	*In the Negative.*
Mr. Ridley, Ch. Ch.	Mr. Ruskin, Ch. Ch.
Mr. Northcote, Exeter.	Mr. Moncreiff, Balliol.
Mr. Tate, University.	

MR. RIDLEY, Ch. Ch. replied.

DIVISION.

Ayes 25
Noes 10
Majority . . . 15

THURSDAY, MAY 24, 1838.

Wyatt's Rooms.

Mr. LAKE, Balliol, President, in the Chair.

Mr. GOULBURN, Balliol, moved:

That the reading of good and well-written Novels is neither prejudicial to the moral nor to the intellectual character.

SPEAKERS.

In the Affirmative.	*In the Negative.*
Mr. Goulburn, Balliol.	Mr. Robertson, Brasen-nose.
Mr. Collyns, Ch. Ch.	Mr. Highton, Queen's.
Mr. Ruskin, Ch. Ch.	
Mr. Moncreiff, Balliol.	

Neutral.
Mr. Newman, Oriel.

MR. GOULBURN, Balliol, replied.

DIVISION.

Ayes 35
Noes 4
Majority . . . 31

THURSDAY, MAY 31, 1838.

Wyatt's Rooms.

MR. LAKE, Balliol, President, in the Chair.

MR. MONCREIFF, Balliol, moved:

That Votes for Members of Parliament ought to be taken by Ballot.

SPEAKERS.

In the Affirmative.	*In the Negative.*
Mr. Moncreiff, Balliol.	Mr. Landon, Worcester.
Mr. Gee, Wadham.	Mr. Campbell, Exeter.

MR. BRODIE, Balliol, then moved the Adjournment of the Debate, which was carried.

FRIDAY, JUNE 8, 1838.

Wyatt's Rooms.

ADJOURNED DEBATE.

MR. LAKE, Balliol, President, in the Chair.

MR. MONCREIFF, Balliol, moved:

That Votes for Members of Parliament ought to be taken by Ballot.

SPEAKERS.

In the Affirmative.	*In the Negative.*
Mr. Brodie, Balliol.	Mr. Northcote, Exeter.
	Mr. Collyns, Ch. Ch.
	Mr. Tate, University.

MR. MONCREIFF, Balliol, replied.

DIVISION.

Ayes 7
Noes 67
Majority . . . 60

WEDNESDAY, JUNE 13, 1838.

Wyatt's Rooms.

Mr. LAKE, Balliol, President, in the Chair.

Mr. RUSKIN, Ch. Ch. moved:

That Intellectual Education as distinguished from Moral Discipline, is detrimental to the interests of the Lower Orders of a nation.

SPEAKERS.

In the Affirmative.
Mr. Ruskin, Ch. Ch.
Mr. Highton, Queen's.

Mr. MONCREIFF, Balliol, moved an Adjournment of the Debate, which was carried on a division by a large Majority.

FRIDAY, JUNE 15, 1838.

Wyatt's Rooms.

ADJOURNED DEBATE.

. Mr. LAKE, Balliol, President, in the Chair.

Mr. RUSKIN, Ch. Ch. moved:

That Intellectual Education as distinguished from Moral Discipline, is detrimental to the interests of the Lower Orders of a nation.

SPEAKERS.

In the Affirmative.	*In the Negative.*
Mr. Tate, University.	Mr. Moncreiff, Balliol.
Mr. Newman, Oriel.	The President.

Mr. RUSKIN, Ch. Ch. replied.

The Motion was then put, and carried without a division.

Mr. TATE, University, moved the following Rider to the Motion:

But that we can expect no permanent advantage from either or both of these, unless they be grounded on pure religious principles.

The Rider was also carried without a division.

WEDNESDAY, JUNE 20, 1838.

Wyatt's Rooms.

MR. LAKE, Balliol, President, in the Chair.

MR. LANDON, Worcester, moved:

That corporal punishment, both in the army and in education, merits warm support.

SPEAKER.

In the Affirmative.
Mr. Landon, Worcester.

DIVISION.
Ayes 54
Noes 11
Majority . . . 43

THURSDAY, OCTOBER 25, 1838.

Wyatt's Rooms.

MR. LAKE, Balliol, President, in the Chair.

MR. RUSKIN, Ch. Ch. moved:

That theatrical representations are upon the whole highly beneficial to the character of a nation.

SPEAKERS.

In the Affirmative.	*In the Negative.*
Mr. Ruskin, Ch. Ch.	Mr. Robertson, Brasen-nose.

MR. RUSKIN, Ch. Ch. replied.

DIVISION.
Ayes 28
Noes 9
Majority . . . 19

THURSDAY, NOVEMBER 1, 1838.

Wyatt's Rooms.

Mr. HIGHTON, Queen's, President, in the Chair.

Mr. MONCREIFF, Balliol, moved:

That the present Ministry, by the Conservative tone of their recent policy at home and in the Colonies, have forfeited the confidence of the Country.

SPEAKERS.

In the Affirmative.	*In the Negative.*
Mr. Moncreiff, Balliol.	Mr. Tate, University.
	Mr. Fox, Wadham.

Mr. MONCREIFF, Balliol, replied.

Mr. TATE, University, moved the following Amendment:

That the present Ministers have never forfeited (because they never possessed) the confidence of any party, save of those who believed them to be both able and willing to sacrifice the institutions of the Country; whose politics have happily been confounded.

The Amendment was carried without a division.

THURSDAY, NOVEMBER 8, 1838.

Wyatt's Rooms.

Mr. HIGHTON, Queen's, President, in the Chair.

Mr. ROBERTSON, Brasen-nose, moved:

That the true objects of Poetry have been more realized by modern than by ancient writers.

SPEAKER.

In the Affirmative.
Mr. Robertson, Brasen-nose.

DIVISION.

Ayes	11
Noes	9
Majority	2

THURSDAY, NOVEMBER 15, 1838.

Wyatt's Rooms.

Mr. HIGHTON, Queen's, President, in the Chair.

Mr. EMERIS, University, moved:

That the means by which the restoration of the Bourbons was effected in France, and the principles on which they proceeded to act, could never have been expected to produce any happy and lasting state of things; while, on the contrary, the principles on which the present Dynasty was founded, and on which it professed to act, do hold out a reasonable hope of permanent good order in that Country.

SPEAKERS.

In the Affirmative.	*In the Negative.*
Mr. Emeris, University.	Mr. Tate, University.
Mr. Arnold, Magdalen Hall.	

Mr. EMERIS, University, replied.

The Motion was lost without a division.

THURSDAY, NOVEMBER 22, 1838.

Wyatt's Rooms.

MR. BUCKLEY, Brasen-nose, Treasurer, in the Chair.

MR. HIGHTON, Queen's, moved :

That the circumstances of the present times demand more than ever the immediate repeal of the Catholic Emancipation Bill.

SPEAKER.

In the Affirmative.
Mr. Highton, Queen's.

MR. HODSON, Merton, moved the following Rider :

That it is in direct violation of all the principles of the Constitution, to admit any but Members of the Established Church to a place in the Legislature.

In the Affirmative.	*In the Negative.*
Mr. Hodson, Merton.	Mr. Fox, Wadham.
Mr. Tate, University.	Mr. Fawcett, University.
Mr. Stevens, Ch. Ch.	Mr. Emeris, University.
	Mr. Hotham, Ch. Ch.

MR. HIGHTON, Queen's, replied.

DIVISION ON THE ORIGINAL MOTION.

Ayes 20
Noes 13
Majority . . . 7

DIVISION ON THE RIDER.

Ayes 17
Noes 18
Majority . . . 1

THURSDAY, NOVEMBER 29, 1838.

Wyatt's Rooms.

MR. HIGHTON, Queen's, President, in the Chair.

MR. FOX, Wadham, moved :

That the British Government were not justified, either on principles of right or of expediency, in that part of their conduct which led to the American Revolution in the year 1775.

SPEAKERS.

In the Affirmative.	*In the Negative.*
Mr. Fox, Wadham.	Mr. Fawcett, University.

MR. FOX, Wadham, replied.

DIVISION.

Ayes 6
Noes 13
Majority . . . 7

THURSDAY, DECEMBER 6, 1838.

Wyatt's Rooms.

MR. BUCKLEY, Brasen-nose, Treasurer, in the Chair.

MR. COURTENAY, Exeter, moved :

That the neglected condition of our Naval power reflects indelible disgrace on the present Government.

In the Affirmative.
Mr. Courtenay, Exeter.
Mr. Northcote, Exeter.

The Motion was carried without a division.

THURSDAY, JANUARY 24, 1839.

Wyatt's Rooms.

MR. HIGHTON, Queen's, President, in the Chair.

MR. FOX, Wadham, moved:

That Oliver Cromwell was greater than any crowned Monarch that has ever sat on the throne of England.

SPEAKERS.

In the Affirmative.	*In the Negative.*
Mr. Fox, Wadham.	Mr. Tate, University.
Mr. Blackett, Ch. Ch.	Mr. Rawlinson, Trinity.

MR. RAWLINSON, Trinity, moved the following Amendment:

That Oliver Cromwell was the greatest rascal that ever sat on the English throne.

DIVISION ON THE AMENDMENT.

Ayes 38
Noes 8
Majority . . . 30

THURSDAY, JANUARY 31, 1839.

Wyatt's Rooms.

MR. ROBERTSON, Brasen-nose, Treasurer, in the Chair.

Mr. HIGHTON, Queen's, moved:

That the proper policy to be pursued towards Ireland is to behave towards the Irish people at once with kindness and firmness; to shew, that while on the one hand we are ready to make any sacrifices on their behalf, which are consistent with our principles, we are on the other determined to maintain the authority of the Queen and her laws; and, above all, to uphold, with uncompromising attachment, the Established Protestant Church in that Country.

SPEAKER.

In the Affirmative.
Mr. Highton, Queen's.

The Motion was carried without a division.

THURSDAY, FEBRUARY 7, 1839.

Wyatt's Rooms.

MR. ROBERTSON, Brasen-nose, Treasurer, in the Chair.

MR. LAKE, Balliol, moved:

That the jacobinism of the present disturbers in England is essentially different from the struggle at the close of the last century, and would therefore be much more easily resisted in this Country than it was in France.

SPEAKERS.

In the Affirmative.	*In the Negative.*
Mr. Lake, Balliol.	Mr. Tate, University.
Mr. Blackett, Ch. Ch.	Mr. Ward, Ch. Ch.
Mr. Arnold, Magdalen Hall.	Mr. Wood, Oriel.

MR. LAKE, Balliol, replied.

DIVISION.

Ayes 30
Noes 13
Majority . . 17

THURSDAY, FEBRUARY 14, 1839.

Wyatt's Rooms.

MR. ROBERTSON, Brasen-nose, Treasurer, in the Chair.

MR. GEE, Wadham, moved:

That the policy pursued by our Government towards Spain, since the death of King Ferdinand, is a disgrace to the British Nation.

SPEAKER.

In the Affirmative.

Mr. Gee, Wadham.

The Motion was carried without a division.

THURSDAY, FEBRUARY 21, 1839.

Wyatt's Rooms.

Mr. MONCREIFF, Balliol, President, in the Chair.

Mr. ARNOLD, Magdalen Hall, moved:

That the conduct of Lord Durham in leaving Canada was unconstitutional, unmanly, and detrimental to the interests of both England and her Colonies.

SPEAKERS.

In the Affirmative.	*In the Negative.*
Mr. Arnold, Magdalen Hall.	Mr. Northcote, Exeter.

Mr. NORTHCOTE, Exeter, moved the following Amendment:

That the retirement of Lord Durham from Canada is unmanly and unconstitutional; and though in itself rather an advantage than otherwise, yet, as a precedent, is fraught with most pernicious consequences.

DIVISION ON THE AMENDMENT.

Ayes 80
Noes 16
Majority . . . 64

THURSDAY, FEBRUARY 28, 1839.

Wyatt's Rooms.

Mr. MONCREIFF, Balliol, President, in the Chair.

Mr. ROBERTSON, Brasen-nose, moved:

That in the administration of the affairs of India by a British Legislature, a one-sided toleration has been in effect an intolerance unparalleled in the policy of Heathen Nations.

SPEAKER.

In the Affirmative.
Mr. Robertson, Brasen-nose.

DIVISION.

Ayes 76
Noes 62
Majority . . . 14

THURSDAY, MARCH 7, 1839.

Wyatt's Rooms.

Mr. MONCREIFF, Balliol, President, in the Chair.

Mr. RAWLINSON, Trinity, moved :

That the active contrivers of the Revolution of 1688 are deserving of the severest reprobation.

SPEAKERS.

In the Affirmative.	*In the Negative.*
Mr. Rawlinson, Trinity.	Mr. Brooke-Jones, Wadham.
Mr. Northcote, Exeter.	

Mr. RAWLINSON, Trinity, replied.

DIVISION.

Ayes 37
Noes 13
Majority . . . 24

THURSDAY, APRIL 18, 1839.

Wyatt's Rooms.

Mr. MONCREIFF, Balliol, President, in the Chair.

Mr. NORTHCOTE, Balliol, moved :

That the present system of Corn Laws is based on sound principles of politics and justice.

SPEAKERS.

In the Affirmative.	*In the Negative.*
Mr. Northcote, Balliol.	Mr. Forster, Worcester.
Mr. Paterson, Wadham.	Mr. Townend, Oriel.

Mr. TOWNEND, Oriel, moved the following Amendment :

That sound principles of politics and justice require that an investigation into the present Corn Laws should take place, in order to know whether they have not operated to the deterioration of Commerce and Manufactures.

For the Amendment.	*Against the Amendment.*
Mr. Blackett, Ch. Ch.	Mr. Landon, Worcester.
Mr. Wood, Oriel.	Mr. Northcote, Exeter.

The Debate was then adjourned till the following Thursday.

THURSDAY, APRIL 25, 1839.

Wyatt's Rooms.

ADJOURNED DEBATE.

Mr. LAKE, Balliol, Librarian, in the Chair.

SPEAKERS.

In the Affirmative.	*In the Negative.*
Mr. Giffard, University.	Mr. Gee, Wadham.
Mr. Fawcett, University.	

Mr. NORTHCOTE, Balliol, replied.

DIVISION ON THE AMENDMENT.

Ayes 8
Noes 72
Majority . . . 64

The original Motion was then carried without a division.

THURSDAY, MAY 2, 1839.

Wyatt's Rooms.

Mr. LAKE, Balliol, Librarian, in the Chair.

Mr. NORTHCOTE, Exeter, moved :

That the arguments of Pitt, on the Regency Question, are more sound and constitutional than those of his opponent, Fox.

SPEAKER.

In the Affirmative.
Mr. Northcote, Exeter.

DIVISION.

Ayes 70
Noes 22
Majority . . . 48

E e

THURSDAY, MAY 9, 1839.

Wyatt's Rooms.

Mr. SULIVAN, Balliol, President, in the Chair.

Mr. BLACKETT, Ch. Ch. moved :

That in the present state of the Empire, it is the duty of an enlightened Government to propose a free and liberal measure of National Education.

SPEAKERS.

In the Affirmative.	*In the Negative.*
Mr. Blackett, Ch. Ch.	Mr. Hodson, Merton.
	Mr. Northcote, Corpus.

Mr. NORTHCOTE, Corpus, moved the following Amendment :

That National Education, to be conducted on any sound and efficient principles, ought to be carried on in connection with the National Religion.

The Debate was then adjourned till Thursday.

THURSDAY, MAY 16, 1839.

Wyatt's Rooms.
ADJOURNED DEBATE.

MR. SULIVAN, Balliol, President, in the Chair.

SPEAKERS.

In the Affirmative.   *In the Negative.*
Mr. Townend, Oriel.   Mr. Tate, University.

MR. ARNOLD, Magd. Hall, moved the following Amendment:

That it is an universally acknowledged principle, that the State is bound to provide for the education of her members; so, since the alteration of our Constitution by the Acts of 1828 and 1829, the Government is bound to provide for all those Nonconformists, who, by our present Constitution, are members of the State, such education as they can accept, and as seems most calculated to improve the condition of our lower classes; and further, that it is the bounden duty of every individual, who would promote the peace and welfare of every society, to further such education.

MR. RAWLINSON, Trinity, moved the following Amendment:

That in the present circumstances of the Empire, it is the duty of an enlightened Government to strengthen and support the National Church in the efforts which she is making to adapt her Educational System, and the existing wants of the Nation.

FOR MR. RAWLINSON'S AMENDMENT, AND AGAINST THE ORIGINAL MOTION.

Mr. Wiggin, Exeter.
Mr. G. Wood, Oriel.
Mr. Courtenay, Exeter.

FOR THE ORIGINAL MOTION.
Mr. R. Congreve, Wadham.

MR. BLACKETT, Ch. Ch. replied, and expressed his wish to agree to Mr. Arnold's Amendment.

MR. NORTHCOTE, Corpus, moved for leave to withdraw his Amendment, which was granted.

DIVISION ON MR. ARNOLD'S AMENDMENT.
Ayes 7
Noes 24
Majority . . . 17

DIVISION ON MR. RAWLINSON'S AMENDMENT.
Ayes 30
Noes 7
Majority . . . 23

MR. RAWLINSON's Amendment was consequently carried, and the original Motion lost.

WEDNESDAY, MAY 22, 1839.

Wyatt's Rooms.

Mr. SULIVAN. Balliol, President, in the Chair.

Mr. RAWLINSON, Trinity, moved:

That by the desertion of true Tory principles, the so-called Tory party fully merited and partly caused their precipitation from power in 1831.

SPEAKERS.

In the Affirmative.	*In the Negative.*
Mr. Rawlinson, Trinity.	Mr. Forster, Worcester.

Mr. FORSTER, Worcester, moved the following Amendment:

That the fall of the Tories from office in 1831, is to be attributed to the hostility which they evinced to those measures of progressive reform, which the spirit of the age and the voice of the country alike required.

Against the Amendment.
Mr. G. Wood, Oriel.
Mr. Northcote, Exeter.

Mr. NORTHCOTE, Exeter, moved the following Amendment:

That the Duke of Wellington, in his concession to the Dissenters and Roman Catholics, was actuated by the purest motives, and a belief in the promise that those concessions would make them peaceable and loyal subjects.

Mr. RAWLINSON replied.

Mr. FORSTER's Amendment was lost without a division.

DIVISION ON MR. NORTHCOTE'S AMENDMENT.
Ayes 5
Noes 21
Majority . . . 16

DIVISION ON THE ORIGINAL MOTION.
Ayes 19
Noes 6
Majority . . . 13

THURSDAY, MAY 30, 1839.

Wyatt's Rooms.

Mr. SULIVAN, Balliol, President, in the Chair.

Mr. TATE, University, moved:

That the consequences of the attempted invasion of the rights of the Legislature of Jamaica (had it succeeded) would have been prejudicial alike to the interests of the Planter, to the Colonial Trade of the Mother Country, and to the improvement of the Negro Population itself.

SPEAKERS.

In the Affirmative.	*In the Negative.*
Mr. Tate, University.	Mr. Blackett, Ch. Ch.
Mr. Rawlinson, Trinity.	Mr. Lake, Balliol.

Mr. BLACKETT explained.

Mr. LAKE moved the following Amendment:

That however we may doubt the expediency of so strong a measure as suspending the Constitution of Jamaica, we cannot too strongly denounce the infamous system which they have for many years pursued towards the Slave Population.

Mr. RAWLINSON explained.   Mr. TATE replied.

DIVISION ON MR. LAKE'S AMENDMENT.

Ayes 12
Noes 9
Majority . . . 3

The Amendment was consequently carried, and the original Motion lost.

THURSDAY, JUNE 6, 1839.

Wyatt's Rooms.

Mr. NORTHCOTE, Exeter, Treasurer, in the Chair.

Mr. FORSTER, Worcester, moved:

That the return of Lord Melbourne to office was fully justified by the circumstances under which it took place.

SPEAKERS.

In the Affirmative.	*In the Negative.*
Mr. Forster, Worcester.	Mr. A. Hope, Trin. Coll. Camb.
Mr. Gee, Wadham.	Mr. G. Wood, Oriel.
Mr. Sulivan, Balliol.	Mr. Courtenay, Exeter.

Mr. FORSTER replied.

DIVISION.

Ayes 14
Noes 73
Majority . . . 59

THURSDAY, OCTOBER 24, 1839.

Wyatt's Rooms.

Mr. SULIVAN, Balliol, President, in the Chair.

Mr. NORTHCOTE, Balliol, moved:

That the troubles of Canada are in great measure attributable to the unworthy treatment which Sir Francis Head received from the Home Government during his Administration

SPEAKERS.

In the Affirmative.	*In the Negative.*
Mr. Northcote, Balliol.	Mr. Kilpin, Worcester.

Mr. KILPIN moved the following Amendment:

That we have not at present sufficient information before us, to enable us to pronounce an impartial opinion on the affairs of Canada.

Mr. NORTHCOTE replied.

DIVISION ON THE AMENDMENT.

Ayes 11
Noes 28
Majority . . . 17

DIVISION ON THE MOTION.

Ayes 28
Noes 14
Majority . . . 14

THURSDAY, OCTOBER 31, 1839.

Wyatt's Rooms.

Mr. LAKE, Balliol, Librarian, in the Chair.

Mr. CONGREVE, Wadham, moved:

That from the renewal of the War with France in 1803, till its close in 1815, the direction of the resources of England was in the hands of men who were unequal to the task; and, consequently, that for the success of that war they deserve no credit.

SPEAKERS.

In the Affirmative.	*In the Negative.*
Mr. Congreve, Wadham.	Mr. Townend, Oriel.

Mr. TOWNEND moved the following Amendment:

That to the plan laid down by Mr. Pitt, and followed up by his successors, Europe was indebted for her freedom, and that the final overthrow of Napoleon may be attributed to those measures.

The Amendment was carried without a division.

THURSDAY, NOVEMBER 7, 1839.

Wyatt's Rooms.

MR. ARNOLD, Magdalen Hall, Treasurer, in the Chair.

MR. BLACKETT, Ch. Ch. moved:

That the excellent administration preserved at home, and the glory which the British name acquired abroad, during the Protectorate of Cromwell, call upon us to admire that period in itself, and to consider it as infinitely more creditable to our national character than the succeeding reigns of the restored Stuarts.

SPEAKERS.

In the Affirmative.	*In the Negative.*
Mr. Blackett, Ch. Ch.	Mr. Northcote, Exeter.
Mr. Sanderson, St. Mary Hall.	Mr. Ward, Ch. Ch.
	Mr. Poynder, Brasen-nose.

MR. NORTHCOTE moved the following Amendment:

That the glory which the British name acquired abroad during the Protectorate of Cromwell calls upon us to regret that his government was founded on usurpation, and distinguished, as far as his internal administration was concerned, by a direct violation of the principles of the British Constitution.

MR. WARD moved the following Amendment:

That whatever may have been the external success of the British arms under Cromwell, we cannot but recognise the total disregard of right and wrong, of law and order, exhibited during that period, and in the succeeding profligacies of the reign of Charles the Second; a just retribution upon this unhappy Country, for having basely betrayed, deposed, and murdered their lawful Sovereign.

The Debate was adjourned till the following Thursday.

THURSDAY, NOVEMBER 14, 1839.

Wyatt's Rooms.

ADJOURNED DEBATE.

Mr. BUCKLEY, Brasen-nose, President, in the Chair.

SPEAKERS.

In the Affirmative.	*In the Negative.*
Mr. Townend, Oriel.	Mr. Rawlinson, Trinity.
Mr. Congreve, Wadham.	Mr. Buckley, Brasen-nose.

Mr. RAWLINSON moved the following Amendment:

That we consider the difference between an hereditary monarch and a self-raised usurper to be such as to preclude us from venturing to institute a comparison between them; but that, in fact, we see nothing either in the domestic or in the foreign policy of Cromwell, that can justify us in admiring the period of his Protectorate, or in looking upon it as otherwise than most disgraceful to our character as a nation.

Mr. NORTHCOTE's Amendment was negatived without a division.

Mr. WARD's Amendment was not put, being declared irrelevant by the President.

DIVISION ON MR. RAWLINSON'S AMENDMENT.

Ayes 33
Noes 25
Majority . . . 8

THURSDAY, NOVEMBER 21, 1839.

Wyatt's Rooms.

Mr. BUCKLEY, Brasen-nose, President, in the Chair.

Mr. TOWNEND, Oriel, moved:

That justice demanded that Slavery should be abolished in the British colonies; and that eternal gratitude is due to the Administrations which carried the several measures necessary to that object.

SPEAKERS.

In the Affirmative.	*In the Negative.*
Mr. Townend, Oriel.	Mr. Rawlinson, Trinity.

The Debate was adjourned to the following Thursday.

THURSDAY, NOVEMBER 28, 1839.

Wyatt's Rooms.

ADJOURNED DEBATE.

Mr. BUCKLEY, Brasen-nose, President, in the Chair.

SPEAKERS.

In the Affirmative.	*In the Negative.*
Mr. Sanderson, St. Mary Hall.	Mr. Courtenay, Exeter.
Mr. Blackett, Ch. Ch.	
Mr. Coleridge, Balliol.	
Mr. Forster, Worcester.	

Mr. COURTENAY moved the following Amendment:

That justice demanded that Slavery should be abolished in the British colonies; and that the eternal gratitude of the nation is due to the many individuals who exerted themselves to obtain it.

Also, as a Rider:

That any effort to destroy the Slave trade by commercial intercourse with Africa, would deserve the nation's strongest support.

Mr. TOWNEND replied.

DIVISION ON THE AMENDMENT.

Ayes 11
Noes 22
Majority . . . 11

The original Motion was then carried without a division.

The Rider was not put, being declared irrelevant by the President.

THURSDAY, DECEMBER 5, 1839.

Wyatt's Rooms.

Mr. BUCKLEY, Brasen-nose, President, in the Chair.

Mr. MOORE-STEVENS, Ch. Ch. moved :

That the recent appointments of Papists to the Privy Council is a measure deeply to be regretted, as a severe blow and heavy discouragement to the British Constitution as in Church and State established.

SPEAKERS.

In the Affirmative.	*In the Negative.*
Mr. Moore-Stevens, Ch. Ch.	Mr. Blackett, Ch. Ch.
Mr. Powles, Exeter.	Mr. Coleridge, Balliol.
Mr. Rawlinson, Trinity.	Mr. Forster, Worcester.
Mr. Lemprière, St. John's.	Mr. Congreve, Wadham.
Mr. Dickenson, Brasen-nose.	Mr. Townend, Oriel.
	Mr. Sanderson, St. Mary Hall.

Mr. FORSTER moved the following Amendment :

That religious opinions ought not to be made a disqualification for civil office; and that so far from regarding the elevation of Roman Catholics as injurious to our Constitution in Church and State, we view it as carrying out the great principle established by the Emancipation Act of 1829, which, by uniting all classes in their defence, afforded the best security for the support of our institutions.

Mr. SANDERSON moved the following Amendment :

That the late appointment of our fellow-subjects of the Romish persuasion to seats in the Privy Council is a measure greatly to be rejoiced at, as agreeable to our Constitution in Church and State, and more particularly to the great constitutional settlement and improvement of 1829 : and further, that both the appointments of 1839 and settlement of 1829 were alike a heavy discouragement to the cause of bigotry and despotism in Church and State, which can only be preserved by disuniting their own and its interests; and by effecting such gradual and progressive reforms as they each and respectively require.

Both the Amendments were negatived without a division.

DIVISION ON THE MOTION.

Ayes 46
Noes 12
Majority . . . 34

THURSDAY, JANUARY 30, 1840.

Wyatt's Rooms.

MR. BUCKLEY, Brasen-nose, President, in the Chair.

MR. SANDERSON, St. Mary Hall, moved :

That capital punishments being in principle barbarous and inhuman, and practically useless and inefficient for the prevention of crime, ought forthwith, and in all cases, to be abolished by the Legislature of this and every other civilized country.

SPEAKERS.

In the Affirmative.	*In the Negative.*
Mr. Sanderson, St. Mary Hall.	Mr. Northcote, Balliol.
	Mr. Northcote, Exeter.
	Mr. Courtenay, Exeter.

MR. BLACKETT, Ch. Ch. during the Debate made some remarks in favour of the Motion, but declined voting.

MR. SANDERSON replied.

DIVISION.

Ayes 3
Noes 30
Majority . . . 27

THURSDAY, FEBRUARY 6, 1840.

Wyatt's Rooms.

MR. BUCKLEY, Brasen-nose, President, in the Chair.

MR. BOUCHERETT, University, proxy for MR. WIGGIN, Exeter, stated that he was not prepared with a speech in support of MR. WIGGIN's Motion:

That the treatment which Mary Queen of Scots met with at the hands of Queen Elizabeth is highly to be condemned.

MR. BODE, Ch. Ch. then moved that the Question be adjourned.

DIVISION.

Ayes 43
Noes 24
Majority . . . 19

THURSDAY, FEBRUARY 19, 1840.

Wyatt's Rooms.

ADJOURNED DEBATE.

Mr. BUCKLEY, Brasen-nose, President, in the Chair.

Mr. WIGGIN, Exeter, moved:

That the treatment which Mary Queen of Scots met with at the hands of Queen Elizabeth is highly to be condemned.

SPEAKERS.

In the Affirmative.	*In the Negative.*
Mr. Wiggin, Exeter.	Mr. Clements, Oriel.
Mr. Phillimore, Ch. Ch.	Mr. Debary, Lincoln.
Mr. Fox, Wadham.	Mr. Powles, Exeter.
Mr. Seymour, Ch. Ch.	
Mr. Clerk, Trinity.	
Mr. Coleridge, Balliol.	

Mr. POWLES, moved the following Amendment:

That the measures adopted by Queen Elizabeth towards Mary Queen of Scots, after her flight into England, are greatly to be regretted.

Mr. WIGGIN replied.

DIVISION ON THE AMENDMENT.

Ayes 8
Noes 19
Majority . . . 11

DIVISION ON THE MOTION.

Ayes 17
Noes 10
Majority . . . 7

THURSDAY, FEBRUARY 20, 1840.

Wyatt's Rooms.

MR. BLACKETT, Ch. Ch. President, in the Chair.

MR. POWLES, Exeter, moved:

That the principles on which the Athenian Government was conducted after the death of Pericles, are a strong illustration of the evils of democracy.

SPEAKERS.

In the Affirmative.	*In the Negative.*
Mr. Powles, Exeter.	Mr. Congreve, Wadham.
Mr. Clements, Oriel.	Mr. Coleridge, Balliol.
	Mr. Sanderson, St. Mary Hall.

MR. SANDERSON moved the following Amendment:

That the democratic element was combined with oligarchical principles in the so-called republics of Greece and Rome, in such a manner and to such a degree, that these have afforded no fair criterion of the workings of a democracy, to which, therefore, the disorders occasioned by its collision with a rival, and equally powerful and prevailing interest, ought not to be ascribed: and further, that had those States been established on pure democratic principles instead of mixed theories of government, the great advances which European modern society has made, the effects of civilization, of Christianity, of improvements in all science, but more especially in the science of government, would not allow us to derive from the evils of an ancient, any inference unfavourable to the character and consequences of a modern, democracy.

MR. POWLES replied.

The Amendment was negatived without a division.

DIVISION ON THE MOTION.

Ayes 13
Noes 9
Majority . . . 4

THURSDAY, FEBRUARY 27, 1840.

Wyatt's Rooms.

MR. COURTENAY, Exeter, in the Chair.

MR. RAWLINSON, Trinity, moved :

That the recent proceedings of the House of Commons in professed vindication of their privileges, are utterly subversive of the true principle of the Constitution.

SPEAKERS.

In the Affirmative.	In the Negative.
Mr. Rawlinson, Trinity.	Mr. Wynn, Ch. Ch.
Mr. Coleridge, Balliol.	Mr. Debary, Lincoln.
Mr. Parnell, St. John's.	Mr. Townend, Oriel.
Mr. Alban, St. John's.	

DIVISION.

Ayes 56
Noes 9
Majority . . . 47

THURSDAY, MARCH 5, 1840.

Wyatt's Rooms.

MR. BLACKETT, Ch. Ch. President, in the Chair.

MR. LEMPRIERE, St. John's, moved :

That an hereditary legislative body is an essential element of a good form of government, and is well calculated to preserve the Constitution against the inroads of popular interference.

SPEAKERS.

In the Affirmative.	In the Negative.
Mr. Lempriere, St. John's.	Mr. Sanderson, St. Mary Hall.
Mr. Parnell, St. John's.	
Mr. Northcote, Exeter.	

MR. PARNELL moved the following Rider :

And that, at the same time, no check more effectual can be devised for preventing the possibility of a limited Monarchy degenerating into the worst form of tyranny.

MR. LEMPRIERE replied.

The Motion and Rider were both carried without a division.

THURSDAY, MARCH 12, 1840.

Wyatt's Rooms.

Mr. BLACKETT, Ch. Ch. President, in the Chair.

Mr. KINLOCK, St. Mary Hall, moved:

That the cession of the Roman Catholic claims in 1829, was a measure as little calculated to check agitation in Ireland, as it was to promote the welfare of the Protestant Church.

SPEAKERS.

In the Affirmative.	In the Negative.
Mt. Kinlock, St. Mary Hall.	Mr. Alban, St. John's.
Mr. Lempriere, St. John's.	Mr. Sanderson, St. Mary Hall.
Mr. Rawlinson, Trinity.	Mr. Seymour, Ch. Ch.
Mr. Courtenay, Exeter.	Mr. Brine, St. John's.

Mr. ALBAN declined voting.

DIVISION.

Ayes 18
Noes 5
Majority . . . 13

THURSDAY, MARCH 19, 1840.

Wyatt's Rooms.

Mr. BLACKETT, Ch. Ch. President, in the Chair.

Mr. CLEMENTS, Oriel, moved:

That the British Government in 1746 was not justified in setting a price upon the head of Prince Charles Edward, &c.; and that the measures then taken for the suppression of the insurgents are to be reprobated for their harshness and rigour.

SPEAKERS.

In the Affirmative.	*In the Negative.*
Mr. Clements, Oriel.	Mr. Debary, Lincoln.
Mr. Clerk, Trinity.	Mr. Parnell, St. John's.
Mr. Rawlinson, Trinity.	Mr. L. Carden, University.

Mr. RAWLINSON moved the following Rider:

But that still we do not intend to assert that Charles Edward was justified in his attempt, or that any subjects of the British Crown were justified in supporting him.

Mr. CLEMENTS replied.

DIVISION.
Ayes 16
Noes 16

The President gave his casting vote against the Motion.

THURSDAY, MARCH 26, 1840.

Wyatt's Rooms.

MR. BLACKETT, Ch. Ch. President, in the Chair.

MR. POWLES, Exeter, moved:

That the collision of nations, caused by the warlike spirit of the middle ages, tended to advance the civilization of Europe.

SPEAKER.

In the Affirmative.
Mr. Powles, Exeter.

DIVISION.

Ayes 50
Noes 8
Majority . . . 42

THURSDAY, MAY 7, 1840.

Wyatt's Rooms.

MR. BLACKETT, Ch. Ch. President, in the Chair.

MR. CONGREVE, Wadham, moved :

That of the various parties which divide the Country, the Conservative is the least entitled to our respect and confidence.

SPEAKERS.

In the Affirmative.	*In the Negative.*
Mr. Congreve, Wadham.	Mr. Seymour, Ch. Ch.
The President.	Mr. Coleridge, Balliol.
Mr. Sanderson, St. Mary Hall.	Mr. Clements, Oriel.

MR. SEYMOUR moved the following Amendment:

That the party truly conservative of our ancient institutions, is that which all good men must join; but that those Radicals and Revolutionists are most deserving of our abhorrence and contempt, who seek to substitute Anarchy for Government, Atheism for Religion.

MR. CLEMENTS moved a second Amendment:

That the Conservative party is worthy of reprobation: and that a strict adherence to Tory principles is the only firm basis for a Government really adapted to the emergencies of all times.

The Debate was then adjourned on the motion of MR. HOTHAM, Ch. Ch.

THURSDAY, MAY 14, 1840.

Wyatt's Rooms.

ADJOURNED DEBATE.

Mr. BLACKETT, Ch. Ch. President, in the Chair.

SPEAKERS.

In the Affirmative.	*In the Negative.*
Mr. Debary, Lincoln.	Mr. Hotham, Ch. Ch.
	Mr. Rawlinson, Trinity.

Mr. FOX, Wadham, moved the adjournment of the House, which was carried without a division.

SATURDAY, MAY 16, 1840.

Wyatt's Rooms.

ADJOURNED DEBATE.

Mr. BLACKETT, Ch. Ch. President, in the Chair.

SPEAKERS.

In the Affirmative.	*In the Negative.*
Mr. Fox, Wadham.	Mr. Parnell, St. John's.
*Mr. McIntosh, Corpus, Cambridge.	Mr. Chase, Trinity.
Mr. Forster, Worcester.	Mr. Brine, St. John's.
	Mr. Alban, St. John's.
	Mr. Portal, Ch. Ch.

Mr. SEYMOUR, Ch. Ch. obtained leave to withdraw his Amendment.

DIVISION ON MR. CLEMENTS' AMENDMENT.

Ayes 22
Noes 16
Majority . . . 6

* Honorary Member.

THURSDAY, MAY 21, 1840.

Wyatt's Rooms.

Mr. BLACKETT, Ch. Ch. President, in the Chair.

Mr. FOX, Wadham, moved:

That the political character of John Milton is worthy of our highest admiration.

SPEAKERS.

In the Affirmative.	*In the Negative.*
Mr. Fox, Wadham.	Mr. Clements, Oriel.
Mr. Parnell, St. John's.	Mr. Courtenay, Exeter.
Mr. Sanderson, St. Mary Hall.	
Mr. Forster, Worcester.	

DIVISION.

Ayes 9
Noes 11
Majority . . . 2

THURSDAY, MAY 28, 1840.

Wyatt's Rooms.

Mr. RAWLINSON, Trinity, President, in the Chair.

Mr. PARNELL, St. John's, moved:

That the adoption of the alteration in the law of Copyright, contemplated by the Bill of Mr. Serjeant Talfourd, would be utterly inexpedient.

SPEAKERS.

In the Affirmative.	*In the Negative.*
Mr. Parnell, St. John's.	Mr. Marshall, Ch. Ch.
	Mr. Clerk, Trinity.

DIVISION.

Ayes 5
Noes 24
Majority . . . 19

THURSDAY, JUNE 4, 1840.

Wyatt's Rooms.

Mr. RAWLINSON, Trinity, President, in the Chair.

Mr. BLACKETT, Ch. Ch. moved:

That the conduct of James the Second, on his coming to the Throne, afforded ample justification of the policy of those who supported the Exclusion Bill.

SPEAKERS.

In the Affirmative.	*In the Negative.*
Mr. Blackett, Ch. Ch.	Mr. Portal, Ch. Ch.
Mr. Debary, Lincoln.	Mr. Clements, Oriel.
Mr. Fox, Wadham.	

Mr. PORTAL moved the following Amendment:

That the Exclusion Bill is opposed both to law and conscience; for that no religion, no law, no fault of the Sovereign, can alter or diminish the divine and fundamental right of hereditary succession.

Mr. BLACKETT replied.

DIVISION ON THE AMENDMENT.

Ayes 21
Noes 15
Majority . . . 6

THURSDAY, JUNE 11, 1840.

Wyatt's Rooms.

MR. RAWLINSON, Trinity, President, in the Chair.

MR. SANDERSON, St. Mary Hall, moved:

That bribery and intimidation at Parliamentary Elections are mainly attributable to the system of open voting; and that the opposite, or secret system, commonly called the vote by Ballot, affords the only efficient remedy for the evils complained of.

SPEAKERS.

In the Affirmative.	*In the Negative.*
Mr. Sanderson, St. Mary Hall.	Mr. Powles, Exeter.
Mr. Congreve, Wadham.	Mr. Coleridge, Balliol.
Mr. Blackett, Ch. Ch.	Mr. Phillimore, Ch. Ch.
	Mr. Forster, Worcester.

MR. FORSTER moved the following Amendment:

That the existing laws have proved utterly ineffectual for the suppression of bribery and intimidation; and that it is expedient that a trial be given to the system of taking the votes by Ballot for the Election of Members to serve in Parliament.

MR. SANDERSON replied.

DIVISION ON THE AMENDMENT.

Ayes 6
Noes 28
Majority . . . 22

DIVISION ON THE ORIGINAL MOTION.

Ayes 5
Noes 28
Majority . . 23

THURSDAY, JUNE 18, 1840.

Wyatt's Rooms.

Mr. RAWLINSON, Trinity, President, in the Chair.

Mr. COLLYNS, Ch. Ch. moved:

That in the present circumstances of the Church, it is the bounden duty of the State to take such measures as shall enable it to meet the calls of an increasing population.

SPEAKERS.

In the Affirmative.
Mr. Collyns, Ch. Ch.
Mr. Seymour, Ch. Ch.

The Motion was carried without a division.

THURSDAY, JUNE 25, 1840.

Wyatt's Rooms.

Mr. RAWLINSON, Trinity, President, in the Chair.

Mr. POWLES, Exeter, moved:

That the public life of Cicero is deserving of high admiration.

SPEAKERS.

In the Affirmative.	*In the Negative.*
Mr. Powles, Exeter.	Mr. Northcote, Balliol.
Mr. Coleridge, Balliol.	
Mr. Blackett, Ch. Ch.	
Mr. Congreve, Wadham.	

DIVISION.

Ayes 24
Noes 8
Majority . . . 16

THURSDAY, OCTOBER 22, 1840.

Wyatt's Rooms.

MR. RAWLINSON, Exeter, President, in the Chair.

MR. CLEMENTS, Oriel, moved :

That the Monastic Institutions of Europe have had a most beneficial influence upon Society, and have contributed largely to the increase of civilization.

SPEAKER.

In the Affirmative.
Mr. Clements, Oriel.

The Debate was adjourned till the following Thursday.

THURSDAY, OCTOBER 29, 1840.

Wyatt's Rooms.

ADJOURNED DEBATE.

MR. RAWLINSON, Exeter, President, in the Chair.

MR. CAZENOVE, Brasen-nose, moved the following Amendment:

That while we freely acknowledge a debt of gratitude to the Monks for many literary and general benefits conferred by them, we cannot give our decided approbation to the system on which their institutions were founded and conducted.

The Debate was adjourned till the following Thursday.

THURSDAY, NOVEMBER 5, 1840.

Wyatt's Rooms.

ADJOURNED DEBATE.

Mr. RAWLINSON, Exeter, President, in the Chair.

SPEAKERS.

In the Affirmative.	In the Negative.
Mr. Scratton, Ch. Ch.	Mr. Coke, Brasen-nose.
Mr. Courtenay, Exeter.	Mr. James, Queen's.
Mr. Blackett, Ch. Ch.	

Mr. CLEMENTS replied.

Mr. Cazenove asked leave to withdraw his Amendment.

DIVISION ON THE QUESTION OF GRANTING LEAVE.

Ayes 24
Noes 11
Majority . . . 13

DIVISION ON THE MOTION.

Ayes 22
Noes 11
Majority . . . 11

THURSDAY, NOVEMBER 12, 1840.

Wyatt's Rooms.

Mr. ARNOLD, Magdalen Hall, President, in the Chair.

Mr. CLERK, Trinity, moved :

That the Foreign Policy of Great Britain during the last ten years has been such as to render the Nation contemptible in the eyes of the whole world.

SPEAKERS.

In the Affirmative.	In the Negative.
Mr. Clerk, Trinity,	Mr. Blackett, Ch. Ch.
Mr. Gladstone, Magdalen Hall.	Mr. James, Queen's.
Mr. Alban, St. John's.	
Mr. Douglas, Exeter.	

Mr. CLERK replied.

DIVISION.

Ayes 28
Noes 11
Majority . . . 17

THURSDAY, NOVEMBER 19, 1840.

Wyatt's Rooms.

MR. ARNOLD, Magdalen Hall, President, in the Chair.

MR. COLERIDGE, Balliol, moved:

That the rise of Chartism was natural, and that its increase is to be expected.

SPEAKERS.

In the Affirmative.	*In the Negative.*
Mr. Coleridge, Balliol.	Mr. Forster, Worcester.
Mr. Courtenay, Exeter.	
Mr. Parnell, St. John's.	
Mr. Congreve, Wadham.	
Mr. Tate, University.	
Mr. Mayo, Oriel.	
Mr. Mackintosh, University.	
Mr. Chase, Oriel.	

MR. FORSTER moved the following Amendment:

That the present aspect of affairs affords no grounds for our supposing that Chartism is on the increase, and that the surest way of suppressing it is to redress the wrongs and ameliorate the condition of those classes in which its supporters chiefly exist.

MR. TATE, University, moved the following Rider to the Motion.

Unless the State forthwith provide that the limits of the influence of the Church be co-extensive with its responsibilities.

MR. COLERIDGE, Balliol, replied.

The Amendment was unanimously rejected.

The original Motion and the Rider were carried unanimously.

THURSDAY, NOVEMBER 26, 1840.

Wyatt's Rooms.

MR. ARNOLD, Magdalen Hall, President, in the Chair.

MR. CHASE, Oriel, moved :

That the late interference of the Legislature with the Cathedral Establishments was unjust and impolitic, and is to be considered as a sacrifice of principle to temporary expediency.

SPEAKER.

In the Affirmative.
Mr. Chase, Oriel.

DIVISION.

Ayes 37
Noes 3
Majority . . . 34

THURSDAY, DECEMBER 3, 1840.

Wyatt's Rooms.

MR. POWLES, Exeter, Treasurer, in the Chair.

MR. FORSTER, Worcester, moved :

That the claims of the Jews to a participation in the same civil privileges as have been granted to the Roman Catholics cannot be with justice refused.

SPEAKERS.

In the Affirmative.	*In the Negative.*
Mr. Forster, Worcester.	Mr. Clements, Oriel.
	Mr. Coke, Brasen-nose.
	Mr. Humbert, St. John's.
	Mr. Gladstone, Magd. Hall.
	Mr. Congreve, Wadham.
	Mr. Alban, St. John's.
	Mr. Parnell, St. John's.

MR. FORSTER replied.

DIVISION.

Ayes 3
Noes 30
Majority . . . 27

THURSDAY, DECEMBER 10, 1840.

Wyatt's Rooms.

Mr. ARNOLD, Magdalen Hall, President, in the Chair.

Mr. CAZENOVE, Brasen-nose, moved:

That the annals of Venice in the middle ages afford strong arguments against oligarchical governments.

SPEAKERS.

In the Affirmative.	*In the Negative.*
Mr. Cazenove, Brasen-nose.	Mr. Seymour, Ch. Ch.

Mr. CAZENOVE replied.

DIVISION.

Ayes 7
Noes 23
Majority . . . 16

THURSDAY, JANUARY 28, 1841.

Wyatt's Rooms.

Mr. ARNOLD, Magdalen Hall, President, in the Chair.

Mr. JAMES, Queen's, moved :

That there is no Reign in English history so disgraceful as that of Charles II. in both its foreign and domestic policy, nor one that has more tended to debase the national character.

SPEAKERS.

In the Affirmative.

Mr. James, Queen's.
Mr. Cazenove, Brasen-nose.
Mr. Lempriere, St. John's.
Mr. Clerk, Trinity.
Mr. Sanderson, St. Mary Hall.
Mr. Carey, Oriel.
Mr. Clifford, Ch. Ch.

Mr. CAZENOVE moved the following Rider :

And that the majority of its faults may be traced to the excesses of the Puritans and Roundheads during the great Rebellion.

Mr. CLERK moved a second Rider, as follows :

And also that we may consider the evils of the Reign of Charles II. as a judgment on the nation for their previous misconduct and rebellion.

Mr. JAMES replied.

DIVISION ON THE MOTION.

Ayes 22
Noes 9
Majority . . . 13

ON THE FIRST RIDER.

Ayes 16
Noes 15
Majority . . . 1

ON THE SECOND RIDER.

Ayes 18
Noes 16
Majority . . . 2

THURSDAY, FEBRUARY 11, 1841.

Wyatt's Rooms.

MR. CLEMENTS, Oriel, Treasurer, in the Chair.

MR. MAYO, Oriel, moved :

That the power of the United States of America is of a nature calculated to experience a speedy decay.

SPEAKERS.

In the Affirmative.	*In the Negative.*
Mr. Mayo, Oriel.	Mr. Humbert, St. John's.
Mr. Bucknill, Trinity.	Mr. Sanderson, St. Mary Hall.
Mr. Chase, Oriel.	

MR. MAYO replied.

DIVISION.

Ayes 21
Noes 9
Majority . . . 12

THURSDAY, FEBRUARY 18, 1841.

Wyatt's Rooms.

Mr. POWLES, Exeter, President, in the Chair.

Mr. LOWDER, Exeter, moved:

That a Country is not justified in colonizing a new world with its convict population.

SPEAKERS.

In the Affirmative.	*In the Negative.*
Mr. Lowder, Exeter.	Mr. Clements, Oriel.
Mr. James, Queen's.	Mr. Carey, Oriel.
Mr. Marshall, Ch. Ch.	Mr. Tripp, Worcester.
Mr. Evans, Trinity.	Mr. Chase, Oriel.

Mr. CLEMENTS moved the following Amendment:

That a Country then only is justified in colonizing a new world with its convict population, when it provides the means of religious instruction for those whom it banishes, and at the same time manifests on all occasions an earnest zeal for their welfare.

Mr. LOWDER replied.

DIVISION ON THE AMENDMENT.
Ayes 20
Noes 29
Majority . . . 9

DIVISION ON THE ORIGINAL MOTION.
Ayes 27
Noes 27

The President gave his casting vote against the Motion.

THURSDAY, FEBRUARY 25, 1841.

Wyatt's Rooms.

MR. POWLES, Exeter, President, in the Chair.

MR. CLEMENTS, Oriel, moved :

That the political character of Lord Strafford deserves the admiration of posterity.

SPEAKERS.

In the Affirmative.	*In the Negative.*
Mr. Clements, Oriel.	Mr. Sanderson, St. Mary Hall.
Mr. Tate, University.	Mr. Phillimore, Ch. Ch.
Mr. Giffard, University.	Mr. Marshall, sen. Ch. Ch.
	Mr. Humbert, St. John's.
	Mr. Congreve, Wadham.

MR. HUMBERT moved the following Amendment :

That the Sentence and subsequent Execution of Lord Strafford is deserving of the detestation of posterity.

MR. CLEMENTS replied.

The President declared the Amendment to be inadmissible.

DIVISION ON THE MOTION.
Ayes 33
Noes 9
Majority . . . 24

THURSDAY, MARCH 4, 1841.

Wyatt's Rooms.

MR. POWLES, Exeter, President, in the Chair.

MR. MARSHALL, jun. Ch. Ch. moved :

That the Poor Law Amendment Act is unjust in principle, and that its working has an injurious effect upon the relations between the richer and poorer classes.

SPEAKERS.

In the Affirmative.	*In the Negative.*
Mr. Marshall, Ch. Ch.	Mr. Lingen, Trinity.
Mr. Vansittart, Oriel.	Mr. Mansel, St. John's.
Mr. Portal, Ch. Ch.	Mr. Blackett, Ch. Ch.
The President.	Mr. Seymour, Ch. Ch.
	Mr. Mayo, Oriel.

MR. MARSHALL replied.

DIVISION.
Ayes 22
Noes 26
Majority . . . 4

THURSDAY, MARCH 11, 1841.

Wyatt's Rooms.

MR. POWLES, Exeter, President, in the Chair.

MR. BLACKETT, Ch. Ch. moved:

That a comparison between the present state of England and of most of the other Countries of Europe, affords a strong argument in favour of the great popular Leaders during the Reigns of the Stuart family.

SPEAKERS.

In the Affirmative.	*In the Negative.*
Mr. Blackett, Ch. Ch.	Mr. Northcote, Exeter.
Mr. Sanderson, St. Mary Hall.	
Mr. James, Queen's.	

MR. NORTHCOTE moved the following Amendment:

That so far from being indebted to the popular Leaders during the Stuart family for any advantages England may at present possess over the other nations of Europe, we must lay to their charge the democratical tendency of most of our institutions, with the pernicious consequences they involve.

MR. BLACKETT replied.

DIVISION ON THE AMENDMENT.

Ayes 21
Noes 16

Majority . . . 5

THURSDAY, MARCH 25, 1841.

Wyatt's Rooms.

MR. CLEMENTS, Oriel, Treasurer, in the Chair.

MR. SEYMOUR, Ch. Ch. moved:

That the United Provinces of the Netherlands were justified in revolting from Philip II. of Spain.

SPEAKERS.

In the Affirmative.

Mr. Seymour, Ch. Ch.
Mr. Doughton, Ch. Ch.
Mr. Sanderson, St. Mary Hall.

MR. SEYMOUR replied.

DIVISION.

Ayes 26
Noes 12

Majority . . . 14

THURSDAY, APRIL 29, 1841.

Wyatt's Rooms.

Mr. POWLES, Exeter, President, in the Chair.

Mr. NORTHCOTE, Exeter, moved :

That the events connected with the French Revolution shew that nations no less than individuals are subject to the retributions of Justice.

SPEAKERS.

In the Affirmative.	*In the Negative.*
Mr. Northcote, Exeter.	Mr. Cross, Ch. Ch.
	Mr. James, Queen's.
	Mr. Blackett, Ch. Ch.

Mr. CROSS moved the following Amendment :

That states as well as individuals are subject to the retributions of Justice, but that the events connected with and subsequent to the French Revolution are up to the present period of the history of that Country an exception to the rule rather than an instance of it.

Mr. JAMES moved a second Amendment :

That without at all justifying the French Revolution, we are bound to consider it an instance of national retribution on the previous misgovernment and corruption of the Monarchy and privileged Orders.

Mr. NORTHCOTE replied.

The first Amendment was lost without a division.

DIVISION ON THE SECOND AMENDMENT.
Ayes 9
Noes 12
Majority . . . 3

DIVISION ON THE MOTION.
Ayes 7
Noes 11
Majority . . . 4

THURSDAY, MAY 13, 1841.

Wyatt's Rooms.

Mr. POWLES, Exeter, President, in the Chair.

Mr. PARNELL, St. John's, moved :

That the imperfections and anomalies in the Representative and Elective systems at present employed in the formation of the House of Commons are such as to deserve the attentive consideration of every Statesman.

SPEAKERS.

In the Affirmative.	*In the Negative.*
Mr. Parnell, St. John's.	Mr. Blackett, Ch. Ch.
Mr. Gladstone, Magdalen Hall.	Mr. Congreve, Wadham.

Mr. PARNELL replied.

The Motion was carried unanimously.

THURSDAY, MAY 20, 1841.

Wyatt's Rooms.

Mr. LANDON, Worcester, President, in the Chair.

Mr. CAREY, Oriel, moved :

That the interests of Religion, and the character of the Nation, demand that some immediate measures be adopted to enforce the Order of the Hon. the Board of Directors of February 20, 1833, regulating the connection between the British subjects and Indian Idolatry.

SPEAKERS.

In the Affirmative.

Mr. Carey, Oriel.
Mr. Humbert, St. John's.

Mr. CAREY replied.

DIVISION.

Ayes 21
Noes 17
Majority . . . 4

THURSDAY, MAY 27, 1841.

Wyatt's Rooms.

MR. LANDON, Worcester, President, in the Chair.

MR. FRITH, Exeter, moved:

That our system of Colonization is defective in principle and most injurious in tendency.

SPEAKER.

In the Affirmative.
Mr. Frith, Exeter.

DIVISION.

Ayes 19
Noes 11
Majority . . . 8

THURSDAY, JUNE 3, 1841.

Wyatt's Rooms.

MR. LANDON, Worcester, President, in the Chair.

MR. TOWNEND, Oriel, moved :

That the present Corn Laws are alike impolitic and unjust, and that the best interests of the Country, more especially with reference to commerce and manufactures, require an immediate alteration of them.

SPEAKERS.

In the Affirmative.	*In the Negative.*
Mr. Townend, Oriel.	Mr. Gladstone, Magdalen Hall.
Mr. Congreve, Wadham.	Mr. Plumptre, University.
	Mr. Tristram, Lincoln.

MR. PLUMPTRE moved the following Amendment:

That the repeal of the existing Corn Laws would confer no permanent benefit on the manufacturing Classes, and would be detrimental to the general interests of the Country.

MR. TOWNEND replied.

DIVISION.

Ayes 29
Noes 3
Majority . . . 26

THURSDAY, JUNE 17, 1841.

Wyatt's Rooms.

Mr. LANDON, Worcester, President, in the Chair.

Mr. TATE, University, moved:

That the domestic Policy of the Whig Ministers of 1835 has been both in principle and practice ruinous to the Country.

SPEAKERS.

In the Affirmative.
Mr. Tate, University.
Mr. Coleridge, Balliol.

In the Negative.
Mr. Congreve, Wadham.
Mr. Sanderson, St. Mary Hall.

The Debate was adjourned till the following Saturday.

SATURDAY, JUNE 19, 1841.

Wyatt's Rooms.

ADJOURNED DEBATE.

Mr. LANDON, Worcester, President, in the Chair.

SPEAKERS.

In the Affirmative.
Mr. Giffard, University.
Mr. Carey, Oriel.
Mr. Vernon, University.
Mr. Cazenove, Brasen-nose.
Mr. Gladstone, Magdalen Hall.

In the Negative.
Mr. Sanderson, St. Mary Hall.
Mr. Blackett, Ch. Ch.
Mr. Debary, Lincoln.

Mr. TATE replied.

DIVISION.

Ayes 21
Noes 5
Majority . . . 16

www.ingramcontent.com/pod-product-compliance
Lightning Source LLC
Chambersburg PA
CBHW080513090426
42734CB00015B/3037